Contents

Acknowledgments

The author and publisher would like to thank the following for permission to reproduce material:

- Marks & Spencer Corporate Press Office for the extract on p. 4.
- Rainier PR for the extract on p. 182.

Every effort has been made to contact copyright holders and we apologise if any have been overlooked.

Photo credits:
Collections/Eric Lewis (p.8, top)
Digital Vision 15 (NT) (p. 6, top left)
Image Club 2 (NT) (p. 217, left and right)
Image Library V2 CD6/Ingram (NT) (p. 282)
Image State (p. 138)
Jeff Moore (jeff@jmal.co.uk) (p. 7, middle, right and bottom; p. 210; p. 214, bottom)
Lesley Garland Picture Library (p. 6, top right)
Paul Ridsdale/Lesley Garland Picture Library (p. 7, left)
Photodisc 5 (NT) (p. 216; p. 237, left)
Photodisc 26 (NT) (p. 208, top; p. 213, bottom)
Photodisc 66 (NT) (p. 130)
Photodisc 68 (NT) (p. 18; p. 22; p. 29; p. 50; p. 62; p. 80; p. 116; p. 177; p. 243)
Photodisc 69 (NT) (p. 202)
Photodisc 73 (NT) (p. 24; p. 36; p. 155, left; p. 174; p. 237, right)
Rex Features (p. 45)
Science Photo Library (p. 209; p. 211; p.215)
Science & Society Picture Library (p. 208, middle and bottom; p.237, bottom)
Stockbyte 6 (NT) (p. 82; p. 134)
Stockbyte 31 (NT) (p. 135; p. 213, top; p. 214, top)
Stockpix 6 (NT) (p. 57; p. 101)
Topham Picturepoint (p. 6, bottom; p. 8, bottom; p. 157, left and middle)
Vodafone (p. 157, right)
Microsoft® screenshots are reprinted with permission by Microsoft Corporation.

Introduction

Successful businesses have powerful, efficient and trustworthy systems that rely on effective and accurate methods of communication, controlled and run by well-trained, informed and motivated people.

This book informs candidates of Business and Communication GCSE about effective communication systems and the roles and responsibilities of the people who design, operate and update them. The book seeks to explain the importance of accurate and efficient systems in the success or failure of a business's response to the customer and the stakeholder of the business. It will provide opportunities for the candidate to apply their knowledge of systems in a variety of different contexts and to practise and develop skills in the different software applications.

The emphasis is on the development of a clear understanding of the importance of communication. As well as discovering the functions of different businesses and their wider context within industry, the text will analyse the kinds of barriers and constraints that exist to deny some businesses success.

This book is structured to take the candidate step by step through the Business and Communication Systems qualification. It has followed the headings in the specification and you will find information about every aspect of the course in these pages.

The business environment

IN THIS SECTION YOU WILL INVESTIGATE ...

- **Types of business organisations**
- **Aims and objectives of business organisations**
- **Stakeholders**
- **Meeting objectives**

INTRODUCTION

KEY TERMS

Products A general term used to describe goods or services offered by a business

Services A general term used to describe everything other than products that may be sold by a business

We live in a world where we rely on a number of different businesses to provide us with the **products** and **services** that we need to survive. These include food, water, the homes we live in and the clothes we wear. However, we live in a society where we want more than just to satisfy our basic needs, so there are many different businesses attempting to provide us with what we want and what we think we need. However large or small the business and however well known it is, it has to be organised to serve its customers well if it is going to survive in the business environment.

Action Points

What is it about some businesses that make them stand out in our minds? Visit your local High Street and take photographs or use the internet to gather images of some well-known businesses that you are very familiar with. A few that spring to mind are:

- Marks and Spencer.
- McDonald's.
- Tesco.
- Superdrug.

1 Write down five reasons why you think they are so successful at making us, as customers, remember their image.

2 Why do you think businesses that have a high profile and are instantly recognisable are sometimes known as 'household names'?

KEY TERMS

Local business A business which tends to operate only in its immediate area

Suppliers Other businesses or organisations that provide items to a business

Raw materials Items bought by a business which need to be processed before they can be sold as a product

Distributors Individuals or an organisation that work with a business to help ensure that their products and services are as widely available as possible

Demand The desire for a product or service

Market research The gathering of information to help make decisions

Needs Essential products and services required by customers

Wants Products or services desired by customers

Market Either an area or a country in which products or services are required, or the number of units sold or money spent on those products and services

Competitors Other businesses or organisations offering similar products or services

Some businesses start small and grow to become household names that are familiar to everyone. Marks and Spencer started as a market stall run by two friends called Mr Marks and Mr Spencer. Coca-Cola started with one man who invented a drink and sold it to local people in his home town for its 'medicinal properties'. Many other businesses are not as successful as these and remain small, never really growing or developing into more than just what we would call a **local business**.

Making a success of a business starts with having a good idea. The problem with having a good idea is that others might try to copy that idea if it is seen to be successful and, even worse, they may make a better job of it. So in order to achieve success, a good business will attempt to:

- Plan its business activities carefully – whatever the nature of the business, it needs to plan carefully to make sure that everything is in place before the business is launched, which means that it needs to have:
  - found its **suppliers** (those who provide the business with the **raw materials** they need to make a product, or those who provide the business with products which are going to be sold under their company name);
  - found its **distributors** (those who transport the product from the business itself to its customers);
  - obtained the equipment and machinery needed in order to make the product (or simply shelves and cash registers in the case of a shop);
  - found good, reliable and efficient staff to represent the business in the best possible way.

- Research the market – whatever the business offers to the customer it must first find out if that product or service is going to be popular and sell. The business will attempt to find out if there is a **demand** for its products by:
  - carrying out some **market research**. This will help the business to find out the **needs** and **wants** of the customer and how large the **market** might be;
  - looking at what people who sell similar products or services are doing. These are the business's **competitors** and they may already successfully be providing a similar product or service, which could present a problem.

KEY TERMS

Costs A business's financial commitments arising out of its operations

Expenditure Payment for something which immediately benefits the business

Profit What is left from income after costs have been deducted

Income Funds coming into a business

Quality Ensuring that products or services are produced to a high standard so that the customer is satisfied

Skills Abilities of employees which help them carry out their work

Motivated An individual who enjoys work and wishes to do a good job

- Keep the cost of running the business to a minimum. A business must keep a careful eye on how much is being spent on running costs. If **costs** are too high the business may not succeed. There will always be costs associated with running a business. However, the prudent business will watch these carefully and avoid waste or unnecessary **expenditure**.

- Make a **profit** – in the same way that a business needs to control how much it spends, it must also make sure that it generates an **income** that is greater than the running costs. In other words, the business needs to make a profit from the sales of its products and services. Obviously the income that a business receives from the sales of its products and services needs to be greater than the money it has to pay out in order to make the product or provide the service.

- Make sure that the customer is treated well – all businesses need to have customers to buy their products and services in order that they can generate the income needed to cover costs and make a profit. The business needs to look closely at the kind of service it gives to its customers. The business wants customers to keep coming back and it does not want them to be unhappy with the products they buy or the service they receive. Happy customers may recommend the business to their friends, but unhappy customers will most definitely tell others and the reputation of the business will be affected. The business will want to:
  - make sure the product or service is produced to the highest possible **quality**. If the product or service is faulty or of poor quality the business will gain a bad reputation and will not be as successful or be recommended to others;
  - have well-trained and efficient staff. A good business will value its people and make sure all of its employees know how to do their job efficiently. The business will want to develop their employees by providing training in all aspects of the work they do, giving them opportunities to learn new **skills** and understand new technology. When a business invests time and money in the people who work for them, their employees will be happy and **motivated** and the business will have more chance of succeeding.

Action Points

18,000 Jobs up for Grabs at Marks & Spencer

Marks & Spencer are looking to recruit at least 18,000 new employees in its stores in the run up to and over the busy Christmas period.

Matthew Brearley, Head of Human Resources for UK Retail at Marks & Spencer, said: 'Christmas and New Year is the peak in many retailers' calendar and this year will be no different. We have a fantastic shopping experience in store for our customers as well as some amazing products, so we want the best team in place, fully trained and raring to go before the rush begins.'

The jobs, which involve both serving customers and behind the scenes work, are available across most departments, including the food and coffee shop areas. Many different shift patterns are available including early mornings and night shifts.

All seasonal employees will be offered a good salary and benefits package – which includes a staff discount.

Matthew continued, 'We have started looking for our people early as we want to attract the pick of the bunch. We need hard working, dedicated individuals who have a natural affinity with our customers and can meet our high standards. These positions are available to anyone but would be ideal for students, busy parents who require flexible working patterns or people looking to get back into employment after a career break.'

Source: www.marksandspencer.com

Read the press release and then answer the following questions:

1 Why has Marks & Spencer started advertising for Christmas temporary staff early?

2 How will the package that part-time staff are offered help Marks & Spencer in its quest for success?

3 What kind of skills and attributes does Marks & Spencer want from the people it is trying to recruit?

4 Why will these skills and attributes help the business?

● Plan for growth and the future development of the business. Nearly all businesses need to think about how they will develop and grow. The owners of the business will probably want the business to make them money and to provide them with security for the future. In order for this to happen, they need to think carefully about the best way to develop, whilst making sure that they still take into account all of the issues we have already discussed. All businesses need to plan carefully in order to ensure that they can grow successfully.

To summarise, a successful business needs to ensure that it has effective procedures in place to:

● Provide its customers with the right product or service.
● Provide its customers with an efficient service.
● Manage income and expenditure in order to make a profit.
● Ensure that the quality of the product or service is maintained.
● Ensure that staff are trained and developed.
● Have effective short-term and longer-term planning.
● Set achievable targets for the future development of the business.

Action Points

1 Produce a table on your computer using the following headings to gather your information:
   Business name   Main activities
   The type of people who are customers

2 Make a list of 10 different businesses that operate in your town or the area around your school.

3 In the second column include an explanation of the main activities of the business, for example what they make or what service they provide.

4 In the final column add a description of the customers they serve.

5 Now choose two of the businesses from your list and carry out the following:
   ● Write a description of the business, the product or service it provides and the customers it serves.
   ● Describe any other businesses that produce the same product or provide the same service.
   ● Give an account of your impression of the business. Is it well organised? Is it well known? Is it popular and successful?
   ● Explain how you think the business might improve the service that it provides to its customers.

TYPES OF BUSINESS ORGANISATIONS

When we consider business organisations in general, we also need to consider the term 'industry'. Industry comprises all of those business organisations which make things or produce raw materials, but it also includes banking, insurance and retailing. Industry is divided into three categories, known as industrial sectors, which are:

- Primary – these industries are concerned with producing raw materials and include agriculture, fisheries, forestry and mining.
- Secondary – these industries are concerned with the making (manufacturing) or processing of products and include car making, food processing and iron and steel working.
- Tertiary – these are the service industries. They do not actually produce the products but they sell them. This category of industry is commonly known as the service sector and includes banking, all of the **retailing** and distribution businesses, and tourism.

KEY TERMS

Retailing A shop or chain of shops selling direct to the public

Examples of primary, secondary and tertiary industries

There are many ways in which a business organisation can be organised and this is known as the 'business ownership'. Basically, the business ownership could be one of the following:

- Sole trader – this is, perhaps, the most common type of business organisation, although in recent years the number of such businesses has been declining. Some of the best examples of sole traders are plumbers, decorators, electricians and window cleaners. Sole traders work for themselves and usually carry out all of the activities of the business alone, although they may employ other people.
- Partnerships – this type of business organisation is often formed in order to overcome any problems that a sole trader may have encountered, for example in raising money. A partnership consists of between two and 20 people who set up in business together and share the responsibility for that business. Good examples are accountants, solicitors and dentists.
- Private limited company – a private limited company has the word 'Limited' or 'Ltd' written after the company name. Private limited companies are usually family concerns, or were originally so, and this form of organisation is often chosen when a sole trader wants to expand but still wishes to retain control of the company.
- Public limited company – this is a larger type of organisation and will have 'PLC' after the company name. These companies raise money by selling **shares** on the **Stock Exchange**, and those who buy the shares are the business's **shareholders**.

KEY TERMS

Shares A certificate which entitles the owner to receive a portion of the profits of the business

Stock Exchange A marketplace where shares are sold and bought

Shareholders Individuals who own a part of a business because they have bought shares in it

- Franchise – this type of business organisation originated in America and has become very popular as a way of starting a new business quickly. Franchising involves allowing another company to trade under your business's name for a sum of money. A good example of a franchise organisation is McDonald's. Franchises may be sole traders, partnerships or limited companies.

 Think about it!

Find out a little more about what is involved in franchising, particularly what is meant by the terms 'franchiser' and 'franchisee', and identify three examples of franchises other than McDonald's.

- Charities – these types of business organisation do not necessarily exist in order to make a profit, but their aim is to obtain money for their cause. Good examples of charities are Help the Aged and Oxfam and the majority of their employees work on a voluntary basis, meaning they give their time for no payment. The management and administration of charities is usually carried out by full-time professionals who are paid for the work.

Whatever the type of business ownership, or the industrial sector to which that business belongs, there are two more types of sector that we need to consider before moving on. These are known as the 'private sector' and the 'public sector' and it is necessary to distinguish between the two.

Generally the private sector is made up of organisations that are independent of the Government and will include:

- Sole traders
- Partnerships
- Private limited companies
- Public limited companies
- Franchises.

The public sector consists of organisations that are either owned or controlled by the Government. The most common forms of public sector organisation are:

- Government departments or the civil service, which are responsible for running Government activities in a specific area, such as the Department of Trade and Industry, which assists businesses.

- Local government, such as County, Metropolitan, District or Borough Councils, which provide services to the community, assist business and promote their local area.
- Public corporations or enterprises, such as the Bank of England and the National Health Service, which provide services essential for everyone and are known as nationalised industries.
- Quangos (Quasi-Autonomous Non-Governmental Organisations) which are funded by the Government to provide services. Examples of Quangos include OFTEL (which monitors the communications industry) and the Arts Council (which provides grants to artists, theatres and film makers).

Whether you live in a city, a town or in the countryside, there is a network of business organisations to cater for nearly all of your immediate needs. Some may be part of the public sector (such as refuse collection or health care), other services will be provided by the private sector (such as supermarkets, newsagents and chemists).

A wide variety of organisations operate on a **national** basis in the UK, such as banks, building societies, travel agents and supermarkets. These medium to large organisations have created national networks to cover the whole of the UK population.

Many large organisations have become **international** or **multinational** by building up their businesses all over the world. Good examples of these are:

- Oil companies (Shell, Esso)
- Computer manufacturers (Dell, Compaq)
- Retail organisations (Marks and Spencer, British Home Stores)
- Franchise organisations (Body Shop, Games Workshop)
- Manufacturing organisations (Ford, General Motors).

They have enormous buying power but have to spend huge sums of money on their communication methods. Communication technology such as video conferencing, email and fax machines have gone a long way towards solving past communication problems, as we will discover in later chapters of this book.

It is probably easier to think of an example of a business organisation than to try to define what a business organisation actually is. Although, as we will see, business organisations can differ enormously, they do have some common features. These are:

- They often use resources that are in limited supply, such as humans, money and materials.

KEY TERMS

National A business which tends to operate only in one country

International A business which trades around the world

Multinational A business which manufactures or produces products in a number of different countries

- They provide something, either a product or a service.
- They normally compete with other organisations.

Each organisation must undertake a wide variety of different activities in order to ensure that they operate well in their own area. Some of these activities, or functions, include:

- Managing employees.
- Selling products or services.
- Distributing products or services.
- Buying the products or services of other businesses.
- **Marketing** products or services.
- Keeping records.
- Observing regional, national or international laws.

Organisations must ensure that when they make a decision they make the correct decision, whether this involves a new product or the employment of more staff.

> **KEY TERMS**
>
> **Marketing** The process of offering the right products or services at the right place, at the right time and at the right price

AIMS AND OBJECTIVES OF BUSINESS ORGANISATIONS

So far we have examined the different types of business organisation and ownership and what the owners can do to help make a business successful. As discussed above, a great deal of thought needs to be given to how best to organise each area of the business to make sure that it all runs smoothly.

The owners need to have specific aims and objectives, and these need to be communicated clearly and effectively to the employees who will take the appropriate action to achieve these. The employees who work in the business need to be clear about their roles and responsibilities in making sure that the aims and objectives are met. They also need to be aware of the best methods to use in order to meet the business's aims and objectives and what resources are available to them, such as time, money, training and equipment.

Everyone involved in the business needs to have clear deadlines and targets so that it is easy to judge when the objective has been met and a new set of aims and objectives should be considered. Aims and objectives need to be SMART, which stands for:

- **S**pecific (clear)
- **M**easurable (they can be calculated)
- **A**chievable (practical)
- **R**ealistic (reasonable)
- **T**ime specific (deadlines).

Think about it!

- If there are no goal posts you cannot really know where to score the goal.
- If you do not know how many goals the opposition have scored you cannot know whether or not you have won the game.
- If the game does not have a finish time you will not know when to stop playing.
- If you do not know the rules you will not know when you have made a mistake.

Action Points

1 Write down your own five-year plan.

2 What are your goals?

3 What do you want to achieve in the next year, two years and five years?

4 Set yourself three goals and for each goal write down next to it how you are going to achieve it, who will help you, what are the barriers that might stand in your way and what resources you will need to make sure you achieve it. Are they SMART?

5 What is the difference between an aim and an objective? Find a definition for both and check your own aims and objectives.

KEY TERMS

Business plan A detailed report of a business's future proposals. This will help persuade investors of its potential

Many businesses begin by setting out their aims and objectives in a **business plan**, which is a formal statement of their goals. However, in reality, the way in which these goals are achieved may differ from the business plan because organisations do not exist in isolation and the business environment in which they operate is constantly changing. Once an organisation has established its goals it must find methods of achieving them. These are known as:

- Strategies – which are the major ways of achieving the objectives and tend to be fairly long term in their approach, for example, 'We want to increase the sales of our products by 50 per cent over the next 10 years'.
- Tactics – which are more short term and flexible. These are the individual parts of the strategy, for example, 'In order to increase sales of our products by 50 per cent over the next 10 years we need to find cheaper suppliers'.

So strategy states what the organisation needs to do, and tactics describe how to achieve the strategy. The setting and meeting of the business's aims and objectives will help the owners achieve their main purposes of existence in a number of different ways, including:

- Judging success – this means that the owners will be able to estimate how successful the business is at the present time. Obviously, if there is some indication that the business is not trading successfully or is not receiving good feedback from its customers, then the business will take steps to improve the way it works and it will set new aims and objectives.
- Profitability – if the aims and objectives set by the business are successful, then hopefully it will be making a profit. Certainly the business will monitor carefully the difference between how much something has cost to produce and how much it is sold for.
- Wealth creation and growth – the owners of the business will be interested not only in profit but also in the future. They will want to keep track of sales and the number of employees they have so that they avoid the risk of becoming too big too fast, as this may mean that the business cannot control what it is doing.
- Job creation and job security – certainly the owner of the business will want to keep his or her own job, but they will also want their employees to be secure in their job roles (security often means a motivated workforce). If one of the aims is for the business to grow, then the owners will want to create new job roles and will see that as a success.
- Market share – a business will strive to increase the amount of products it sells and so enlarge its share of the market. Obviously the business will hope to increase this slowly in stages and gradually increase its market share by beating its competitors.

Businesses need to think ahead in everything they do. Forward planning is essential to sound organisation and good communication. A well-organised business will have short-term and long-term plans. There will be **contingency plans** in case unforeseen circumstances stop the original plan from being carried out.

Some businesses have strategic plans that plan the future of the business for the following 12 months, two years and five years. The plans are reviewed regularly and adjustments are made to take into account changes that might have occurred or events

KEY TERMS

Contingency plan A backup plan to help a business prepare for the unexpected that might happen that alter the plan and its outcomes. Long-term plans might involve the business opening up new branches or creating new product lines. They might include extending markets by selling to Europe or to countries worldwide. Sometimes plans might involve shrinking the business operation as well as planning for it to grow. In order for a business to achieve long-term aims and objectives that have been set in the planning process there need to be a series of shorter-term plans that lead to the achievement of the longer-term aim. The following Table gives some examples.

Long-term planning	Short-term planning
Expand business into Europe	Investigate different countries and their markets Find suitable premises Select and recruit staff for overseas
Develop a new product line	Investigate the potential market Research possible competition Plan to buy new machinery Select and recruit new staff Change the production process to accommodate new product line
Become the market leader	Investigate quality in order to improve the product or service Investigate what the competition is doing Increase the sales team Embark on a massive advertising campaign
Reduce waste by 50%	Find out how much waste is produced now Develop strategies for improving waste management Investigate how other companies, countries and individuals deal with waste

It is all well and good having a plan, whether it is a long-term plan or a short-term one, but the secret is to make sure that the plan is carried out. Everyone makes plans but not everyone sees them through. How many times have you made a New Year's resolution and have not even managed to get through New Year's Day before it is broken? How many times have you made a serious promise to achieve something by a certain time only to break that promise?

In business, broken promises and unfulfilled plans can have a serious effect on the success of the business and all the people influenced by the success of the business. It is therefore essential that the planning process is effective and that everyone understands their role in carrying out the actions contained within the plan. Effective plans will state clear aims and set out measurable and achievable objectives that provide a pathway for the successful implementation of the plan. One of the keys to ensuring that plans are followed through is to place realistic deadlines against each of the stages and try to keep to these as far as possible.

Think about it!

We all need to be organised in order to make sure that life runs fairly smoothly. Before you leave the house in the morning to go to work, school or college you need to make sure you have everything you need – keys, books, homework, etc. Before you go on a journey you need to think carefully about where you are going, how much it will cost, how you are going to get there, how long will you stay, what to do while you are there. Some people are more organised than others. Those people who are organised are usually more successful and achieve more than those who are disorganised.

Action Points **W**rite down 10 ways in which you would like to become more organised, then choose one of your 10 and answer these questions:

1 What actions will I have to take in order to ensure that my resolution to be more organised can succeed?

2 By what date can I make sure I have succeeded in being more organised?

3 Who will help me in my quest to be more organised?

4 What resources (time, money, people, actual items) will I need in order to achieve my goal?

5 Are my plans and goals realistic and achievable?

6 What will I gain by succeeding in my plan to be more organised?

STAKEHOLDERS

Stakeholders are all those people who are affected in some way by the activities of the business or have an interest in the operations of the business. For example:

- The local community might be affected by the business because of fumes or traffic congestion, or local people might welcome the business because it brings jobs to the area.
- The Government imposes rules on business and collects taxes from businesses which they use to help run the country.
- Local government may be called upon to judge whether a business should be granted planning permission for new buildings.
- Suppliers, from whom the business regularly buys products and services, rely on that business in order to continue to be successful themselves.
- Distributors rely on the business for their own income.
- The business's competitors also have an interest in what the business is producing, how much it is charging for the products and how customers view the products.

All businesses need to be aware of the wider group of stakeholders and the **constraints** that they may place on the business in its quest for success. Keeping everyone with an interest in the activities of the business happy can be difficult and time consuming. Ultimately it is down to effective and accurate communication, as well as careful consideration of stakeholders' reactions and what they need to know.

In any business, however large or small, there are both internal and external stakeholders, apart from the employee and the customer.

KEY TERMS

Constraints Issues and demands that might affect the way a business is allowed to operate

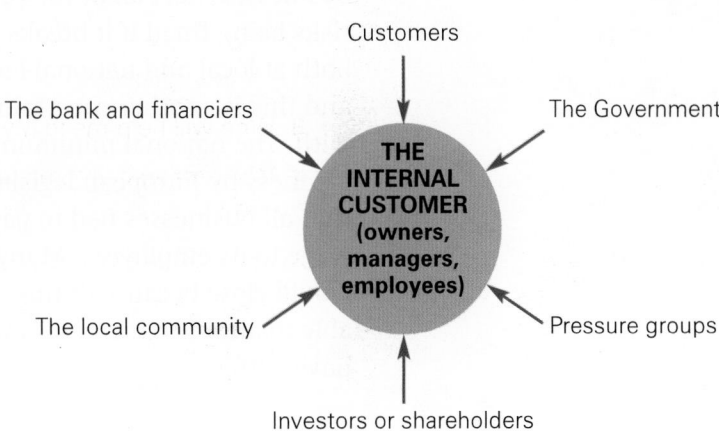

Figure 1.1

KEY TERMS

Advertising Paid-for communication in the media about a business and its products

Stakeholders can place some constraints on a business and these include:

- The need to ensure profitability – all businesses need to be profitable to satisfy their **shareholders** or to make money for the owners. A business that struggles to make a profit will not be able to spend money on effective **advertising** and it will be unable to make a good impression. Marks & Spencer are a very good example of how easy it is to fall from grace when profits begin to drop. The business had to look very closely at why customers were staying away. Improved profitability in 2002 led the Chief Executive to say:

> I am very pleased with these results, delivered against our own weak comparatives and in buoyant High Street conditions. The improvements made to date in clothing appeal, store ambience, food innovation and home products have been appreciated by our customers and are delivering results. We expect High Street conditions to normalise as the year progresses but we know we can do even more to create a better shopping experience for our customers and to recover lost ground.

> Source: Marks & Spencer Annual Report 2001, Luc Vandevelde, Chairman and Chief Executive

- Government legislation – there is an ever increasing constraint being placed on business by the imposition of legislation (laws that the Government imposes on business). These constraints can be imposed by local by-laws, the UK Government or by EU legislation. It is very costly for a business that does not comply with the legislation, and there are many regulators or inspectors employed by the Government to make sure businesses meet all of the rules and regulations. A business risks being fined if it breaks laws or regulations. Government, both at local and national level, imposes taxes on business and this is another constraint that the business has to work with. The national minimum wage was imposed on British business by European legislation in April 1999. This meant that all businesses had to pay more than a stated minimum wage to its employees. Many businesses thought they would close because of this; however, it seems that most were able to afford to increase wages and few businesses appear to have suffered.

- Employee organisations – there are many trade unions and employee organisations that exist to support employees at work. Trade unions exist to advise and help employees who feel they have been unfairly treated or who feel exploited or unsafe. It is the right of every employee to be a member of a trade union. Employers usually work closely with trade union representatives to make sure there is a good working relationship.

- Pressure groups – sometimes a business does something dangerous or controversial. There are a number of pressure groups that lobby businesses, as well as the Government, to try and change the way businesses operate. There are many examples of the pressure these groups exert on business; for example there have been objections to businesses using cheap labour from poorer countries to produce their goods. Pressure has also been brought on the nuclear industry to try and make sure that it is safe, and concern has been voiced about building companies that use wood from threatened rain forests. Pressure groups may be local, in the case of noise or problems with a business in the neighbourhood, national in the case of groups trying to change the way a whole industry operates, or international in the case of pollution or the use of national resources.

Stakeholders

Think about it!

Visit the websites of Greenpeace and Friends of the Earth and find out about their activities (www.greenpeace.org.uk and www.foe.org.uk).

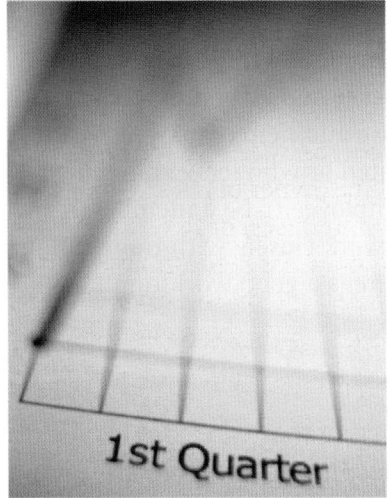

1st Quarter

Business exists to serve a wider community. All businesses need customers – without them a business would have no income. The business would not be able to buy vital equipment and supplies or pay wages to employees and eventually the business would have to close. Every function inside the business has to work towards meeting the needs and expectations of the customer, as well as dealing with the demands of the other stakeholders. Often, the demands of the stakeholders are opposed; for example shareholders may be concerned only with profits, employees may be concerned with salaries, and the Government with the effects of pollution, and a business needs to tread carefully in satisfying all of them.

The image that the business presents to its customers is vital in creating a good impression so that the customer will want to continue using the business. The way the business communicates its image and culture to the customer leaves a clear impression of the quality of the services it provides. Many businesses use questionnaires and feedback sheets. Barclays Bank offer advice on making a complaint. A business with a poor reputation and bad image can often fail; even an inappropriate statement can cause ruin. In the 1990s Gerald Ratner, the owner of a chain of retail jewellers, referred to the products that his stores sold as 'rubbish'. Subsequently customers refused to shop at Ratners and within a short time the whole chain closed.

Action Points

1 In groups discuss your role as a customer.

2 Make a list of all the times in one day that you are a customer of a business.

3 Discuss with members of the group any occasion when you have been unhappy with the service you have received.

4 Consider how this might have been avoided.

5 How could the service be improved in the future?

6 Write a list of do's and don'ts for businesses that have direct contact with their customers.

7 Use a computer to create a poster to present your list.

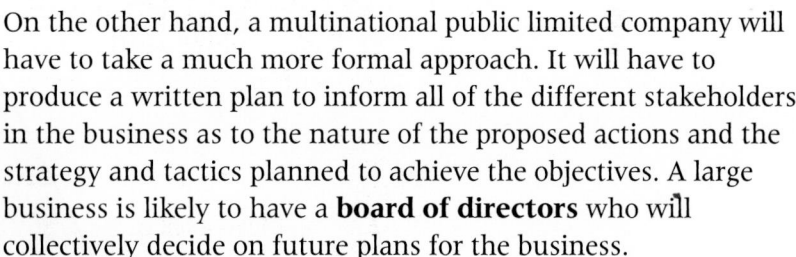

MEETING OBJECTIVES

Planning starts at the top, so the owners of the business need to communicate effectively their goals for the business. The owner may have a clear vision of where he or she wants that business to be in one year or five years, but that is useless if the vision is not communicated effectively to all concerned. The goals need to be explained firstly to the managers and then to the employees who are responsible to the managers. After all, it is the managers and the employees who are going to try and ensure that the plan succeeds.

The owner or owners of the business make decisions regarding the long-term future. For example, the owner of a small shop may plan to increase sales, find new premises, or take over a rival shop to eliminate the competition. A large multinational company, with shareholders and shares sold on the stock market, might want to expand into new markets, develop new products or open new branches in order to keep shareholders happy by increasing profits in the longer term.

The owner of the smaller, more informal business may simply have these plans in his or her head. There may be only a few employees in this type of organisation and they will hear the plans from the owner and work closely with him or her to help put the plans into practice. It is unlikely that the plan will be written down in any formal way. Nevertheless, if the business wanted to approach a bank for a loan to help it expand, it would need to put its plans in writing.

On the other hand, a multinational public limited company will have to take a much more formal approach. It will have to produce a written plan to inform all of the different stakeholders in the business as to the nature of the proposed actions and the strategy and tactics planned to achieve the objectives. A large business is likely to have a **board of directors** who will collectively decide on future plans for the business.

KEY TERMS

Board of directors
A decision-making committee of senior managers

Business structures

It is important to consider some of the different ways that an organisation will structure itself, as this has an impact on the way the owners can communicate with their employees. The structure of an organisation will vary depending on a number of factors, including:

● The size and nature of the market in which it operates (are there many customers and where are they?).

- The type of activity in which it is involved (what is made or sold?).
- The need to maintain good communications (how are communications carried out?).
- The size of the organisation (the number of employees).
- The number of branches or sites involved (locations).
- The type and number of customers (consumers or other businesses).
- How much it is affected by Government legislation (laws relating to the business).
- The impact of new technology on the business (the use of machines and computers).
- Its past and current structure (the way that it has grown and restructured, and the way in which the business is managed).
- Its future plans (short, medium and long term).

Hierarchical structures

The best way to understand what a hierarchical structure looks like is to imagine a pyramid. At the top of the pyramid are the owners, who make the decisions, but as you look further down the pyramid the shape widens. As the shape widens, more and more employees are involved, so the majority of the employees are at the base of the pyramid. The responsibility, power and authority are all much greater at the top of the pyramid and communication flows down from the top to the bottom. This type of structure would have the owners or the directors at the top, the departmental managers next, and the more junior employees at the bottom.

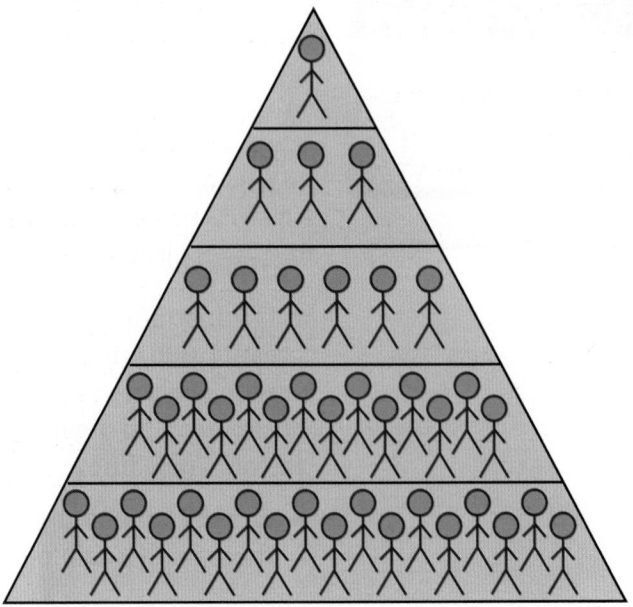

Figure 1.2 Hierarchical structure

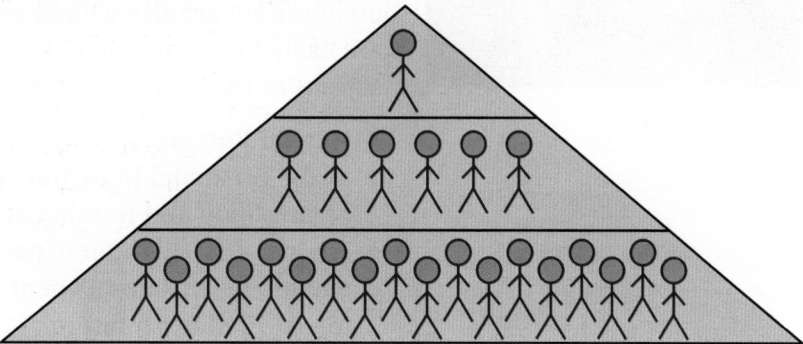

Flat structures

This type of organisation has reduced the number of layers involved in a hierarchical structure. The theory behind having fewer layers in the pyramid is that decisions can be made quickly and efficiently. Each layer is able to communicate easily with the other layers and this type of structure is often found in organisations that operate from a single site where all employees can meet with each other readily.

Figure 1.3 Flat structure

Communication

There are two further terms that we need to understand when considering the business structure and communication flows. These are:

KEY TERMS

Chain of command An indication of how a business explains how to get things done

Span of control The number of employees who are controlled by one manager or supervisor

- **Chain of command** – this is the structure of the organisation which shows how many levels of management there are and how information or instructions are passed up and down the organisation.
- **Span of control** – this relates to the number of individuals who report directly to a single manager.

However large or small the business and whatever type of organisational structure is in place, it is important that the owners communicate the plan to those who will carry it through. A plan is most certainly more effective if it is written down, making it clear as to the nature of the actions, the timescales involved and the way in which the plan is likely to be implemented. It is not good practice for the owner of any business, however small, to pass on information only via word of mouth as this can be an unreliable form of communication. Each individual who hears the plan may not understand all of the details or may mishear what is being said.

The manager's role

A manager is someone who takes responsibility for running the business on a day-to-day basis. In a very small business the managers may also be the owners and they will be responsible for every aspect of the business. However, in larger businesses the owner and/or the board of directors will communicate the plan to the individual managers who will help to implement it. It is worth mentioning at this stage that the managers of a large organisation are also usually employees of the business. There are likely to be a number of managers in charge of different aspects of the business activities, including:

- Human Resources – this department or function, also known as the Personnel Department, deals with the recruitment, organisation and training of the employees of the business.
- Finance – in addition to paying the wages and salaries of the employees, this department or function also monitors the income and expenditure of the business.
- Production – this department is involved in all functions related to producing the products or services for the customer to buy.
- Purchasing – this department is involved in buying all of the materials required for the business to function.
- Distribution – is responsible for ensuring the safe storage of the business's products and the transportation of them to the customers.
- Sales and Marketing – sometimes these are two separate departments, but their main responsibilities lie in making sure that the customer is aware of the products that the business offers and then selling them to the customer.
- Administration – this department of a business controls all of the paperwork and supports the other departments by servicing their needs for secretarial work, e.g. filing, mailing, handling information, etc.
- Research and Development – if this function exists within the business it will work closely with the marketing department by keeping a constant check on the products being offered for sale by competitors. It also develops new products or services for the business to sell. In some businesses this function is carried out by those in marketing.
- Quality Control – often part of the Production Department, this section of the business tries to maintain a consistently high-quality product.
- Computer (IT) Services – this department has responsibility for the hardware and software that the business uses, as well as the maintenance of telecommunications and other technological office development. It will ensure that the

employees are using the most appropriate equipment and that they are trained in any new technology that the business acquires.

The manager's role in any of the above departments or functional areas is to interpret and then communicate the plan to his or her employees. Without effective communication at this level the individual employees will not have a clear understanding of their roles and responsibilities in carrying out the plan. The manager needs to make sure that the employees all understand:

- The nature of the task they are expected to undertake.
- The timescales involved.
- The resources available, such as the right equipment and tools, the amount of time and finance, a place to work, etc.
- The expected outcome.

If the manager fails to communicate the plan and its associated tasks, the employee is unlikely to be able to complete the work successfully. Remember, if there are no goal posts it's unlikely that goals can be scored; if the rules are not clear then these may be broken or ignored; and if there is no clear deadline then it is difficult to work to an effective time plan.

It is therefore the manager's role to:

- Communicate effectively the tasks that need to be undertaken.
- Give clear instructions as to the time the task should take.
- Provide the resources available to carry out the work.
- Give a clear indication as to what the end result should look like.
- Seek feedback from the employee that he or she understands the nature of the task and the associated issues relating to how it will be completed.

Another role of the manager is to ensure that those employees who are expected to meet the objectives are trained and instructed effectively. If an employee is unable to complete the task because of lack of training, then not only will the objectives not be met, but the employee may become what is known as **demotivated**.

The role of the employee

Ultimately it is the role of the employee to carry out the tasks set for them by the managers and/or the owners of the business. The way that the business is structured will have an effect on the different roles of managers and employees. In some businesses

KEY TERMS

Demotivated Those who lack an enjoyment of work and therefore carry out their job less effectively

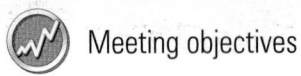
the role of manager is much less obvious. A flat structure will mean that there are fewer managers and much of the decision-making and the distribution of tasks is done through teams working together. In organisations with a much more hierarchical structure, the manager will have a clear role in managing a group of employees where the task is delegated from senior manager to manager and then to employee. In some businesses there may be a layer of **supervisors** between the managers and the employees. Supervisors tend to be the next level down in an organisation structure, below managers. They are team leaders or organisers of specific projects or functions of the business and will usually answer to a manager.

In a well-run business it will be possible for the employees to agree that the tasks set out before them are within their capabilities. An employee should be able to ask for training or instruction if it is necessary. An employee should also be able to negotiate as to resources of time, money and equipment if the job is to be completed satisfactorily.

An employee should be able to work with others in a team or group where this is expected and should be able to lead or follow as is required. Sometimes an employee should be able to work quietly and alone on specific tasks. It is also important that all employees at whatever level are safe in their working environment and that they make sure the work they do is not a danger to themselves or to others. Again, in some instances employees should be able to ask for training or instruction in Health and Safety issues.

KEY TERMS

Supervisor Someone in charge of a group or team of workers who makes sure the instructions of the manager are carried out

Think about it!

Mary Molloy had worked for Doolittle and Dally solicitors for 10 years. She was the general administrator. 'Truth be told,' she had said to a friend, 'I am the only one in that firm that knows where everything is.' She kept a manual filing system where everything was neat and tidy. She could put her hand on client names and addresses, their files and their correspondence. She was proud of the way she worked. It came as a great shock to her when the Practice Manager said that a computer was to be installed. She would have to put all the data on to the computer and develop new systems. She complained bitterly and resisted the change fiercely. However, it was no good, the decision was made.

The computer arrived and Mary was expected to begin by developing a database of all the clients. She was given a manual to help her and she was then left to her own devices. After two weeks of trying she had made very little progress. The Practice Manager called her into the office and was not very pleased to hear she had made such little progress. 'I thought you would have finished by now,' he said. 'I was hoping you could move on to developing a spreadsheet for the accounts.' Mary handed in her notice at the end of the week, much to the surprise of the senior partner and the other partners in the firm. Mary was going to be difficult to replace.

- Why do you think the partners in the firm decided that it would be good idea to computerise the different administration functions?
- Why did Mary not succeed in completing the task she had been set?
- How could Mary have helped the situation?
- How could the Practice Manager have helped Mary to succeed in completing the task?

Whatever the plan and whatever the tasks that will make the plan happen, it is ineffective unless those involved in delivering it have received clear instructions and guidance as to what to do next. Poor communication of the message in any situation will lead to demotivation, misunderstanding and a poor response. It is therefore crucial to good business practice to look carefully at the way that the message is communicated. There are many ways in which the aims and objectives outlined in a plan might be effectively passed on to those who are to carry out the tasks. Although we look in more detail at each of these methods of communicating information in a later chapter of this book, it is useful to look at them briefly here as they are the major ways that the owners and managers of a business transfer the information to the employees and receive feedback from them. These might include:

- Formal board and management meetings
- Team meetings or briefings
- Meetings of the whole staff
- Newsletters and fact-sheets
- Mission statements
- Formal and informal interviews
- Appraisal interviews.

Formal board and management meetings

The Directors and senior management of a medium to large business will almost always have a system of regular meetings when the group will consider how the business is moving forward. These meetings will address issues that affect the way that the business is run. Those attending the meeting may look at the needs and demands of the many stakeholders, both inside and outside the business, and make decisions about how best to deal with them.

There will be a person present who will take minutes of the meeting (the Minutes Secretary). All of the main issues and decisions will be recorded in these minutes and after the meeting has taken place a copy will be sent to each person that attended. Decisions made at a formal board meeting need to be acted upon. If the meeting is to be meaningful and useful, it is essential that where actions need to be taken after the meeting it is clearly stated who will be responsible for taking those actions as discussed and agreed. The actions need to be defined clearly in order to make sure there is a positive result. After a formal board meeting it is likely that each Senior Manager or Director will **cascade** the information and **delegate** certain tasks to managers in their department or functional area.

This redistribution of tasks and information is likely to take place at a meeting of managers. Well-structured management meetings should follow the same procedures as board meetings, with well-documented minutes. Each member of the meeting should be clear as to their role and responsibilities after the meetings.

KEY TERMS

Cascade Passing information down the levels of an organisation

Delegate Passing authority and responsibility down to others of lower rank in the organisation

 Think about it!

Find a business definition of the terms cascade and delegate. Why is it so important for managers to cascade information and delegate tasks to others?

Action Points

1 Set up a meeting of a group of your fellow classmates. You are going to have a debate about an issue that is important to you as a group. Some ideas might be:
   - Should there be a ban on television advertising of children's toys?

- Should the age at which young people can drive be lowered to that of the USA?
- Should there be a relaxation of the law on taking drugs?
- Should the school day or the school year be changed?

There are many topics that arouse strong feelings in all of us.

2 Ask members of the group to present an argument for and against the motion you have chosen to debate. Conduct the debate in a formal way. You will need to elect a chairperson and a person to take the minutes. Each member of the group should have the opportunity to speak on the motion.

3 At the end of the debate discuss how well the meeting was conducted. Did everyone have the opportunity to speak? Were all the issues fully discussed? What conclusion was arrived at, if any?

 Think about it!

You are on the Board of Directors of Bridgesouth Limited, a chain of fast-food outlets across the south of England. At the last board meeting it was agreed that the business should expand by opening another restaurant in the northern town of Leeds. A suitable site has been located; however, it is in a conservation area and planning permission might be tricky. In your role as Operations Director you have agreed to organise the planning and design of the interior, the entrance and car parking arrangements for the new premises. You agree to come back to the meeting with suitable plans and an idea as to the cost of the new venture.

At the next board meeting you arrive with a set of plans and a document outlining the cost of the operation. Other members of the board are unhappy with your contribution. The Finance Director is unhappy with what he considers to be high costs. The Marketing Director is unsure about the concept of the entrance which is not the same as the others in the chain. The Managing Director is critical of the plan because it is only on paper and is not a 3D model.

- What do you think went wrong at the original meeting to make your fellow directors so unhappy?
- How could you have made sure you were clear as to their needs?
- What do you think can be done to sort out the problems?

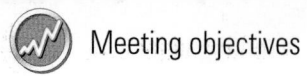

Team meetings and briefings

It is important for the manager to make sure that the tasks entrusted to him or her are carried out. A good manager will delegate responsibility to a number of different teams and individuals within the functional area or department. If a business decides to market a new product to a new sector and wants to send out a leaflet to **a targeted audience**, it would be unlikely that the manager would be involved with filling the envelopes or inputting the data into the computer. However, it is vital that the manager is aware of progress, can help if there are problems, and can offer positive and constructive feedback on the way the task is progressing. Regular team meetings or briefings possibly once a week, but in some cases every day, should take place to make sure the job is done satisfactorily. These meetings are important for the employee. It is a time when people can meet together and talk about issues that affect their work.

Meetings of the whole staff

Occasionally there needs to be a meeting of all of the staff. There are many issues that cross different departments of a business and the employees involved need to have the opportunity to raise issues that affect the business as a whole, such as the achievement of the aims and objectives. Staff meetings can also be opportunities to welcome new staff, discuss major changes taking place in the business or consider issues such as health and safety or the refurbishment of a building that might affect everyone in the business.

Newsletters and fact-sheets

These can be used successfully to reinforce issues that have been raised in other meetings. They are useful as a tool to pass on information about staff achievements, new staff or staff that may be leaving the business. The newsletter can also be a useful means of starting a discussion or passing on information about an issue in the firm as it gives staff time to consider the matter before a formal meeting. A fact-sheet can inform about issues such as Health and Safety, training or new technology.

Mission statement

This is a simple statement that tries to convey what the business is trying to achieve.

KEY TERMS

A targeted audience A particular share of the market –

- teenagers
- pensioners
- homeowners
- people with high incomes
- females

Action Points

1 Use the internet or visit your local shopping centre and collect some mission statements and company logos to make a collage for the classroom wall.

2 Does your school have a mission statement? If yes, add this to your collage; if not, have a discussion to come up with a suitable mission statement that says what your school is trying to achieve.

3 Find out if other local schools also have a mission statement and add some of these.

Formal and informal interviews

One-to-one meetings are important for many reasons. Formal interviews take place when a manager is trying to find out if a candidate is suitable for a job or for a promotion. A formal interview may take place if a person is to be disciplined. This type of interview may require more than one person to be present to make sure everything is conducted properly.

Informal interviews may take all sorts of forms – a chat over a sandwich, a discussion at a desk between a manager and an employee about a problem that has just occurred, etc.

It is important that the manager and the employee are clear as to when the interview should be informal and when the issue under discussion is important and therefore requires a more formal setting.

Appraisal interviews

These are also formal interviews. However, they deserve to be considered separately. An appraisal is an opportunity for the manager to discuss with an employee how well he or she is doing in the job, and what training and development they may need to progress and improve their performance. The employee can also appraise the performance of the manager by suggesting improvements in the way the manager communicates his or her needs or whether resources are sufficient for the employee to complete the tasks set. The appraisal is usually conducted after the manager and the employee have completed a form of some kind which will become a discussion document that can be used during the formal interview. The manager and the employee will agree targets for improvement over a period of time, usually 12 months. The targets will be about performance, training and

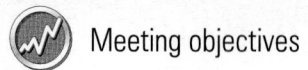
development, the release of resources such as time, money and equipment, and support on both sides. The interview and the feedback given in any written document should always be constructive and not negative.

Action Points

1 Find a definition of the word 'appraisal'.

2 Encourage a discussion with your form tutor or subject teacher about your performance and how you might improve.

3 Consider how the teacher might help you to achieve more in the future. Remember to be constructive!

Workplace organisation

IN THIS CHAPTER YOU WILL INVESTIGATE ...

- **The working environment**
- **New working practices**
- **Health and safety**
- **Data preparation, storage and retrieval**
- **Security of data**
- **Effective use of resources**

THE WORKING ENVIRONMENT

There are as many different working environments as there are businesses. Each type of workplace organisation has to be designed so that the work can be done safely, accurately and efficiently. Although each environment will be organised differently, there are certain aspects of the workplace that will be the same.

It is not very easy to work at a computer without a desk and a chair. There needs to be space to lay out plans or books and charts if the business activity demands this. A business involved in cutting out cloth or rolling metal will need to have the space and the equipment set up efficiently in order that the activity can take place satisfactorily and safely.

Some business activity requires a quiet place to work, whilst other activities require that people work together in groups or teams. In some businesses there is a need for both **interactive** spaces and quiet spaces. In the **Marketing** Department a team may work together to come up with an idea to **promote** a new product. The team may need to be working in the same room so that ideas can be discussed, drawings and plans drafted and redrafted. A sales person may need to work in a quiet space, talking to customers on the telephone to find out their needs and successfully sell the product or service on offer without being disturbed or distracted by background noise.

KEY TERMS

Interactive To act and respond to each other

Marketing The process of offering the right products or services at the right place, at the right time and at the right price

Promote Making a product known to customers by using the media to advertise it

The open plan office environment

Many businesses have chosen, or have been forced, to design their office space so that people work in what is known as an open environment. This means that the business has probably decided to make the best use of the space that they have available and to reduce the number of individual offices.

There are definite advantages of working in this way, including the following:

- It promotes team working and gives employees and managers the opportunity to discuss work issues immediately without having to find someone in another office. Work can be moved freely from one person to another without the need to walk from office to office.
- Employees feel less alone than if they were confined to a separate office.
- Equipment can be shared, for example individuals can share telephone handsets, faxes, printers and other office equipment.
- It can help individuals to understand the work done by others within the business.
- Managers may be more accessible to their team.
- There can be more immediate communication across different **functional** areas of the business.
- It is often a light and airy atmosphere whereas partitioned offices might be dark and small.
- Managers can see clearly the work that is taking place.
- It is cheaper than a series of smaller rooms from the point of view of lighting, heating and cleaning.

KEY TERMS

Functional The different job roles or duties within a business organisation, for example the role of different departments

Think about it!

Find a definition of the word 'confidentiality'. Find some examples of when a business would need to make sure there was somewhere for confidential activity to take place.

However, there are disadvantages to an open plan office, including the following:

- It can be noisy and distract those who need to concentrate, particularly if there are several other employees moving around the office.
- There may be nowhere to go if privacy is needed or the work being undertaken is confidential.
- An employee might think that he or she is being watched and this might make him/her feel uncomfortable.
- Individuals can be possessive about their own space and feel annoyed if it is invaded by other workers.
- It is easier to lose or mislay important documents if more than one person has access to the same space.
- There is an increased possibility of theft, both of equipment and of information. Certainly it is worth considering that some individuals may be able to access information when they are not entitled to do so.
- Infection can spread more easily in this type of office environment, particularly colds, therefore employees might be absent from work more often.
- There could be problems regarding the amount of heating or lighting that individuals prefer, as one person's taste and preference is not the same as another's.
- The office may feel as if it does not really belong to anyone and this could make it an impersonal place to work.

Action Points

1 Visit local branches of banks and building societies and observe the way they operate. Many have moved to a more open plan environment. Observe the activities taking place. There may be people waiting to pay money into the bank or to draw money out, people with queries or enquiries about loans, savings or mortgages, etc.

2 How do the different organisations deal with issues such as privacy and confidentiality?

3 Is the environment neat and organised?

4 Give some examples of how the business organises paperwork.

5 Are the customers well served?

6 Write an account of your observations of one of the places you have visited.

7 In your opinion, how might the environment be improved for the following:
- Staff?
- Customers?

The cellular office

Putting one person or a few people into small offices is a much more traditional approach to workplace organisation. This more traditional space is referred to as the cellular office, although even in open plan environments it is likely that some of the more senior members of the business will have their own private office or working space.

Advantages of the cellular office environment might include:

- A quiet and more private environment which would enable the employee to work with the minimum amount of disturbance.
- It offers privacy both to the occupant of the office and to other employees who visit.
- Meetings can be held privately, particularly with customers of the business.

- The work and associated papers and equipment are contained and belong only to the person or persons working in the office. However, noisy equipment could be situated outside the office itself in order to reduce disturbance.
- It offers the individual the opportunity to make the office more personal. This can help the employee feel more comfortable in their work environment.
- Security is improved because the individual offices are often lockable. This is as important for access to information as it is for access to equipment. Confidential information can be kept secure and valuable equipment is safe when the office is not occupied.

However, there are also some disadvantages to the cellular office and these might be:

- The employee or group of employees within the office is not constantly supervised by a manager so there could be times when they are not working to their full potential.
- Equipment will be needed for each office and it could be that it is only used infrequently. This means that from the business's point of view it is not always **cost effective**.
- An individual can be very possessive of their own office space.
- The individual employee could feel isolated and out of touch with the rest of the business.

KEY TERMS

Cost effective Something is said to be cost effective if it does not cost too much to do and has benefits to the business that equal the cost of putting the process or equipment in place

KEY TERMS

Chartered accountant A person who has achieved a recognised accountancy qualification

Think about it!

Mike had worked for many years for Des who was a **chartered accountant**. Mike was not really trained as an accountant, but he had picked up how to balance the books and put the information into the correct order. He worked in a small office next to Des. There was a receptionist, but she worked in the reception office and did not really have very much to say. Mike worked methodically. He was quite happy until Des decided to sell his practice to a larger, much more modern, firm. Mike was to be part of the deal. He was OK about this until he started work at the new firm. He was working in a large open plan office with lots of other accounts clerks. Telephones rang and people shouted. Mike became conscious of the fact that he was used to working in a mess and was constantly told to tidy up his area. He was also unhappy about the fact that people in the office used his pens and his paper.

What do you think Mike should do about his situation?

Workplace policies and practices

Regardless of the type of office environment used in an organisation, the business will have a number of set procedures or policies in place to ensure that the working environment is safe and pleasant for its employees. Safety is something that an organisation has to be very aware of by law. So, too, is the health and comfort of the employees. The organisation will have set procedures in place to cover the following aspects of the working environment:

- The health and safety of employees. This is a legal requirement which we will look at in some detail below.
- The safety of machinery and equipment being used by employees. The business will not want accidents to occur because they have not been thorough in their instructions regarding the use of machinery and equipment. Employees who use machinery and equipment on a regular basis as part of their job have to be well trained in its use. The business also needs to ensure that the machinery or equipment is regularly serviced or maintained by a qualified person.
- There may be a no smoking policy within the organisation. This will be in place in order to make the working environment more comfortable for non-smokers and also to reduce the risk of fire.
- There may be a no eating or drinking at desk policy in place. This will reduce the risk of the spillage of liquids near expensive equipment, such as computers, and will also reduce the risk of food being left around the office. Obviously if food is left in a waste basket overnight there is a chance that mice will be attracted to the premises and this could be a health risk to employees.
- Policies will also be in place regarding alcohol and drugs. Obviously the business will not want to be associated with the use of either on the premises, but there will be procedures for dealing with employees who arrived for work in an unfit state because they had used these substances.
- The business should ensure that all employees are fully aware of what to do in the case of an emergency at the organisation. These procedures will cover emergency situations such as fire, flood, leaks of dangerous substances and security alerts.
- Personal presentation and dress code is one area where an organisation may enforce stringent rules. This means that

employees have to ensure that they dress for work and behave in an appropriate manner at work. This is important in order to make a good impression on customers and only fair on other employees. For those employees who regularly come into contact with customers, the business may make an allowance of money for their clothing or supply them with a uniform. This ensures that the employees are well presented and the customer forms a good impression of the business.

Planning for working

Businesses will want their employees to give them value for the money they are paying them and will do all they can to ensure that daily tasks are done in the shortest possible time. In order to help their employees, the business will have a number of policies in place to reduce the amount of time spent on different tasks.

It is in the employees' interests, as well as the interests of the business, that efficient and effective office systems are used. It is worth remembering, however, that all offices have their own work loads and demands and no one office is the same as another. However, all offices would want to ensure that:

- Employees know how work is planned and by whom.
- Employees know how work is organised and scheduled.
- Each employee knows how his or her own work area is organised.
- Each employee knows where other employees are situated within the business.
- Employees know how machinery and equipment is taken care of, by whom and why.
- Employees know about the Government laws regarding health and safety.

Being organised is very important for everyone who has a job, whatever it involves. These organisational skills, as they are known, can include any of the following:

- Being neat and tidy in your own desk area.
- Keeping a diary up to date, particularly if the job involves several meetings. This could be a normal desk diary or it could be an electronic one. Some offices also use wall planners, wall charts and planner boards to keep their employees informed on forthcoming meetings or key dates.
- Storing materials and paperwork in an efficient way to ensure that they can always be found when needed. This also applies to the way in which files are stored on a computer system.

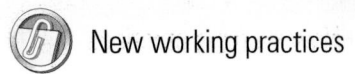
● Managing time efficiently and being aware of the need to make the best use of the time spent at work and not wasting too much time.

Team working

Communication between departments and individuals within an organisation is vital if a business is to succeed. Employees working in an organisation rarely work alone and more often than not teams are created to carry out certain tasks. A team is a group of individuals working together towards a single common objective. When working as a member of a team, people need to know which members of the team have the power and authority. In other words, who is actually in charge of the efforts of the team? It is common to find a supervisor fulfilling this role. Businesses have recognised the advantages of building teams and many pay for their employees to attend training programmes to encourage a particular way of working.

Teams communicate in several different ways and members of a team require many different communication skills. This is discussed in some detail in Chapter 4 of this book, but basically, to be a successful team member, the following skills are required:

● The ability to communicate.
● An understanding of the objective of the task.
● The ability to carry out a variety of tasks within the team.
● The ability to co-operate and work well with others to finish the tasks set.

Teams are encouraged within the organisation for the following reasons:

● Teams give employees a sense of belonging.
● Individual employees can help one another by sharing goals and objectives.
● Individual employees can share common interests and ideas.
● Teams often get noticed by management, whereas individuals can often go unnoticed.

NEW WORKING PRACTICES

Although, traditionally, work meant going off to the office or factory every day, in more recent years this has changed. Nowadays many people consider work to be quite different from this traditional view and businesses have had to adapt in order to attract new employees and keep their existing ones. The working environment has changed in the following ways.

Hot desking

In hot desking (which is also sometimes called 'location independent working', 'virtual office' or 'hotelling') the employees do not have their own desks but are given work space to use according to the needs of the task that they are working on. They keep their own belongings in a filing cabinet or locker, but share office furniture and equipment with other employees. This system of working is most commonly used by businesses whose employees spend a lot of time out of the office, possibly visiting their customers or working from home. By not giving them a permanent desk space or telephone the business can reduce **costs** and use the space they would have taken up.

KEY TERMS

Costs A business's financial commitments arising out of its operations

Working from home and teleworking

There is a definite shift in working practices taking place in some organisations and this needs to be considered carefully. It is likely that as time goes by the nature of work and the relationship between home and work will change dramatically. Generations of workers have been used to leaving home in the morning to do a day's work, returning home in the evening leaving work firmly behind them. This is changing and many people work from home at least some of the time. This is particularly true of those people that work with computers. The ability to use email and the internet has provided the opportunity for information to be sent at the touch of a button all over the world. Individuals can keep in touch with people at the office and with their customers and suppliers. Mobile telephones mean that people can communicate when they are anywhere – on the train, walking the dog, even when they are in the bath.

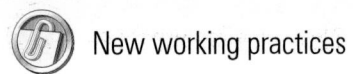

There are distinct advantages to working from home as opposed to attending a workplace every day, including:

- Travelling time for the employee is reduced or eliminated and this saves money and time and reduces the effect on the environment.
- There may be less distraction and fewer demands on the employee.
- There is time to concentrate on specific projects or reports.
- The employee has less need for formal work-style clothes.
- Work can be combined with other aspects of life such as family commitments.

However, talk to anyone who does work from home and there are definitely disadvantages:

- It can be very lonely and the employee might find it difficult to become **motivated**.
- There are many distractions that allow the individual to put off starting to work.
- It is easy to lose touch with important events happening in the workplace.
- There is less of a distinction between home time and work time, so it is difficult to know when to work and when to 'be at home'.
- Other people, such as friends and relatives, will telephone or visit during work hours because you are at home.

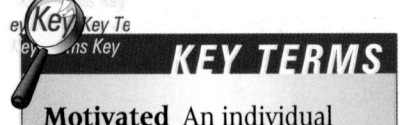

KEY TERMS

Motivated An individual who enjoys work and wishes to do a good job

Think about it!

When Steve was given the opportunity to work from home three days a week he was delighted. The pressure of travelling for two hours a day in rush-hour traffic and the constant interruptions once he arrived at the office had been getting him down. He had a demanding job as a design technician that required a lot of concentration and he needed time and peace to work. So working from home for part of the week would be ideal.

He set up his computer with the **CAD** software he needed as well as more basic office software for day-to-day administration; he had a small telephone system installed, and bought a fax machine and a small photocopying and scanning system. He was all set up.

For the first week or two Steve worked pretty well. He worked at home on Tuesday, Wednesday and Thursday and went into the office on Monday and Friday. He would begin at 9.30am and find himself still

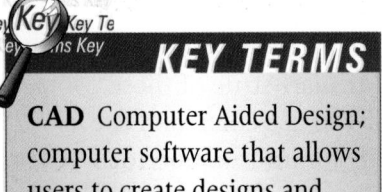

KEY TERMS

CAD Computer Aided Design; computer software that allows users to create designs and edit them

working at 7.00pm. However, after the third week he found he couldn't concentrate on the job he was working on. He found himself taking the dog for a walk, buying the newspaper, telephoning colleagues and friends. He was achieving less and less and becoming lazy about working.

He finally admitted to a colleague who had worked from home for years that he was not enjoying it at all. The colleague had some advice for him.

- Remember at work you have distractions that mean you are not constantly working on the same project. Take regular breaks, just like you would at work and do not feel guilty about it.
- Set yourself a realistic working day. Remember that you can do more at home than at work, so work for a shorter period of time, say three hours in the morning, take an hour for lunch and do another two hours work in the afternoon.
- Set yourself deadlines and targets, make sure they are realistic and achievable, and when you have met them give yourself a reward – read the paper or have a cup of coffee.

1 Explain why you believe Steve had the kind of job that meant he could work from home.

2 Why do you think Steve became less productive after a few weeks?

3 Why do you think Steve's productivity might increase by following the advice he has been given?

Action Points

1 All students have to do some work from home. Think about the advice Steve has been given. In a similar way write down at least three targets that you might give yourself to make sure you are more productive in getting your homework done on time.

2 Do you have a special space where you work at home? If so, produce a diagram to describe how the space works for you. If not, design your ideal workspace at home.

Job sharing

Job sharing allows two employees to divide the working week between them according to the share that they have agreed. Normally this means simply halving the working hours so that one employee works the mornings and the other works the afternoons, although it can be more complicated than that.

Obviously this method of working allows the employees involved to have time at home, perhaps to care for children or an invalid relative. However, there are also some advantages for the business, including:

- They have two employees for the **wage** bill of only one. They also have the energy of two part-time members of staff instead of one tired full-time employee.
- They know that if one of the employees is off sick, at least half of the job will continue to be done during that time.
- Each employee can cover holidays, sickness or when there is a high workload.

However, there are also some disadvantages to this method of working:

- One of the employees might have to work harder than the other because the work load is heavier at different times of the day.
- The two employees may work in slightly different ways or one of the employees might be more efficient and organised than the other.
- The business has a **legal** responsibility for two employees rather than just one.

Shift working

Shift working, or the working of non-standard hours, is often used by businesses that manufacture (make) their products. The **production** process often has to be manned for 24 hours a day as it would not be efficient to switch off the machinery at night. This method of working is also used by the emergency services (police, fire brigade and the ambulance service) as it would not be appropriate for them to operate only from 9am to 5pm.

In order to make sure these employees are available at all times of the day and night they are often paid additional money for working during the night. In some cases employees would work for a number of days and then, after a short break, they would work for a number of nights.

KEY TERMS

Wage An amount of money paid to the employee by the business on a regular basis in exchange for the carrying out of their duties

KEY TERMS

Legal Laws passed by Acts of Parliament

KEY TERMS

Production The department within a manufacturing organisation that is responsible for the making of the product

Action Points

1 Do you know anyone who works shifts? If so, contact them and talk about what the advantages and disadvantages are.

2 Take notes during your conversation and produce your findings in the form of a table on your computer. Head the first column 'Advantages' and the second 'Disadvantages'.

3 Print a copy of your work for your tutor.

Flexible working

Flexible working, also known as 'flexi-time', allows individual employees to arrange their working week to suit themselves and the business. There will usually be a 'core time' during which they will have to be present at work (usually between 10am and 4pm), but the employee can choose to make up the rest of the hours that they have to work when it is most convenient.

Some businesses prefer their employees to work on this basis because they may close at certain times of the week. In that case, employees would work longer hours (say from Monday to Thursday) but have all day Friday off because the business is closed.

Multi-skilling and re-skilling

Multi-skilling is where businesses train their employees to be able to carry out a wide range of different tasks. This means that employees are able to cover for absent colleagues more easily and that problems (such as machinery or equipment breakdowns) can be handled without having to call in specialists. Employees have a wider knowledge of the business and how each job role fits into the overall scheme of the business's activities. Multi-skilling can motivate individuals more as they have a wider variety of jobs and more responsibilities.

Over the years re-skilling has come to mean training employees to do new jobs after their old ways of working have disappeared. In the past employees used to use typewriters and many were employed to copy documents. These jobs have all but disappeared with the development of computers and photocopiers. Therefore, employees had to be re-skilled in order to use these new pieces of equipment. Re-skilling continues as machinery is introduced to do boring and repetitive work that is currently carried out by hand. Individuals are re-skilled to use new equipment as it becomes available to the business. Often less employees are needed as new pieces of technology are brought in.

Core and peripheral workers

Core workers are the essential employees in a business. They are the individuals who carry out all of the most important tasks in the business and are full-time, permanent members of staff. Without these people the business could not hope to function.

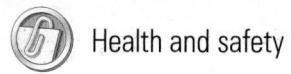

The core workers are supported by numbers of peripheral or freelance workers. These individuals are brought into the organisation, often on a temporary basis, to carry out basic work, particularly when the business is busy. As these peripheral workers tend not to be full time or permanent, they can be used flexibly and are only employed when required. Peripheral workers are typically seasonal staff, who may work during the summer months when core workers are taking their holidays or when the business is busy. Alternatively, they are taken on during the Christmas period, which is often the case in shops.

HEALTH AND SAFETY

However the working environment is organised it needs to be safe for the employees and for the customers who will be involved in the activities that take place there. There are rules and regulations that the business must follow in order to ensure that the environment is safe.

These rules are laid out clearly in the Health and Safety at Work Act 1974. This Act has been updated and altered in various ways to reflect changes that have taken place over time. However, it is known as an 'enabling Act' and remains the main legislation to which all businesses have to adhere.

The main points that the Act deals with are listed below.

The Health and Safety at Work Act 1974

The requirements included in the Health and Safety at Work Act 1974 apply to all workplace environments, however large or small. The Act applies to anyone who is on the premises including employees, managers, customers and even **contractors** who are involved in maintenance or temporary work.

The Act states that:

1 All employers must ensure the health, safety and welfare at work of all their employees as far as 'is reasonably practicable'. Specifically it covers the following points:
   - all entry and exit routes must be safe;
   - there must be a safe working environment and adequate facilities for the welfare of staff (somewhere to make a drink, toilet facilities, a quiet area);
   - equipment must be safe and well maintained;
   - steps should be in place for the safe **transportation** and storage of all articles and substances;

KEY TERMS

Contractors Those individuals or businesses that are paid by the organisation to carry out a particular task or series of tasks although they do not work for the business on a permanent basis

Transportation The moving of a product from the business to the customer by means of a number of different modes of transport

- the provision of **protective clothing** (i.e. protective clothing should be provided where necessary);
- there should be clear information, instruction and training on health and safety with adequate supervision of issues to do with health and safety.

2 Where the business has five or more employees there should be a written statement on health and safety policy for the business. The statement should be written by the employer and continually updated to include any changes. This document must be circulated to all employees.

3 The business should permit a trade union to appoint safety representatives who must be allowed to investigate accidents or potential **hazards** and follow up employee **complaints**. Safety representatives should be given time off to carry out their duties.

All employees must:

- Take responsibility for their own health and safety.
- Take responsibility for the health and safety of others who may be affected by their activities or actions.
- Cooperate with their employer to meet health and safety requirements.

KEY TERMS

Protective clothing This might include:
- hard hats
- gloves
- goggles
- ear plugs
- body protection suits

Hazards Those potential risks that could cause injury

Complaints Those negative comments, often received from customers, about the service/product provided by a business

Action Points

1 All employers must have on display the main requirements of the Health and Safety at Work Act 1974. Somewhere in your school or college there will be a notice for all employees and students to read. Find out where this notice is situated. Does it give any indication as to what you should do if you spot a health and safety problem?

2 Take a clipboard around your school or college and list any potential hazards that you can spot. Write a letter to the Head Teacher or Principal outlining any issues you have spotted.

Before the Health and Safety at Work Act nearly 800 fatal accidents occurred each year in workplaces in Britain. This number had fallen to 257 in 1999. Although it is still far too many, this decrease is a result of the Health and Safety at Work Act and subsequent laws that make it illegal for the employer, the employee and anyone visiting a company to endanger the health and safety of individuals.

There are still far too many work-related accidents and injuries. The Royal Society for the Prevention of Accidents states that each year over 25 million working days are lost and 27,000 people have to give up work because of injury or illness. In 1999 the Health and Safety Commission stated that more than a million people were still being injured at work and 1.3 million people were affected by work-related ill health. The Commission also pointed out that although injuries are more likely to occur in industries such as construction and manufacturing, illnesses were being reported in many 'new jobs' that take place in an office environment such as telesales and computing.

Action Points

1 Visit the website of the Health and Safety Executive at www.hse.gov.uk and find the most up-to-date figures for accidents at work.

2 Put your findings into a table and a graph, alongside the ones stated above, using a spreadsheet package on your computer.

The cost to a business of poor health and safety can be enormous and is not really worth it. Here are some of the problems:

- People may have to take time off with full pay if they have been involved in an accident at work.
- People who are off work with an injury may need to be replaced by more expensive temporary staff.
- There may be a claim for **compensation**. This means that the injured person may request money from the employer.
- The business owners and managers may be taken to court.
- The reputation of the business may be damaged.
- Staff who consider they are not safe at work are unlikely to be motivated and therefore may not work as hard.

Working in administration can be just as hazardous as working in a more physical environment. The computer is an invaluable asset to an efficient working office, but spending too much time huddled over the keyboard can affect both the back and the joints. This can have a long-term effect on the health of the computer operative. Looking at the screen for long periods of time can also cause eye problems.

KEY TERMS

Compensation A sum of money paid to a person who has been damaged or injured by the lack of care of another individual or business

Action Points

Here is some advice taken from an article called 'Health and Safety in the Home Office' from a magazine called *Home Office* (issue 49).

Playing it safe

If you are going to spend several hours typing on a keyboard you should consider taking steps to prevent long-term injuries or aches and pains ... In 1795 a health and safety report warned of the health risks of reading books, listing arthritis, asthma and gout among the dangers. Thankfully these possibilities have all been dismissed and it is tempting to ignore concerns about computer safety in the same way.

However, injuries to the arms, shoulders and back, particularly from repetitive strain injury, are common and the dangers of over exposure to a monitor screen are well documented. You have probably felt a few aches and pains after spending a couple of hours sitting at your desk and these don't go away quickly.

If you feel your back tensing up go for a walk, if your eyes start to feel slightly heavy or glazed, take a break and sit in the garden or somewhere away from the TV or monitor. If you are busy or in a rush to get something finished then you may not think that you can spare the time, but the long term benefits will usually outweigh any short term loss.

1 Produce a poster or a leaflet to reflect the advice given in this article.

2 Use some graphics to illustrate your leaflet.

The Workplace (Health, Safety and Welfare) Regulations 1992

These regulations complement the Health and Safety at Work Act 1974 and provide more details for employees. They are important for those who are responsible for the working environment and all employees should know what is contained within the regulations. The main parts of the regulations are listed below.

Key points relating to the Workplace (Health, Safety and Welfare) Regulations 1992

The main requirements of these regulations are as follows.

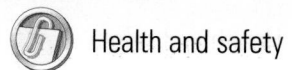

- Work environment:
  - effective ventilation;
  - reasonable temperature;
  - adequate and emergency lighting;
  - sufficient space;
  - suitable workstations;
  - protection from adverse weather conditions for workstations outside a building.

- Safety:
  - traffic routes so that pedestrians and vehicles can circulate in a safe manner;
  - properly constructed and maintained floors;
  - safe windows and skylights;
  - safely constructed doors, gates and escalators;
  - safeguards to prevent people or objects falling from a height.

- Facilities:
  - sufficient toilets and washing facilities;
  - an adequate supply of drinking water;
  - adequate seating;
  - suitable accommodation for clothing;
  - rest areas, including provision for pregnant women or nursing mothers;
  - provision for non-smokers in rest areas;
  - adequate facilities for people who eat at work.

- Housekeeping:
  - proper maintenance of all workplaces, equipment and facilities;
  - cleanliness of workplaces.

There are several other regulations that apply to those working in an office setting and these are listed below.

The Control of Substances Hazardous to Health 1999 (COSHH)

All hazardous substances must be stored in a safe environment and those who use them must wear protective clothing. This would apply to toxic cleaning material used to clean computers and other equipment. An employee using such a substance should wear rubber gloves.

Provision and Use of Work Equipment Regulations 1998 (PUWER)

Employers must ensure that all equipment (such as photocopiers and fax machines) is well maintained and appropriate training and instructions are provided for users.

Manual Handling Operations Regulations 1992

These relate to lifting and handling items. It is suggested that wherever possible an **automated** or **mechanised** process should be used, but employees who have to move items should be trained properly in order to minimise injury. These regulations would apply where an employee might be expected to move heavy boxes of paper or computer equipment.

Display Screen Equipment Regulations 1992

There are also special regulations in place for those using display screen equipment and VDUs (visual display units). A lot of work is done using computers with VDUs so it is important to make sure that anyone using this kind of equipment understands the regulations that are in place. There are many people who are now suffering from what is known as RSI or repetitive strain injury. This can be very painful and cause long-term damage to joints and bones. There is also a danger of serious damage to the eyes if the user does not take regular breaks or works with too much glare. Posture is also an important consideration. The correct furniture at the right height needs to be used and a chair that is specially designed for use with a VDU screen should be provided.

KEY TERMS

Automated The use of machinery to replace human labour, often in order to reduce costs

Mechanised Driven by machinery

Action Points

1 Consider the Display Screen Equipment Regulations below.

2 Carry out a survey of the type of equipment and where it is positioned in your computer room at school or college. Does the room itself and the equipment used meet with the Regulations?

3 Write a letter to the IT coordinator or tutor explaining any problems you might have found. If you cannot find anything wrong write your letter praising the department for its **compliance** with the Regulations.

KEY TERMS

Compliance Fulfilling the requirements of the law

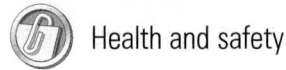

Key aspects of the Display Screen Equipment Regulations 1992

All employers must:

- Ensure that all workstations, related furniture, computer software and the working environment of VDU users meet the minimum requirements of the Regulations.
- Ensure that all users have regular breaks or changes in activity – it is illegal to work continuously at a computer all day.
- Offer eye examinations, on request, to employees who use a VDU for more than one hour a day and provide special spectacles if the tests show that these are needed.
- Provide users with relevant health and safety training.

All equipment must conform to the following standards:

- Display screens must have clear characters of adequate size, a stable image, adjustable brightness and contrast, and be able to tilt and swivel easily. There must be no reflective glare.
- Keyboards must be separate from the screen and it must be possible to tilt them. There should be space in front of the keyboard to provide 'rest' space. The surface should be matt, the keyboard easy to use and the symbols clear on the keys.
- Work surfaces must be large enough for the work being done and must have a low-reflective finish. The equipment must be flexible so that it can be arranged to suit the needs of the user.
- Work chairs must be stable and allow easy movement and a comfortable position. The user must be able to adjust the height of the seat and the seat back – which must provide good back support. A footrest must be provided if requested.
- Working environments for VDU users should provide satisfactory lighting to minimise glare. Windows should have blinds or workstations should be positioned to avoid reflections. Noise and heat levels should be comfortable. Radiation levels must be negligible and humidity should be controlled so that it is constantly at a satisfactory level.
- Software and systems must be appropriate for the task, user friendly and appropriate to the level of knowledge of the user.

Other regulations

There are also regulations to control the use of electricity and regarding the maintenance of electrical systems. Employers must ensure that noise hazards are reduced to a minimum and they should provide ear protectors to employees where necessary. Employers are also obliged by law to provide protective clothing where the environment may endanger the employee.

Who enforces the law?

It is all well and good having rules and regulations, but if there is no one to enforce them then an employer may well choose to ignore them. After all, it is expensive to make sure that all of the right equipment and furniture is in place. Health and safety is monitored and enforced by the Health and Safety Executive (HSE). The HSE has a team of inspectors that operate in every **local authority** in the country. There is an **advisory** service provided by the HSE; this service provides guidance to employers and other people responsible for implementing health and safety legislation. It issues approved codes of practices (called AcoPs) which give advice on how companies can comply with the law.

The Health and Safety Inspector has the power to visit any working environment without warning in order to inspect the premises, or investigate a complaint, or to find out the facts about an accident. If the Inspector has reason to believe that the working practices are unsatisfactory he or she will issue an improvement notice. This explains what is wrong and gives the business a stated amount of time to put things right. If, however, the Inspector fears that the working conditions might endanger the employees who are working there, he or she can issue a **prohibition** notice. If the business is given a prohibition notice the employer must stop operations immediately. If the issues are serious and they are not put right the owners of the business can be fined or imprisoned.

KEY TERMS

Local authority A body charged with the administration of a particular area of the country

Advisory An independent opinion offering advice

KEY TERMS

Prohibition Absolutely not allwed to be used

Action Points

1 Find a copy of the Health and Safety Executive's *An easy guide to the regulations* and *Health and Safety (Display Screen Equipment) Regulations 1992* in the library.

2 Make sure you are familiar with the regulations contained in these booklets. Think about your own health and safety at school or at work if you have a part-time job.

3 Visit the HSE website www.open.gov.uk/hsehome.htm. Find out exactly what services the HSE offers.

4 Download the booklet *Working with VDUs*. This gives some useful information that may be helpful to you.

5 Go to the Risk Education home page of the HSE site and find out how the HSE is helping students studying National Curriculum subjects to minimise health and safety risks at school and college.

Action Points Between 1996 and 2001:

- 54 young people (below the age of 18) were killed in the workplace.

- There were 12,599 serious injuries involving broken limbs, amputations and serious burns.

- There were 46,495 injuries leading to at least three days off work.

- 4 million people each year were hurt at work.

- Injuries and deaths costs the UK £16 billion each year.

- Young people (aged 16–24) faced the highest risk.

- New workers had the highest risk of injury.

Conduct a survey of the health and safety risks at school or college and produce a fact-sheet for other students explaining how to avoid being injured or killed by following the rules and regulations laid down by the different legislation.

Summary

The world is a dangerous place and if we thought too hard about it we would probably never step outside the house. Thinking about it, the inside of our own homes can be just as dangerous as the world outside. We all take risks – we travel by car, by air, sea and rail; we play sport, we visit buildings that have potential hazards at every turn. We are all aware that there is a risk, but we assess that the risk is very small and on that basis we are prepared to take a chance.

In a way that is what a business owner has to do when he or she makes decisions on behalf of employees in his or her employment. It is important that those responsible for others at work minimise the risk of accident or injury. However, the work still has to be done and in some cases there will be danger attached to that work. Employers have a duty to carry out risk assessment by checking that risks are either eliminated or controlled as much as possible. Employees also have a responsibility to inform their employer if a new hazard is identified or if it is thought that the degree of risk has changed in some way.

The office can be perceived as a relatively safe place to work; however, more than 5,000 serious injuries occur in offices every year and many more are never reported. There are a variety of potential hazards in an office and these include:

- Various materials and substances such as cleaning fluid and toner.
- The various machines and equipment being used.
- Electrical plugs and sockets.
- The potential for unsafe working practices.
- The potentially unsafe behaviour of individuals.
- Accidental breakages and spillage.
- Environmental factors such as poor air quality or extreme heat or cold.

Most businesses have specific policies to deal with potential risks. The law requires that a business must have a safety policy, and that policy should include:

- The arrangements made to cover training and instruction.
- The organisation's rules regarding safe working.
- Emergency arrangements or procedures in place for employees to follow.
- The organisation's system or procedure for reporting accidents.
- Details of where the most common risks have been experienced.

Businesses should also have a code of practice that states the procedures that all employees must follow in the event of an emergency, such as a fire, or if an accident occurs. The code of practice should also state who has been appointed as a qualified first-aid employee, where the medical room is and how to contact a doctor or send for an ambulance. Employees should also be aware of how the business's accident report must be completed.

Action Points

Barry and Jo had been working for Clear Crystal Glassware Company for a few months helping the business to update a database of customers by putting the information onto a computer and checking the details of each customer over the telephone. The room they had been given was small but cosy and both Barry and Jo had agreed that it would be fine. It was a little dark, but they could manage. They were given a desk and a chair each, although the desks were very small and the chairs were not very comfortable. In fact, the chairs were borrowed from the canteen; they were kitchen chairs. The Manager, Mr Fowler, had explained that this arrangement was temporary and new desks and chairs were on order. The work was fairly tedious and boring, but both Barry and Jo recognised how much time it would save once the database was updated and computerised successfully. Time passed and no new furniture was forthcoming. Mr Fowler was a little concerned when Jo was off work with severe back pain. He was worried that the database project would not be completed on schedule. His worry turned to panic when Barry complained of having bad headaches and also took time off.

1 Explain what was wrong with Barry and Jo's working environment.

2 How are Barry and Jo protected by the law?

3 If either Barry or Jo were permanently damaged by the badly designed work space, what could they do about it?

4 Write a memo to Mr Fowler explaining to him how he can improve the working environment for Barry and Jo. Explain to him how this present situation needs to be improved and that in the longer term it would be cost-effective for him to do something about it.

DATA PREPARATION, STORAGE AND RETRIEVAL

It has been mentioned above that an organised work area enables the employee to find information quickly and efficiently. This is important when considering the filing of paperwork or documents. But it is as important that information stored on a computer system is organised correctly so that vital details can be found quickly and used by the managers of the business straight away. Many businesses will have a computerised system for handling such information, known as data. They would have chosen a specific data-handling system because it had a number of different facilities that were useful to their own particular range of activities. However, the use of computerised systems has its own set of advantages and disadvantages.

The business will have chosen their system for the preparation, storage and retrieval of data for a number of different reasons. They will then train the employees who will be using this equipment and software in order that they are aware of the following significant issues:

● The importance of accuracy and checking – given the fact that any computerised system is only as accurate as the data it receives, there is always the possibility that the information is inaccurate as a result of human error. Obviously, more sophisticated data-handling systems will have a series of checks and double checks in order to identify potential errors. Accuracy is of paramount importance if the organisation is to rely upon the system, especially given that many decisions will be made on the basis of the information that it handles.

- The importance of cost – most organisations will use data-handling systems in order to cut costs. Bearing in mind that there will be significant costs related to the initial buying and setting up of the system, there needs to be a point at which the data-handling system gives good value for money as far as the organisation is concerned. This can be measured in terms of either the time that can be saved in using the system or the reduction in the number of employees. At other times, cost-cutting benefits could also include the fact that sales are not lost, products are always in stock, or employees are paid the correct amount of salary. The more time that can be saved by not having to repeat tasks or sort out problems, the more money will be saved.

- The importance of speed and accessibility – in most cases, the use of data-handling systems means that information can be processed much faster than it could using a **manual** system. Provided they can rely on the system, employees are free to concentrate on other areas of the business's activities, for example customer service issues or the development of a new product or service. Many organisations have to operate within very strict deadlines, particularly in the banking industry where many millions of financial transactions have to be processed on the same day.

KEY TERMS

Manual A task not carried out by equipment or machinery, but by the skills of the worker

SECURITY OF DATA

When we considered the different types of office layout we mentioned the fact that cellular offices are often more secure than open plan offices. Security can be one of the biggest considerations for an organisation. This does not mean just installing burglar alarms or having lockable filing cabinets. A business should consider all or some of the following issues, depending on the type of business activity they are involved in.

Personal security and security of vital information

All employees want to keep their personal property safe from theft or misuse by another individual. Businesses feel the same way about their own property and about that of their employees.

Technological advances over recent years have made it much easier for individuals and organisations to make their premises more secure. At home, we use a variety of different security systems to ensure that we are safe. Organisations also use these security systems on their buildings or warehouses to ensure that unwanted visitors are detected at the earliest stage possible so that assistance can be sought. Very often their security-control systems are connected directly to the emergency services so that the police, for example, are notified instantly of any security threat or situation.

However, there are regular, day-to-day checks that employees and owners of a business could take to ensure that their organisation's data is safe and secure, including:

- Locking rooms when they are not being used.
- The secure storage of disks containing data that could be useful to another person or business.
- The ultraviolet (UV) marking of keyboards and monitors so that they can be identified should they be found by the police after having been stolen.

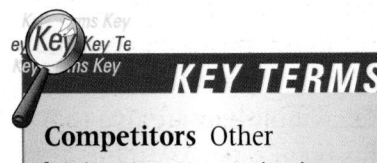

KEY TERMS

Competitors Other businesses or organisations offering similar products or services

All organisations have to be security conscious as all of the information they hold, whether on computer or manually, is useful to their **competitors**. A sensible organisation will have a series of security checks in operation in order to make sure that no important information is lost from its computer files. Although it would seem safe to assume that the cost of losing its computer equipment would be of prime importance to an organisation, it is often the case that it is more costly and time consuming if the data is lost, mainly because this may be irreplaceable or at least extremely difficult to replace.

The loss of data could occur in the following circumstances:

KEY TERMS

Corruption of data The act of making data useless, or the loss of data

- A fire at the premises of the organisation.
- The theft or **corruption of data** by employees or intruders.
- Accidental damage to data by employees who overwrite or delete files.

Organisations need to be particularly vigilant to ensure that no individual gains unauthorised access to either their premises or their computer systems. They must ensure that systems are in operation which restrict access to their data because:

- Confidential material held on a computer system could be very useful to competitors or any person or organisation wishing to cause the business damage.

• The Data Protection Act 1984 (see below) requires the organisation to keep the information that they hold regarding their employees, customers and suppliers in a secure manner.

Obviously, any information which an organisation or an individual holds on a computer system should be backed up onto a CD or floppy disk. The main advantage of this is that an exact copy of the data is made, and the organisation will often store this in fireproof cabinets or in an alternative building so there is less likelihood of damage as the result of fire.

Organisations will protect their confidential data by limiting access to authorised personnel only and by ensuring that wrongful access is highlighted immediately. One way of limiting access to such information is by the use of passwords. This means that each individual will have a unique password which he or she has to key into the computer before access is allowed. Obviously, all passwords will have to be kept confidential, in the same way that **PIN numbers** for bank or building society accounts are secret. Such passwords will allow the user only certain levels of access to the data. More senior members of staff will probably have full access to any high-security data, whereas those in a more junior position will only be allowed into the less confidential and more routine material. It is also important that those users who are allowed access to the confidential material do not have the option to make any changes to the data contained in the files: some files should be 'read only' (i.e. they should be locked so that they can be read but not changed). An organisation will also need to be able to identify all those personnel who have accessed the files during the course of a given period of time. This is known as an **audit trail** of users.

Another way of restricting access to information is by means of encryption. This means that an individual can gain access to the information only via a user name and password. **Encryption** should prevent unauthorised individuals gaining access to sensitive or confidential information. Businesses with websites, particularly those designed to allow customers to make purchases online, will have a secure encrypted area so that unauthorised individuals cannot discover customers' credit card details, addresses or other private information.

KEY TERMS

PIN – Personal Identity Numbers A unique number used by one person only to access information and money

Audit trail A means of tracking a series of events or transactions

Encryption A password or code only available to those authorised to have access to sensitive information

Viruses, hackers and firewalls

One of the most common threats to a business's computer system is a computer virus. This is a small program that can copy itself to other computers. Viruses can spread quickly from one system to the next and may range from harmless messages to viruses that will erase all data. In order to avoid viruses it is essential to purchase virus protection software. This software will routinely scan all incoming emails and check them for viruses. Another source of viruses is programs downloaded from the internet. Files attached to emails which may include the letters .exe, .com or .vbs should be avoided as they will start a program and may contain a virus.

A hacker is a computer programmer who enjoys exploring computer systems. Hackers consider the security on business computer systems to be a challenge and will use any means to break into those systems. In some cases hackers only wish to prove that they can break into a system, whilst others search for secret information or wish to erase the data on a business's computer system.

A firewall is a program or a piece of hardware which checks information coming through an internet connection. If the information does not pass routine checks then it will not be allowed through to the computer. Firewalls filter and analyse data which may damage a business's computer systems. They also prevents hackers from gaining access to data stored on a computer system.

The Data Protection Act 1984 and the Computer Misuse Act 1990

These two pieces of Government legislation were introduced to protect those individuals whose information is stored on computer systems. They also protect businesses and individuals who are using computer systems to store information because they give strict guidelines for them to follow. The main aspects of these two laws are given below.

The Data Protection Act 1998

The law requires that data relating to individuals is protected: this cannot be ignored.

The Data Protection Act 1998 reinforces legal rights, established under the Data Protection Act 1984, for individuals concerning the use of data held about them. The Data Protection Act 1998 also extends the limits of coverage to include data held in relevant, manual filing systems.

The Act also requires that data users (data controllers) register their activities, and honour eight principles of good practice. These data protection principles are as follows:

- Data shall be obtained and processed fairly and lawfully.
- Data shall only be held for specified, lawful, registered purposes.
- Data held shall be adequate, relevant and not excessive in relation to the purposes for which it is processed.
- Data shall be accurate and, where necessary, up to date.
- Data shall not be kept for longer than is necessary.
- Data shall be processed in accordance with the rights of data subjects, i.e. an individual (data subject) is entitled to be informed by the data controller as to whether data is held about them, and to have access to such data with the right to have the data corrected or erased.
- Data should be secure against unauthorised access, alteration, disclosure and destruction (including accidental loss or destruction).
- Personal data shall not be transferred to a country or territory outside the European Economic Area unless certain data protection rights exist in that country or territory.

The Computer Misuse Act 1990

Under Section 1 of the Computer Misuse Act 1990 a person is guilty of an offence if:

- He or she causes a computer to perform any function with intent to secure access to any program or data held in any computer.
- The access he or she intends to secure is unauthorised.
- He or she knows at the time when he or she causes the computer to perform the function that this is the case.

The intent a person has to have to commit an offence under this Section need not be directed at:

- Any particular program or data.
- A program or data of any particular kind.
- A program or data in any particular computer.

The Act defines that a person found guilty of this offence shall be liable on conviction to a maximum prison sentence of six months or a maximum fine of £2,000, or both.

It is an offence to gain unauthorised access to a computer system. This includes causing a computer to perform a function with intent to secure access to any program or data, knowing that the access is unauthorised. Note that this is an offence regardless of whether the motives for access were well meaning or malicious. Access to any program or data held in a computer system is a wide definition and includes altering/erasing the program or data, copying it, moving it, using it and having it output from the computer in which it is held. Examples of such offences could include unauthorised use of another person's username and password, persistently trying to guess a username and password, and laying a trap to obtain a password or password file.

Section 3 of the Computer Misuse Act 1990 states that it is an offence to cause unauthorised modification of computer material. The Act defines that a person found guilty of this offence shall be liable on conviction to a maximum prison sentence of five years or an unlimited fine, or both. Examples of offences under this Section would be deleting another user's files, modifying system files, introducing viruses, or deliberately generating information to cause a complete system malfunction.

Action Points

1 Consider, from a personal point of view, the Data Protection Act and try to assess the range and amount of information about you which may be stored by different organisations.

2 Who could have personal information about you?

3 What kind of information do they have?

4 Write a list of any considerations you can think of, and then compare your list with those of the remainder of your group. How much do they vary?

EFFECTIVE USE OF RESOURCES

If a business is to survive and thrive, it needs to ensure that it is making the best use of those resources available to it. As well as ensuring that the business's data is secure, that employees are working in an appropriate and efficient work environment, and that all Government legislation is being complied with, a business also has to think about its effectiveness from a resource point of view.

This final part of the chapter looks at how a business ensures it is using its resources effectively. The specific resources considered here are human beings, or, in other words, the employees of the business.

Human resources

The effective use of human resources begins with a business needing to know what tasks have to be undertaken in order to effectively run its operations. Against each of the tasks a series of duties need to be identified. These can form the basis of a **job description**. The business then needs to work out the kind of person it requires to carry out these tasks. What experience would a person need? What skills? What qualifications? Above all, will there be sufficient work for the individual to be busy all day?

Businesses will try to staff their operations with the minimum number of employees necessary to carry out the work. An earlier chapter considered how businesses identify core workers who are at the heart of their operations and always available to carry out the basic, key tasks required. Should there be a need for additional workers, then part-time or temporary staff can be taken on. The last thing that a business wants to have is a large number of staff and insufficient work for them. The efficient use of staff, particularly in larger organisations, is the responsibility of the Personnel Department or Human Resource Department and, on a day-to-day basis, each functional manager who directs what the individuals do each day.

For most businesses the largest cost is the wages and salaries bill. It is not unusual for this to account for as much as 75 per cent of all expenditure. Therefore, it is essential that this expensive resource is used to its maximum potential.

Wastage and recycling

Increasingly, businesses are becoming aware of the cost of waste and they are being encouraged by the Government to cut down

KEY TERMS

Job description This explains what the job involves and is useful for matching the right person to that job

on this. Certain levels of waste are unavoidable, particularly in the case of businesses who deal with products which have a limited shelf life. Supermarkets, for example, do their utmost to ensure that they sell products before their sell-by date. It is sometimes impossible to do this and the food is wasted.

In other types of business, waste is generated from all parts of the operations. Paper is wasted when printers fail or photocopiers jam, energy is wasted by employees leaving their computers turned on overnight or by lights left on in rooms which are not occupied. Manufacturers will often waste raw materials or components, not to mention those which are damaged or broken whilst they are being made.

Businesses are constantly reminded of the costs of this waste and, in the last few years, many have begun to realise that this is an unnecessary expense. Governments and pressure groups also recognise that resources are being wasted. There is now pressure upon businesses to try to ensure that waste is reduced to a minimum and that, where possible, these vital resources are recycled. Paper can be reprocessed into new sheets; metal can be melted down and used again; but, above all, energy can be conserved by simple measures such as installing better insulation, turning off machines when they are not being used, and using renewable energy such as solar or wind power.

Eco-friendly hardware and consumables

There have been developments in hardware and consumable products that allow them to be used either with less energy or in ways that mean they can be recycled easily. Most computers will routinely shut down to standby mode if they are not being used. This reduces the energy (electricity) being used by the machine. Employees are encouraged to turn off printers and other machines if they are not being used, particularly overnight. Even printer cartridges and other consumable items can now be refilled or recycled. This helps not only the planet in terms of conserving natural resources, but it also assists the business in that it can purchase refills or recycled consumables at a lower cost than brand new ones.

Human resources and finance

THE HUMAN RESOURCE FUNCTION

People are vital to the success of any business, however large or small it may be. People at work need to have certain qualities so that the business can be efficient, effective and successful. As we have already mentioned, these qualities include:

- The right skills to be able to do the job.
- The right abilities to do the job.
- A commitment to work hard and do the job properly.
- The ability to work with other people.
- The ability to be able to finish the tasks they are asked to do.
- The ability to deal with customers successfully.

It is the job of the Human Resource (also known as Personnel) Department of the business to make sure that the right people are employed so that the organisation can work effectively. It is also their role to ensure that once employed those people are well looked after, receive effective training and are happy and safe in their jobs. In a small business the person who carries out

these functions may be the owner of the business or one of the few people employed there. In a larger business there will probably be a Human Resource Department or function. The role of the human resource function is as follows:

- Planning where there is a need for staff to be employed.
- The management and monitoring of employees to ensure they are working in the right place, at the right time and in the right way.
- The training and development of employees to make sure they are able to perform their duties to a satisfactory standard.
- Dealing with any **grievances** the employees might have or the management might have about the employees. It is inevitable that problems of this nature will arise between employers and employees and the business will have a set of procedures in place to deal with these.
- Dealing with any discipline problems with employees. The business will have a set **disciplinary procedure** to deal with any problems that arise in the business, and the employees will be aware of the steps the employers will take to sort out such difficulties.
- Ensuring employees are aware of the business's health and safety policy and that all aspects of the business's activities are carried out in line with Government laws.
- Carrying out staff **appraisal** interviews in order to assess the performance of individual employees in their jobs and to gain information from the employees about their opinions of the jobs they do.
- Dealing with the **dismissal** or **redundancy** of employees.
- Keeping accurate and up-to-date information on employees in line with the regulations in the Data Protection Act 1984.

KEY TERMS

Grievances Complaints which an employee may have against the employer or vice versa

Disciplinary procedure Action taken by an employer to punish an employee who has broken the rules or regulations of the business

Appraisal A method employers use to measure the effectiveness of an employee. This is carried out by comparing actual performance against agreed goals

Dismissal Being dismissed or sacked from a job because the rules or regulations of the business have not been kept

Redundancy When an employee's job role no longer exists he or she may be made redundant

 Think about it!

Find a definition of the words redundancy, grievance and appraisal. By talking to friends, family or someone you work with, find examples of what happens when a person is made redundant, has a grievance at work or is undergoing an appraisal at work.

Each of the above functions of the Human Resource Department is considered in more detail a little later in this chapter. However, in order to make sure that the human resource function can carry out its roles and responsibilities, there needs to be a set of clearly defined roles and responsibilities for all members of the department. They need:

- Someone who is in charge and who can lead other members of the team to success in the tasks they carry out.
- The right people in the team so that there is a good spread of sufficient skills and experience to enable them to carry out all the different tasks and activities required of them.
- The right resources and equipment so that those in the team are able to do their job properly.

The team of people who work in the Human Resource Department have to communicate effectively with each other as well as with other departments in the business. They also have to deal with some complicated and often confidential information. A successful and effective Human Resource Department will:

- Hold regular meetings to decide what needs to be done.
- Decide, at the meetings, how the objectives of the team will be met.
- Decide, at the meetings, who will carry out the different tasks needed to meet the objectives of the team.
- Decide, at the meetings, the deadlines involved in the team meeting their objectives.

KEY TERMS

Feedback The passing on or receiving of comments and information

There will then be regular **feedback** meetings where each member of the team will report on their progress in completing the tasks and activities that were agreed.

The Human Resource Department exists to make sure that the right staff are employed, that the right number of people are employed and that they have the skills and abilities to do a good job in a safe and secure environment. It is therefore essential that people who work in the human resource section of a business:

- Discuss with all other sections of the business their needs regarding the number of employees that they require and the different skills each of those employees should have.
- Make sure all employees are trained to do the job expected of them. This is not just for the sake of the business, but also for the employees, who will feel much more confident if they have been effectively trained for a particular job.
- Make sure that everyone is safe and secure in the workplace. This applies just as much to visitors to the business as to those employed within the business.

- Make sure that the employees are aware of the business's procedures for dealing with problems. Such problems could include a grievance or disciplinary matter, but could also involve procedures for coping with an emergency situation.
- Make sure everyone has a chance to develop and grow within their job. This is important if employees are to continue to give the business value for the money it is paying them. A happy employee is one who feels that their job is going to develop and not stay in the same place for years to come. The opportunity for **promotion** within the job and the possibility of a pay increase are often important factors.
- Make sure that employees have the opportunity to make their wishes known to the employers through an appraisal interview. These interviews give both the employer and the employee the opportunity to discuss freely their views about where the job is going and to voice any problems they have noticed in the past year.

KEY TERMS

Promotion When an employee is awarded a more senior role in a business

INTERNAL AND EXTERNAL RECRUITMENT

Human Resource Department managers often have to look outside the business to find the right staff to fill vacancies, and they have to decide where to look to find the most suitable employees. If they advertise a job inside the business this is known as 'internal recruitment', but if they advertise outside the business this is known as 'external recruitment'. Once they have received applications from individuals who want to join the business, they go through what is called a 'selection process'.

They also have to keep up to date with the latest qualifications and training programmes. It is their responsibility to be aware of any changes in the law that affect the business, and they will need to be well informed about the availability of new employees.

How does the human resource team know when there is a vacancy? There are various ways for this information to be passed to the human resource function:

- A meeting might be set up between the manager of the department requiring the new employee and the Human Resource Manager to discuss all the details (formal communication).
- A **memo** (**memorandum**) or note might be sent to the Human Resource Manager from the manager of the department requiring the new employee (formal communication).

KEY TERMS

Memo (memorandum) A standard way of passing on written information within an organisation

- The manager of the department requiring the new employee might simply telephone his or her request to the human resource section (informal communication).
- The manager might meet a person from the human resource team in the corridor and explain his or her requirements (informal communication).

It is essential that the message sent is accurate and all the details are correct. It is much more likely that this will happen if the information is passed on by means of a formal communication rather than an informal one.

Action Points

1 Make sure you know the difference between a letter and a memo. Find out how to lay out a memo correctly.

2 You work as a manager in the production department of a large bakery. You have identified that there is a need for a bakery assistant to work on a new product line. You are going to send a memo to the human resources function with your request. You need to communicate the following information:
- The person you want needs to have experience.
- You will pay £5.00 an hour.
- You will send more details about the job later and want the opportunity to discuss the job itself in more detail with the Human Resource Manager.
- This is a new post.

Design a memo sheet and compose a memo communicating the information above. You will need to explain how soon you would like the appointment to be made.

Internal recruitment

In order to obtain the right employee for the new job, the Human Resource Department will go through their recruitment and selection processes. It might be that the right individual already works for the business and just needs to be informed that the new job is available. In order to ensure that anyone who is interested in the new job is informed at the right time, the Human Resource Department might use a written form of communication. It is as important that the full details are given to an internal applicant as it is that they are given to an external one. To ensure that the full details are given and that all employees have the opportunity of seeing the job advertised at the same time, the Human Resource Manager will instruct one of his team to place an advertisement for the job on the business's notice board.

There are advantages and disadvantages in internal recruitment, both for the business and for the employee. The advantages are:

- The employee already knows a great deal about the business.
- It cheaper to advertise internally than externally.

But the disadvantages are:

- Someone new to a business often brings good ideas that an internal employee might not have.
- Someone new to a business often works harder than an internal employee does.
- The internal recruitment of an employee leaves his or her job to be filled.
- Picking one of several internal employees leaves others thinking they are not highly regarded in the business.

External recruitment

There are a number of stages that need to be followed in recruiting a new employee.

- Deciding that there is a need to find a new member of staff.
- Designing a **job description** (see below) that explains what the job is all about.
- Designing a **person specification** (see below) that explains what sort of person is needed.
- Deciding where to advertise the job.
- Designing the advertisement for the job.
- Looking at all the different **applications** for the job.
- Deciding on a **shortlist** of those who have applied.
- Interviewing those on the shortlist.

KEY TERMS

Job description A detailed statement prepared by the Human Resource Department, which identifies the nature of a job, including tasks and responsibilities

Person specification Also known as a job specification, which identifies the characteristics that an individual would need in order to carry out a particular job

Application A written request by a potential employee for an advertised vacancy

Shortlist Part of the job selection process when the top five or six potential candidates for a job are selected and asked to attend an interview

- Taking up **references** for the successful **candidate**.
- Writing to inform the successful applicant and then the unsuccessful applicants.

Who decides there is a need for a new member of staff?

- The manager may recognise a need to bring someone new into the department.
- Someone may leave and it is necessary to replace them.
- A new order may require more staff to help get the product to the customer.

Whatever the reason, it is essential that the department where the vacancy has arisen tells the right people so that the wheels can be put in motion to find someone suitable as soon as possible.

There may be other things to consider when deciding to recruit new members of staff. The manager may have to ask the following questions:

- Can we afford a new member of staff?
- Is there enough space for this person?
- Do we need new equipment for this person to use?

It may be necessary for the manager to consult the Finance or Accounts Department to check that there is enough money to pay for the new recruit and to pay for any additional equipment they may need.

Job descriptions

A job description explains what the job entails and is useful in matching the right person to the job. A job description will include the following items:

- The job title. In other words, the title of Manager or Supervisor would be included if the job entailed being responsible for and having authority over other employees.
- Where the new employee will fit in within the business. In other words, their position within the structure of the organisation.
- It states the tasks and activities that the person doing the job will need to carry out.
- It explains the roles and responsibilities that are required of the person doing the job.

The amount of detail included will depend on the type of job that is being described. There will probably be more details for a job with management responsibility than for a job for a junior person with few responsibilities. A typical job description will include the following:

- Job title
- Department/function/section
- Wage/salary range
- Main purpose of the job
- Duties and responsibilities
- Responsible to
- Responsible for.

Sometimes there is also a catch-all statement such as: 'Such additional and/or alternative duties as may be assigned by your functional manager or head of department'.

Action Points

1 Have a look in your local newspaper and choose an advertisement for a job that you think you would like to do in the future.

2 From the advertisement see if you can write a brief job description for the job involved. Choose an advertisement that has a lot of detail, although you might be able to think of some hidden duties that are not included in the newspaper.

Action Points

1 Choose one of the following occupations or choose another occupation you are familiar with:
- Supermarket checkout assistant
- Garage attendant
- Assistant to a chef
- Waitress in a restaurant
- Office administrator
- Dental nurse.

2 Find out as much as you can about the job so that you can reproduce the job description template above (i.e. job title, department, etc.) and fill in the job description of the person of your choice. You may find it useful to talk to family and friends who are involved or have been involved in this type of job to ask them some questions about their duties and responsibilities.

Person specifications

A person specification is a description of the qualities the person should have in order to be able to do the job satisfactorily. A person specification is the business's checklist of the ideal person for the job and will include a description of:

- The previous experience the person should have.
- The skills the person should have. For example, a nurse working with sick children would need to demonstrate that he or she is patient and has caring skills.
- The physical characteristics the person needs to have. This refers to things like height, weight, hearing, eyesight, etc., which could affect the person's ability to do the job. So if the job requires that the person can lift heavy objects, then the physical characteristics associated with strength and good health might be important.
- The qualifications the person needs to have. For example, a computer expert would need the qualifications to prove he or she could do the job.
- The personality and temperament the person needs to have. This is important if the job involves working closely with other employees or with customers, or if the job involves the new employee leading a group or members of a team.
- The level of motivation needed for the job. This means that the new employee might have to be capable of working alone and not being supervised by a manager. If so, the business will want to know that the individual will take pride in the work he or she is doing and give the business value for the money it is paying the employee. Where the job requires that someone works many hours doing something repetitive, it is unlikely that the business will be looking for someone with ambitions to be the Managing Director.

Action Points

1 Choose one of the following occupations or choose another occupation you are familiar with:
- Supermarket checkout assistant
- Garage attendant
- Assistant to a chef
- Waitress in a restaurant
- Office administrator
- Dental nurse.

2 Think carefully about the role you have chosen and draw up your own person specification to describe the qualities you think a person doing the job should be able to display.

3 Produce a person specification using a word-processing package.

It is important that the department or functional area that wishes to appoint a new member of staff should have a say in the drawing up of a person specification and a job description. However, it may be that they do not have the same expertise as a member of the Human Resource Department who will know exactly what should be included. The best way to design an effective job description and person specification is for the human resources expert to work closely with the person who is looking for a new recruit.

Advertising the vacancy for the best response

When the decision has been made to go ahead and advertise for a new member of staff, someone in human resources will have to decide where to place the advertisement. There are many different ways of advertising vacancies externally:

- The local newspaper – this method is used to attract local people and is often used for less senior and lower paid jobs.
- A national newspaper – this method of advertising a job vacancy can attract many readers from all over the country who are looking for a job. Applicants who apply will probably be expecting a higher wage or salary than the one they are receiving at the present time, but will have to be prepared to move to the job, which may be in a different part of the country from their present home.
- The Job Centre or Careers Service – there is no charge to place an advertisement in a Job Centre. The unemployed and unskilled, low-paid workers go to these places to look for work. It is unlikely that a business will advertise a highly paid or management position here.
- Recruitment consultants or agencies – there is no charge to the person looking for a new job when they register with a recruitment consultant. The recruitment consultant or agency is informed of the vacancy by the business and they try to match that vacancy with the jobseekers that register with them. There are general recruitment consultants and more specialised ones. Some specialise in management positions whilst others are more general in their service. The most specialist forms of recruitment consultants are known as head hunters – these organisations go in search of very talented people who are employed, and they try to tempt them to go to work for someone else, often offering them large increases in pay to do so.

- The internet – this has become a more common and popular form of advertising job vacancies. All the national newspapers and trade magazines have now designed sections for their websites where applicants can look for work.
- Trade magazines – most of the different industries have their own trade magazine and these are used to advertise specific vacancies in their particular industry. Teachers can look for jobs in the *Times Educational Supplement*, accountants have a magazine called *Accountancy Age*, and those people who work in marketing and advertising have a magazine called *Campaign*.

The best place to advertise will depend on the kind of job. If the job is fairly junior and not very technical, and the pay is not high, then the business will want to look locally. They will want to attract someone who lives near the business in order to keep travelling time and costs to a minimum.

If the business is looking for someone specialised, it is likely that they will want to encourage people to apply from further away and will use a national newspaper, trade magazine or a specialist recruitment agency to help them find the right person.

Action Points

1 Find examples of advertisements for jobs in as many different places as you can. You will probably find a national newspaper in your school library; you should have easy access to a local newspaper; go to a newsagent and obtain a trade magazine on sale there; ask at school if there are any vacancies being advertised just in the school.

2 Visit the internet and look at the kind of advertising for jobs that is taking place there.

3 Visit the Job Centre and a local recruitment consultant and look at how these organisations advertise their vacancies.

4 When you have completed your investigation you will have a number of different advertisements to compare. Make a copy of the Table below using a word-processing software package to compare the different advertisements. Complete the Table giving examples to answer the questions.

The advertising medium	Is the advert for general or specialised jobs?	Does the advert include a business logo?	Is the advert attractive and appealing to the applicant?	Does the advert give enough information to the applicant?
The notice board				
The local paper				
A national paper				
Job Centre				
Recruitment Consultants				
The internet				
Trade magazines				

Action Points

You are now going to produce your own advertisement for the local newspaper. You have been asked to send a copy of the advertisement in a layout that the newspaper can follow. You will need to think carefully about how to make the advertisement as interesting and attractive as possible. It is expensive to advertise for staff and you want to get it right.

1 Your advertisement should be produced using a word-processing package or a publishing package.

2 You will need to choose a suitable job vacancy; use an example from your investigations or an example of a job you are familiar with.

3 You will need to include a suitable company logo. You might like to design a logo or you may have one to scan into the advertisement.

4 Concentrate on the layout of your advertisement. Think about the language you will use. What information do you want to include and what information will you leave out and give at the interview?

Senior Salesperson
PRESTO

Established company seeks an enthusiastic Senior salesperson to take on and grow the existing customer base.

You will have at least 5 years experience and a proven track record in sales.

You will be in charge of a small team of salespeople and will report directly to the Managing Director.

To apply, send your CV with expected salary to:

Presto Products, HR Department, Presto House, Preston, PR2 2RP.

Veterinary Nurse

Busy Vet's practice specialising in small animals requires a qualified Veterinary Nurse to assist in the surgery.

You will be required to work with all types of small animals, and the public, as part of your job will be to advise owners on how to look after their animals after an operatively. This is an exciting opportunity to join one of this area's top Vets. There is a competetive salary and benefits.

Please apply in writing, with your CV to:

Paws Veterinary Surgery, Dog Lane, Kennelworth KN1 2DC

Office Junior

Administration department of a national company seeks an office Junior.

The post would suit a school leaver or those wishing to return to full time employment.

Please apply in writing to the following address, enclosing your CV and marking your envelope for the attention of Ms B Brent.

METHODS OF SELECTION

There are three main ways that an applicant might be asked to apply for the job that has been advertised. The business advertising the job might:

- Ask for a **CV**.
- Ask for a letter of application.
- Ask the applicant to complete an application form.

Curriculum vitae (CV)

It is a good idea for everyone who wishes to find employment to have their own curriculum vitae. This is a document that provides information about you the individual, and is a history of yourself. It should include personal information such as name and address, date of birth, qualifications, work experience and other information such as your hobbies and interests away from work or school. The main headings should be:

- Name.
- Address.
- Date of birth.
- Marital status (single, married, divorced) and number of children (if appropriate).
- Education and qualifications.
- Employment and work experience.
- Hobbies and interests.
- A statement about your good personal qualities or particular achievements.
- Referees who might be approached to verify that what you say is true. These could include the present employer or school/college. Family members should not be used and permission should always be asked before using someone as a referee.

The advantage of using a CV is that the applicant can include information that the business does not ask for in an application form, and the CV can be prepared in advance so it can be sent quickly in response to an advertisement. It is, however, produced by the individual applying for the job and may not include information of great interest to the business. Therefore, it is often not the best way of finding out if the candidate is suitable.

 **Action Points** **W**rite your own CV using a word-processing package. Think carefully about how you can make your CV interesting to an employer, but try to keep it to two sides of A4 paper.

Application forms

A business may prefer to ask the candidate to complete an application form.

The application form is designed by the business and is given to all the candidates that apply for the job being advertised. This means that the business can compare the qualities and experience of each of the candidates and make a decision about who they wish to interview.

The information contained in the application form will often be similar to that which the candidate would include in a CV, but the order and amount of detail might be different. The application form might require specific information, for example, 'Give reasons why you want this job'. This kind of information would not be included in a CV, which would be much more general.

There is usually a large space available somewhere on the application form for the applicant to state in their own words what they think their strengths and qualities are and how these will help them succeed in the job. This needs careful thought; it is often the only place on the form where the applicant can sell themselves to the business as being suitable for the job.

Action Points

1 Use the local newspaper to find a suitable vacancy and request an application form from the business. Complete the application form following these rules:
   - Look after the form carefully, keep it clean and free from creases.
   - Read the form thoroughly and photocopy it. Practise filling in the photocopy before you complete the real application form.
   - Have all the relevant information available, such as dates, addresses, etc.
   - Always use a black pen and write in capitals where you are asked to do so. Your handwriting can say a lot about you!
   - Think carefully about any personal statement you are asked to write. Write it out in rough first and ask someone to check what you have written.
   - If there are sections on the form that do not apply to you, write 'N/A' (for not applicable), do not just leave a blank space.

- Check your work carefully and when you are sure it is completed sign and date the form in the appropriate place.
- Make sure you address the envelope to the correct person. This is often stated in the advertisement.

Remember, first impressions count. Would you want to interview someone who:

- Missed out vital information.
- Had untidy handwriting that was difficult to read.
- Submitted a form that was messy or crumpled.
- Included a personal statement that was incomplete or poorly written.

2 Now obtain some copies of different application forms. You may find examples in the office at your school, or you could ask the local council, your bank or a large local employer for the form they use. In groups discuss how the different forms are laid out and what information each one requires from a candidate.

3 You are now going to design an application form of your own. Using a word-processing or desktop publishing package design your form using the best qualities you have identified from the different forms you have looked at as a group.

The letter of application

Sometimes the advertisement for a job will simply ask for a letter of application. At other times the business will require a letter of application to be written and sent with a CV or a completed application form. Sometimes an advertisement will ask specifically that the letter of application be completed in the candidate's own handwriting. Handwriting can reveal a lot about a person and can be useful to the business in identifying individuals that they wish to go to the next stage of the selection process. Unless the advertisement specifically asks for the letter of application to be handwritten, it is often easier to use a word processor so that a neat and well-organised letter can be produced.

The letter of application should include:

- An opening paragraph that states where you saw the advertisement, what appeals to you about the job and why you are applying for it.

- What qualities and experience you have that make you suitable for the job.
- A closing paragraph that assures the business you are serious and lets them know that you are happy to attend for an interview should they require you to do so.

A letter of application should use a blocked style like the one shown below.

John Fielding
12 The Old Smithy
Stafford
ST12 5TH

Mr G J Balantine   24 May 2002
Parsons Electrical Limited
Clarkson Avenue
Stafford
ST1 2RF

Dear Mr Balantine

I would like to apply for the post of trainee electrician as advertised in the Stafford Evening Chronicle of 23 May 2002.

I am 16 years old and at present I am a pupil at Stafford High School. I am taking six GCSEs and three GNVQ qualifications. I am expected to achieve grade C or above in each of the subjects. I will be leaving school at the end of June and am looking for a suitable training opportunity so that I can continue my education and work at the same time.

I have always wanted to work as an electrician and have proved myself reliable during my time at school. For my design technology coursework I am looking at the use of electricity in the home. Because of my interest in your type of work, I feel I would be a suitable candidate for the post advertised.

I enclose a copy of my curriculum vitae and I am available for interview at your convenience.

Yours sincerely

John Fielding

Enc

 **Action Points**

1 Find an advertisement in your local newspaper that would be suitable for you to apply for when you leave school.

2 Produce a letter of application to send to the organisation that has placed the advertisement.

3 Produce two copies of the letter, one handwritten and one word processed, and discuss with members of your class which is the best method of production and why.

 Think about it!

Find out what is meant by graphology and why it can play a part in the selection process.

Sifting through the applications – who stands out?

The business of finding the right person for a particular job is time consuming and costly. It is therefore important that whoever is finally selected is right for the job, will stay for a reasonable length of time, and has the skills to complete the tasks and activities that are required of him or her. The human resources team will have produced a job description and a person specification that fully describes the person they are looking for.

The human resource team will try to match the skills, qualities and attributes of the different applicants to the requirements of the job. This process is likely to take place during a meeting between a member of the human resources team and the manager of the department where the new employee will be working. Below is a Table that they might use to decide who to interview for a job where a new employee is required to work as part of a team producing specialist engine parts:

	Relevant skill and experience of engine valves	Experience of teamwork	Ability to work to tight deadlines	Ability to demonstrate accuracy and attention to detail
Candidate 1				
Candidate 2				
Candidate 3				
Candidate 4				
Candidate 5				

It will be fairly straightforward to establish which applicants have previous experience of engine valves. The business will know other companies that produce similar products and the applicant may have worked at one of these organisations. However, it is much more difficult to find out if the applicants have the ability to work as part of a team, can work to tight deadlines and pay attention to detail. These qualities are as important as knowledge of the work itself. It is possible for the business to train the candidate to produce engine valves, but it may not be so easy to make him or her into a good team member or to ensure speed and accuracy of work. Sometimes it is possible to recognise these qualities in the candidate at the interview stage of the recruitment and selection process.

An example of how the selection process might identify a good team member could be to check if the candidate plays any sport, such as netball, hockey or football. The candidate may have helped organise a function or a charity event, they may be a member of a school or youth quiz team or belong to a society of some kind. By considering the qualifications that candidates have gained, it may also be possible for the business to identify those who are able to work to tight deadlines. Consideration of coursework results or the completion of project work and good attendance records will give the business an indication of the reliability of the candidate. It will also be interesting for the business during this selection process to consider how quickly the application arrived at the organisation after the advertisement was placed.

The application form, letter of application and CV will help the business to identify how much attention a candidate pays to detail by considering the following:

- How neat and accurate is the information submitted?
- How carefully has the candidate completed the necessary paperwork?

The qualifications that the candidate has gained can also indicate how employable a person is likely to be. A candidate who has worked systematically and used information carefully is likely to achieve higher grades.

The selection process will take a great many different factors into account. It will be necessary for those involved to communicate with different people to find out relevant information. The process of selection will require the Human Resource Department to speak to:

- The department that is to employ the new member of staff.
- The selected candidates to invite them for interview.
- The referees listed on each of the candidates' CVs.

Once the candidates are selected for interview it will be necessary to write to them to ask them to attend on a specific day and at a particular time. The people who are to be involved in the interview will have to be informed, and the referees may also have been contacted before the interview itself, although often these individuals are not contacted until after the candidate has been interviewed.

Action Points

You work in the Human Resources Department of Peabody and Crabtree, a department store. You have been asked to invite two candidates for interview for the job of Administrator in the Accounts Department of the store. Their names and addresses are:

- John Mablethorpe, 26 High Street, High Town, Topshire;
- Denise Powers, The Creek, Low Town, Deepshire.

1 Write a business letter inviting each candidate to attend for an interview on 24 April. The first should attend at 2pm and the second at 3pm. The interviewers have requested that the candidates bring with them any qualification certificates and their records of achievement.

2 Greg Dodds, from the Accounts Department, is going to interview the candidates, so confirm the names, date and times of the interviews with him by memo.

3 You will need to send another memo to the Managing Director's secretary because you would like to use the boardroom for the interviews and this has to be booked into her diary.

INTERVIEWS

The interview is all about face-to-face communication. It is likely that whatever the job there will be some form of interview. For management and senior positions the interview will probably be held on a formal basis, where the candidate (interviewee) may well be interviewed by a number of people who make up a panel (interviewers). Senior teachers and the head teacher of your school will have undergone this kind of interview. Each member of the panel should have prepared carefully before the interview so that they have a clear idea as to the questions to be asked and the kind of response expected. The questions should be the same

for each person being interviewed. This kind of interview can be stressful for the person being interviewed (and often for the interviewers).

The interview has two basic purposes:

● To help the business choose the right employee.
● To help the employee choose the right business.

It is important for the business to structure the interview in such a way as to enable them to find out as much as possible about the candidate. Similarly, this will help the candidate find out as much as possible about the business.

For less senior positions, or in a smaller business, the interview might be informal in nature. It may be that one manager interviews the candidate and this kind of interviewing can be less intimidating for all concerned. However, unlike the formal interview when several opinions are available, in the informal interview there is only one opinion – from the person conducting the interview. It can be advantageous to a candidate to be interviewed by a panel because a one-to-one interview could result in the interviewer disliking the candidate or being more attracted to another candidate for some reason.

However the interview is conducted the issues remain the same. The interview is the best way for the business to find out who is the most suitable person for the job. In order to make sure the interview is conducted in such a way that the interviewer is able to choose the right person, there should be some preparation prior to the interview, for example:

> *What experience do you have working as part of a team?*

> *Where have you learnt how to use a forklift truck?*

> *How would you deal with a difficult customer?*

> *When can you start if you are offered the job?*

> *Why do you believe you have the experience and skills required for this role?*

- It is important to choose the questions carefully beforehand.
- There should be a suitable room available and the room should be set out to suit the kind of formal or informal interview that is taking place.
- All the relevant paperwork should be ready and available.
- A pen and paper should be available in order to take notes.

The most important part of the preparation is to think about the kind of questions to ask in order to reveal the qualities of the interviewee. It is also important to think carefully about how to ask the questions. If you ask a question that starts with 'Do you' or 'Can you', such as, 'Do you use a word processor in your present job?', the candidate can only answer yes or no. If you ask, 'Can you work well as part of a team,' the candidate once again may simply answer yes or no. It is much more informative if the interviewer asks questions that allow the candidate to answer fully with a sentence or two. Words such as:

- Where
- How
- When
- Why
- What

provide the basis for asking what are known as 'open questions'. The following questions would allow someone to give more detailed answers:

- What systems do you use for dealing with written correspondence in your present job?
- What examples can you give to show that you work well as part of a team?

The questions should also help the business to identify what qualities the candidate can offer them. A good interviewer will find out if a candidate is well organised by asking: 'What systems are you familiar with for organising paper work?', or if the candidate can work to tight deadlines by asking: 'How do you make sure you complete a task on time?'

Other questions that might be asked include:

- 'What examples can you give that you work well as part of a team?' The answer to this question will help the business to find out if the candidate works well with other people.
- 'How would you deal with a situation where you had to make a decision because the manager was not available?' This gives the business an idea of whether or not the candidate can think for themselves.

Finding out about the ways in which a candidate spends their leisure time will give the business an idea of whether or not they would fit in with the other employees. Towards the end of the interview there may be a question that seems trivial or does not relate to the job at all, but the interviewer may ask it to gain more of an insight into the personality and interests of the candidate. This kind of question can reveal a lot about a person, for example:

- What newspaper do you read?
- What book are you reading at the moment?
- What is the biggest mistake you have ever made?
- Where do you see yourself in five years time?
- If you had to choose one person, who do you admire the most?

It is usual to take up references from at least two people who have been named by the candidate before making the job offer. The referees should be known to the candidate and be able to give favourable comments about their good character, honesty and ability to do the job. Usually one referee will be personal (e.g. a family friend) and one will be professional (e.g. from work or school). The referee's permission should be given before their details are given to potential employers.

 Think about it!

Find out the meaning of the word 'testimonial'. When might this be a useful document to have in your possession?

Action Points

1 Use the following to apply for one of the jobs that you found advertised earlier:
   - The relevant person specification.
   - The job description you produced in previous activities.
   - The CV you produced earlier.

2 In groups of four plan an interview using the paperwork for the job. You will need to appoint two interviewers, an interviewee and someone to observe and take notes.

3 Produce a set of questions that you wish to ask the candidate, and when you carry out the interview it may be a good idea to video it so that you can see how well each member of the group performs.

4 Having done this, you might want to change roles within the group so that everyone has a turn at interviewing and being interviewed.

5 At the end of the exercise discuss how each member of the group performed in:
● Asking questions.
● Answering questions.
● Giving a good impression of himself or herself.
● Appearing as the most suitable candidate.

Shortlisting is one of the ways that a business will decide who they want to interview. It is also the way they will select, from those interviewed, who they want to see again. Interviewing is an expensive process for the business and they will try to avoid having to call too many candidates back for a second interview, preferring to select a suitable person from the first round of interviews.

Interview techniques

Being a good interviewer can be difficult. It is important that the interview is structured in such a way as to find out the most about the candidate and to give the candidate the opportunity to find out as much about the business as possible. It is good practice for interviewers to:

● Put the candidate at ease. The interview can be opened with some friendly questions about the interviewee's interests.
● Ask open questions which give the candidate the chance to give more than a simple 'yes' or 'no' answer.
● Take notes so that memory does not have to be relied upon after the interview.
● Give the candidate time to think, and then ask follow-on questions to help them give full answers.
● Give the candidate the opportunity to ask questions.
● Close the interview by thanking the candidate for attending and make sure they know when they are likely to hear from the business about the decision.

An interviewee also has to be well prepared. When a letter from the business arrives showing the date and time of the interview, a candidate for a job knows that he or she has got to the interview stage. This is good news for a job applicant and means it is time to begin preparations for the interview. An interviewee should:

● Prepare and plan for the interview – the first step is to reply to the business with a letter or telephone call accepting the interview date. The candidate could also read through all the

paperwork relating to the interview, such as their copy of the application form, to remind themselves about the job and the business.

- Find out as much as they can about the business, which may include:
  - the type of activities they carry out;
  - their range of products or services;
  - the type of customers they have;
  - how big they are;
  - who their competitors are.

This information could be found out from newspapers, libraries, websites or friends and family.

- Make sure they know who they have to ask for when they arrive at the business (this information will be given on the letter of invitation to attend interview).
- Prepare a set of questions that they want to ask at the interview.
- Work out the most reliable route to get to the business. It might be that the candidate needs to have a trial run to make sure they arrive on time on the day of the interview. It is appropriate to arrive for interview about 10 minutes before the time stated in the letter.

At the interview, the interviewee should:

- Show some confidence. This can be done by looking at the person who is asking the questions and trying to be positive when answering questions.
- Listen to questions – concentrate on what is being said and avoid being distracted. Be alert and ready to respond.
- Be clear and ask questions at the right time. Make sure your questions are easy to understand and that they are asked at the right time.
- Dress appropriately for an interview. Do not be tempted to wear clothes that are not suitable for interview just because they are comfortable. If you are unsure of how to dress, before the interview have a look at some of those working for the business and see what they consider to be a suitable 'dress code'.

A candidate might find out there and then if they have been chosen for the job or he or she may have to wait to receive a letter in the post. If told straight after the interview, one would still expect to have this confirmed in writing. So whether the news is good or bad, the facts need to be communicated formally, in writing. This task would probably fall to an administrator or clerk who is employed as a member of the human resource team. For the successful person who is to be offered the job, the letter needs to confirm the following details:

- Start date
- Wage or salary
- Hours of work
- The job title
- Who the new employee should report to on the first day of work.

The letter might be accompanied by a job description and it might explain that the offer of a job is subject to the business obtaining satisfactory references. The offer letter might look similar to the example below.

Davenport & Worfield
Chartered Accountants
The High Street
Weston WV12 5TG

R K Chesterton
12 Water Road
Pendle
WT3 2DF

12th October 2002

Dear Richard

Accounts Clerk Vacancy

Following your recent interview we are very pleased to confirm that we would like to offer you the position of Accounts Clerk within our firm.

We would like you to start on 1 November at a salary of £12,000 per annum payable monthly in arrears. This offer of employment is subject to our receiving satisfactory references.

Please confirm your acceptance to this offer in writing by 21 October.

Before you start we will send you a job description for your information and a contract of employment outlining your conditions of service. Please sign and return the contract to us as soon as you receive it.

We look forward to working with you.

Yours sincerely

G H Cavendish ACA

It is courtesy to inform others who attended the interview but who were unsuccessful. This is known as the 'rejection letter'. It is usually short and to the point and does not necessarily go into detail as to why each individual has not been chosen. The rejected candidate might ask for feedback as to why they have been unsuccessful, but it is unlikely that this information will be given in writing. If feedback is given to the unsuccessful candidate it should be based upon facts about the job and the candidate's unsuitability for the job. It should never be aimed at the candidate's personal qualities or performance generally. It is likely that there will be a standard rejection letter that is sent to all those who are unsuccessful in obtaining employment in a particular business. The main bulk of the letter will be saved as a template and it can be used time and time again with the relevant names and addresses attached in the appropriate places. Where there are a number of candidates to write to this will save time. The person who is responsible for sending the letters will only have to key in the names and addresses and any other relevant information; the body of the letter will not have to be keyed in each time. These letters could be sent out using a mini mail merge facility on standard word-processing software.

Action Points

1 Write a rejection letter and send it to three of your classmates who were unsuccessful in the recent interviews that your group carried out.

2 Set up a mail merge using your computer and input the details for each member of the group who will receive the letter.

3 Print a copy of the standard letter for your tutor.

KEY TERMS

Probationary period A length of time, usually for at least one month, when a new employee is there on a trial basis and both the employer and the employee can decide whether to make the situation permanent

Think about it!

Most businesses appoint people for a trial or **probationary period** before finally making them a permanent member of staff. Why is this is a good idea? What will the business be assessing during this trial period? Find out how long a trial period usually lasts.

CONTRACTS AND EMPLOYMENT

KEY TERMS

Expenses In this sense it means money paid by a potential employee during the process of selection for a job

All employees of a business are entitled by law to have a contract of employment. This is an agreement between the employee and the employer and it is expected that this will be issued to the new employee within 13 weeks of starting the job. Both the employer and the employee have certain rights and responsibilities and the contract of employment takes immediate effect as and when the individual starts work. A contract of employment will usually state the following responsibilities of the employer:

- To pay wages or a salary to the employee.
- To provide work for the employee.
- To pay back to the employee any **expenses** he or she has had to pay in order to carry out their work, for example travel costs. (There are normally strict rules about what will be paid back to the employee.)
- That the employer will give the employee a reference if they require it at a later date.
- That the employer will provide safe working conditions for the employee.
- That the employer will give the employee any information needed about their work, pay, conditions and opportunities within the business.
- That the employer will act in good faith towards the employee.

The employee's responsibilities will include:

- Acting in good faith towards the employer.
- Accounting for any cash received from other sources (this is to make sure that the employee does not accept any bribes or money from other organisations).
- Keeping the business's secrets confidential.
- Obeying any instructions and giving faithful service to the employer.

In addition, the contract of employment will contain the following information, depending on the type of organisation the new employee has joined:

- Details about the company itself.
- Details about the job and the conditions of service.
- Details about issues such as sickness, pensions and trade union membership.
- Details outlining the disciplinary and grievance procedures of the business.

The contract will state the rate of pay, the number of days holiday an employee can have, how much notice the employee will have to give if he or she decides to leave or if the company decides to end their employment. It will explain the procedure to be followed when the employee is ill or is disciplined. The contract of employment is signed by both the employee and employer and it is a legally binding document.

CONTRACT OF EMPLOYMENT

These terms and conditions will apply from 25th January 2005.

1. **Employer**

Robert and Mary England, a partnership trading as Ambrose Trading of Scotley House, Scotley Road, Exmouth ("the Employer")

2. **Employee**

You are Rosy Bowers of 22, High Street, Exmouth.

3. **Job Title**

You are employed as Administration Assistant [your job description is attached]. In addition to the normal duties associated with your post, you may be required to carry out additional tasks as requested from time to time.

4. **Period of Employment**

4.1. Your employment with the Employer begins 25th January 2005.

4.2. No previous employment will be treated as continuous with your employment by the Employer.

4.3. Your employment is for an indefinite period, terminable on notice or otherwise as set out in your job description.

5. **Remuneration**

5.1. Your current basic rate of pay is £15,000 per annum.

5.2. You will be paid in arrears every month, by transfer directly to your bank account on the last working day of each month.

5.3. Employees' rates of pay are subject to review from time to time by the Employer. You are not guaranteed an increase at such a review.

6. **Normal Working Hours**

6.1. Your normal days of work are Monday to Friday.

6.2. Your normal hours of work are 9.00 a.m. to 5.00 p.m.

6.3. You are entitled to one hour for lunch at a time agreed by the Employer, which will not be working time and will not be paid.

6.4. You are, in addition to the above, required to devote whatever additional hours are reasonably required for the proper performance of your duties.

SIGNED...*Mary England*..... (For and on behalf of the Employer)

I confirm that I have read and agree to be bound by the above terms and conditions and I agree to work a 48 hour week on average if necessary.

SIGNED......*Rosy Bowers*.......... DATED........*29/01/05*...........

Rosy Bowers

EMPLOYMENT RIGHTS AND RESPONSIBILITIES

The employer and the employee both have duties to each other. Many of these duties and obligations are enforced by Government law or legislation.

⚙️ Think about it!

Find out the main points outlined in the 1999 Employment Relations Act. This aimed to increase employees' rights.

Laws are made to protect the individual and the organisation. It is important that employees and employers understand the main terms of legislation that applies to the workplace.

Laws are made to protect against:

- Dangerous practices.
- Discrimination of any kind.
- Unfair working practices.

The Health and Safety at Work Act 1974 protects the employer and the employee by ensuring that the organisation and the individual take all realistic precautions against risks to health or safety. Extra regulations were introduced in 1996 to set out minimum standards which employers must maintain in the workplace and in the working environment.

The main provisions of the Health and Safety at Work Act 1974 are:

- Employees must be given all necessary safety equipment free of charge.
- Employers must provide a safe working environment.
- There is an obligation on employees to observe the rules relating to safety within the business.
- Where there are five or more employees there must be a written safety policy on display.
- The business must allow safety representatives to inspect the workplace and investigate the cause of any accidents that occur.

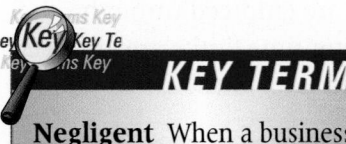

KEY TERMS

Negligent When a business or an individual has failed to do its duty and has caused another individual or business to suffer a loss as a result

It is expensive to make sure that all the regulations are adhered to. It is, however, much more expensive if someone is hurt and the business is found to be what is termed as **negligent**. There can be heavy fines and in extreme cases the business can be closed and the owners imprisoned.

Being safe at work can be comforting for employees and it is important for them to be aware that employers care enough to keep them safe and free from harm. Health and safety issues are controlled by the Health and Safety Executive (HSE), which was set up by the Government. Inspectors from the HSE can visit a firm without notice to check they are not breaking the law. The employer and the employee both have a duty to keep each other safe. The Health and Safety at Work Act (1974), the Workplace (Health, Safety and Welfare) Regulations 1992 and the Display Screen Directives of 1992 are the main pieces of legislation that cover these rights and responsibilities. We covered these laws in some detail in Chapter 2, and you might want to return to this to refresh your memory.

The following are the main examples of other Government laws that have been passed to try to make sure that both the business and the employee obtain their rights and carry out their responsibilities:

- Working Time Regulations 1998 – these came into force on 1 October 1998. The basic rights and protections that the regulations provide are:
  - a limit of an average of 48 hours a week which a worker can be required to work (though workers can choose to work more if they want);
  - a limit of an average of 8 hours in every 24 hours which night workers can be required to work;
  - a right for night workers to receive free health checks;
  - a right to 11 hours rest a day;
  - a right to a day off each week;
  - a right to an in-work rest break if the working day is longer than six hours;
  - a right to four weeks paid leave per year.

In addition there are extra rights for young (adolescent) workers. Rest periods, breaks and annual leave are enforced through Employment Tribunals, and the working time limits are enforced by the Health and Safety Executive and local authorities.

 Think about it!

Get further information about the Working Time Directive by visiting the website www.dti.gov.uk/er/work.

 **Action Points**

1 Find out some information about the rights of adolescent workers.

2 Put the information into a leaflet to give to a number of local employers so that they are well informed as to the rights and responsibilities that the business has to young employees.

3 Use your computer to develop an informative and illustrated leaflet or fact sheet.

Action Points

In most large businesses it is the human resource section that would keep track of all the different legislation within the business, making sure that the business is complying with the law.

1 Write a manual for use by those working in human resources so that they are well informed as to the key facts from all of the main pieces of legislation.

2 Use the information you have been given in this section and any other information you have found from various websites.

- Employment Rights Act 2002 – this Act amends the 1996 Employment Rights Act and the Equal Pay Act of 1970 and its main points are:
  - women are entitled to six months paid maternity leave (fathers get two weeks);
  - the encouragement of flexible working hours (the right to work flexi-hours);
  - more streamlined disciplinary and grievance procedures within a business;
  - introduction of equal pay questionnaires.
- Equal Pay Acts 1970 and 1983 – these Acts state that both sexes should be treated equally when it comes to employment. Both men and women should be paid the same if the job they do is the same.
- Equal opportunities, and the Sex **Discrimination** Act 1975 – the Equal Opportunities Commission was set up to enforce this legislation. The Act requires equality when selecting a new recruit, and covers issues relating to promotion, access to benefits, facilities or services within the business and matters to do with dismissal. The Act states that in all of these areas

KEY TERMS

Discrimination To act unfavourably towards different members of society on the grounds of colour, sex or disability

the employer must not favour a male or female purely based upon their gender.

- Race Relations Act 1976 – this law requires employers to show no discrimination against men or women on the grounds of sex, marital status, skin colour, race, nationality, or ethnic or national origins. This legislation applies when someone is being selected for employment and during the whole time the individual remains employed. The legislation is enforced by the Commission for Racial Equality.

- Disability Discrimination Act 1995 – this Act makes it unlawful to treat disabled people less favourably than anyone else. It also requires the business to make reasonable adjustments to the working environment and working conditions to help provide a suitable place of work for a disabled person. This can be very costly to a business. The rules only apply to businesses with more than five employees. There are many ways that a business can provide a practical working environment for a disabled employee. A ramp or a lift can allow a wheelchair-bound person access to work; a person who is hard of hearing can work using a computer; a blind person can use the telephone.

 **Action Points** **T**ake a clipboard around your school and list the ways you might improve the area in order to accommodate a person in a wheelchair.

EU legislation

As well as laws passed by the British Government, there are also several pieces of legislation that have been the result of discussions within the European Union. These laws have been passed in order to try to make the treatment of individuals who work in the different European countries more similar. In other words, they attempt to harmonise the rights and responsibilities of employers and employees throughout Europe. When the European Parliament agrees new laws these are known as Directives and each country in the European Union must follow these.

Action Points

Government statistics suggest that 3,800 non-fatal injuries occurred in offices between 1998 and 2002. Of these, 620 were major injuries causing serious, long-term problems for those involved. Over 3,000 were less serious but still led to the victim taking more than three days off work. These figures only take into account accidents that were reported. It is estimated that many more serious and less serious accidents happen that are not reported. The most common injuries resulted from items that fell from a height. There were four recorded fatalities (deaths) from this kind of accident. Other injuries and their main cause are given below.

Cause of injury	Major injury %	Less serious injury %
Slipping or tripping	49	26
Falling off a ladder, chair or racking	22	12
Struck by a moving or fixed object	9	12
Handling, lifting or carrying a heavy object	6	29

Source: HSE ©Crown copyright

1 Write a set of procedures that employees could follow to try to avoid these kinds of accidents happening at work.

2 Then write a memo to a manager suggesting the best way to communicate this information to all employees.

Disciplinary and grievance procedures

We have discussed the fact that laws have been passed to give the employees the right to a grievance and disciplinary procedure, and the fact that the job description might contain information about this process. We need to look at both of these in a little more detail and consider the responsibility of the employer as well as the rights of the employees.

It is inevitable that disputes will often arise between the employer and the employees. The procedures employed by organisations and the role of trade unions or external organisations can be crucial to the settlement of such disputes. An organisation known as the Advisory, Conciliation and Arbitration Service (ACAS) has approved a disciplinary procedure, the key points of which are:

- That the disciplinary procedure is written down;
- That all employees have access to the disciplinary procedure;
- That the employees are aware who operates the disciplinary procedure;
- That the employee is entitled to have a friend or colleague present at all disciplinary meetings;
- That the employee has the right to appeal against a disciplinary decision;
- That there will be no discrimination during the disciplinary process.

Usually the disciplinary procedure would be put into place when an individual employee demonstrates a lack of capability or shows poor performance in their job. The main stages in a disciplinary procedure are:

1 Verbal warning – if the employee's conduct, behaviour or performance does not reach an acceptable standard then they will be given their first formal verbal warning. This is the first stage of the procedure and provided they improve it will go no further.
2 Written warning – if the employee does not improve after the verbal warning they will receive a written warning. This is usually written by the employee's supervisor.
3 Final written warning – if the employee continues to fail to improve and the conduct or behaviour has been bad enough, then this warning will threaten dismissal or the employee will be suspended.

4 Dismissal – this is the final stage and to reach this point the employee must have failed all the other stages. The employee will receive a written statement which includes the reasons for dismissal and the date their employment ends. It will also tell them how they may appeal.

5 Appeal – if an employee chooses to appeal they must inform their employer within two working days.

Most large organisations have a grievance procedure in place to deal with problems arising with their employees. The ACAS *Employment Handbook* offers the following advice:

> Grievance procedures should aim to settle a grievance fairly, quickly and as closely as possible to the point of origin, and help to prevent minor disagreements developing into more serious disputes. For this reason, it is usually advisable for the first stage to be between the employee and his or her immediate supervisor or line manager. This can also help to maintain the authority of the supervisor and can often lead to the issue being resolved directly between the parties without the involvement of a representative.

It is not in the interests of either the business or the employee for grievances to carry on for very long. Many organisations have stated that:

- The first stage of the procedure must be completed in 24 hours.
- The second stage of the procedure must be completed within three days.

All organisations would obviously prefer to resolve their own internal disputes. However, in some cases this is not possible and an external organisation may have to be involved or invited in to help settle the issue.

Staff consultative committees and unions

These external organisations help to protect an individual employee and the workforce as a whole during times of dispute. They will assist employees by **negotiating** with employers on the following matters:

- Pay increases.
- Working conditions.
- Working hours.

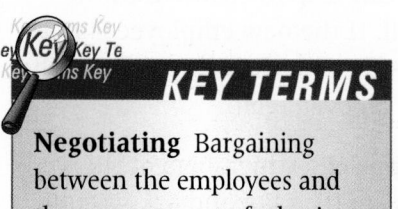

KEY TERMS

Negotiating Bargaining between the employees and the management of a business

- Solving disputes.
- Promoting the interests of the members.
- Protecting the position of the members.
- Bargaining with the employer.
- Bargaining with the Government.
- Seeking benefits for the employees (such as pensions, sick pay and injury pay).
- Monitoring health and safety at the business.
- Ensuring the business is providing a good level of employee welfare.

Think about it!

The term 'employee welfare' covers a number of different issues. Find a definition of the phrase and see how many issues you can think of as a group.

Visit the TUC (Trade Union Congress) website to see what help and advice is available to an employee in trouble.

TRAINING

A new job is exciting and nerve-racking at the same time. It is very important that the business makes the new employee feel welcome and provides the right environment for the employee to be able to perform the job role efficiently. It is equally important that the employee fits in and works hard to fulfil the expectations of the employer.

A good employer will make sure that the employee will have a planned and well-organised start to their working life. This is known as an **induction**. The employee is given a programme of events and activities that will help him or her to fit in and become well informed about the job he or she will be doing.

It costs a lot of money and takes a long time to find the right employees. The induction process can help to ensure that the new member of staff settles in well. If the new employee is not happy he or she may not want to stay with the company and the whole process would have to start all over again.

The induction process is often organised by members of the human resource team who will create the plan and ask various other people in the organisation to help. An induction programme should include the following aspects:

- Initial meeting at the beginning of the first day.
- A tour of the organisation.

KEY TERMS

Induction An introductory training programme for new employees to help them become familiar with the way in which the business operates

- An opportunity to review company documentation such as health and safety documents, departmental manuals or handbooks, the contract of employment and any other documents that are relevant to the job, including the disciplinary and grievance procedures.
- Introductions to the people that the new employee will be working with directly and those to whom they will report.
- Training with new technology or specific machinery that the employee will be using.
- Time to become familiar with the working environment and new colleagues.

The induction can last for just a day or it can be spread over a number of weeks. The length of time of the induction will depend on the nature of the job, its degree of difficulty and how important the role is seen to be within the organisation.

The initial induction should be followed up with some kind of review a few weeks into the job. The new recruit may feel well looked after and be the centre of attention during a planned induction; he or she may feel a bit isolated and insecure if the induction is the only support given. It is also important to make sure that there is some kind of ongoing training and development to ensure that the new recruit can do the job and is able to work with unfamiliar machines or procedures.

A person who feels that he or she is being well looked after and effectively trained will be more motivated and more productive and happy in their job. Good communication is essential to make sure this happens.

Action Points

You work in the Human Resource Department of a supermarket nearby. The supermarket has just recruited three new members of staff. They will work on the tills, stacking the shelves and helping in the delicatessen. It is your job to organise an induction programme for them. You have been asked to:

- Write a schedule for the induction day.
- Ask three people who are already employed at the supermarket to shadow (observe and support) the new recruits and show them around the organisation.
- Prepare a short presentation about health and safety issues.

1 You will need to include in your schedule the following information – arrive at 9.15am, short introduction to be given by the General Manager, tour of the buildings, talk about health and safety issues, opportunity to meet other members of the organisation, time to discuss training needs. The schedule should give precise times for each of the activities that need to take place. Use your imagination about times.

2 You will need to send a memo to inform those who are going to shadow the new recruits.

3 You will also need to send a memo to the General Manager to ask him or her to give a short talk at a stated time.

4 You should also write a letter to each of the new recruits with a copy of the schedule.

Tom's first day

Tom had received a letter telling him he had been successful at the interview. The job as a trainee warehouse manager was his. He was over the moon. He liked the idea of being trained to become a manager and he knew he would be happier working in a large warehouse than in an office environment. He was told in his letter of appointment that he should report to the company at 8.00am on 1 November.

He found it difficult to sleep as he was so excited and nervous and he was up very early on his first day. He made a special effort to look smart and set off in good time to make sure he was not late.

When he arrived he told the receptionist who he was. She looked puzzled and started telephoning different people to ask where she should send him. Tom sat down on the chair he was offered and waited. At 9.30am someone finally came to collect him. The man who came was flustered and abrupt. He said, 'You had better come with me, nobody told me you were coming today. We are really busy and I don't really have the time to deal with you. You will just have to muck in so that this big order goes out on time.'

Tom spent the rest of his first day driving a forklift truck loaded with pallets and then lifting large boxes onto a big truck that had to leave the warehouse before 3.30pm. His new suit was filthy by the time the job was done. He had never driven a forklift truck before, which was scary, and his back and arms hurt from lifting heavy boxes. He did not learn the name of any of the people he was working with. They were all too busy to even give him the time of day. At the end of the day when the panic was over, Tom asked what kind of training he would get in his new job. The others just laughed at him.

1 What is going wrong here?

2 Write an account of how Tom should have been treated on his first day in his new job.

An induction programme is the first introduction a new employee will have to any kind of training and development opportunities. There are very few jobs where some form of training is not essential, especially today when we live in a fast and changing world where new technology dominates. It is in the best interests of the business to make sure that all employees are well trained and able to perform to a high standard in their work. Non-trained or badly trained employees may make mistakes, become a danger to themselves and others, or cause customers to become dissatisfied.

Action Points

It is often said that training can be very motivating and employees work much harder if they believe that, due to the investment in their training and development, they are highly valued. Abraham Maslow carried out a great deal of research about the way people work and what motivates them.

1 Find out about Abraham Maslow's theory of motivation by researching in the library and on the internet.

2 Draw his well-known diagram 'The hierarchy of needs'.

3 Where would training fit into his theory?

The human resource section often has to make sure that the workforce is sufficiently trained to carry out the duties expected of them during their working day, or it may be the role of the manager in specific departments of the business to ensure the staff in his or her section are sufficiently trained. Whoever is responsible for organising training and development, it is important that the right training is given. There should be opportunities for employees to discuss their training needs and there should be chances for review and feedback to make sure the training was adequate, positive and the person involved in the training achieved what they set out to achieve.

This process of staff development is often started through a process known as appraisal. Appraisal is where the individual employee meets with their manager or a supervisor to discuss the employee's performance over a given period of time, usually a year. This form of communication is important. It is usually a formal meeting where both parties can be frank and honest about what each expects from the other.

Often both parties complete an appraisal form or written report that examines the employee's strengths and weaknesses and suggests where improvements can be made. The appraisal process helps to identify issues that might affect the working relationship between different people in a business. It will help to show where there are training and development needs and where there are other issues that might affect performance.

Where two people have a formal opportunity to communicate their needs and aspirations it is far less likely that there will be misunderstandings about performance. The individual will have a chance to ask for training and explain why it is necessary for them in order that they can do their job to the best of their ability.

Action Points **C**onsider your own performance as a pupil at school.

- What aspects of your school work do you think are most successful?
- What aspects of your performance could you improve upon?
- What kind of help would you like so that you can improve your skills?
- Do you have access to all of the tools and resources you need to be successful in your studies?
- Are you performing to the best of your abilities?

1 Write a frank answer to each of the questions listed above.

2 Ask a friend or a teacher to answer the same questions about you.

3 Compare your answers with their answers, then arrange a meeting between the two of you. Discuss in the meeting:
- How you might improve your performance in the future.
- What help you might need in order to improve.
- Who might be available to help you.
- What obstacles are preventing you from improving.
- What your strengths and weaknesses are.

4 Make a list of steps that you are going to take to improve in the future and state what help you will need to do this.

Think about it!

Find a solution to the following problems:

- Raj has been working for the same company for six years as a sales person. His sales figures were consistently high until this year. He seems to have lost his ability, even though he is selling an exciting new product to new customers.
- Candi keeps making mistakes using the new accounting software. She was sent for a day's training but it has not helped. She was so efficient on the old system.
- Don was told to produce a report as soon as possible to present to the Managing Director about the possibility of moving to larger premises. Don is now told that it is wanted for tomorrow's board meeting. Don knew it was urgent but he did not realise it was that urgent, since nobody told him.
- Barri has just handed in his notice; he is the fifth person to do so in the last few weeks. Barri says he is unhappy because he has been told off for not working quickly enough and for not using the new computer software to do his work. He has had no training at all and feels it is unfair that he is being blamed.

How might the appraisal process have helped to resolve some of these issues?

Whether through appraisal or other more informal methods, it is important that staff have access to training and development so that they can do the job successfully. There are all sorts of different kinds of training that can be used in various situations. Training can be divided into two distinct types:

- **On the job training** – where the training occurs at the place of work. Till training will most likely take place at the till where the person being trained is going to work. This is a good way to train a person in practical, hands-on activities. A good example of this kind of training is learning to drive; you are never going to learn to drive by reading a book or listening to someone explaining their experiences of driving a car.

Training that takes place at work can take many forms, including:

- shadowing another member of staff to learn from them. This method might be used where a new member of staff has several jobs to learn;

- mentoring, where another member of staff can be on hand to offer help and advice while a person is learning the job. This method might be used to reassure a new member of staff during their first weeks;

- coaching, where there is someone helping the employee to learn. This method might be used to teach a new recruit about software or a piece of equipment.

  Sometimes the business will use a system known as job rotation. The employee will spend a period of time doing a variety of different jobs. This allows the employee to learn many new skills. He or she can move from job to job within the business, hopefully avoiding boredom and ensuring that the workforce is multi-skilled.

- **Off the job training** – this is all about attending training courses away from the workplace or in a separate environment within the workplace. Management training, sales training, customer service or health and safety training might be taught off the job. Employees like the opportunity to have a day away from work developing their skills and meeting other people with similar jobs.

  There are thousands of different training courses available to businesses who wish to train their staff. Some businesses have their own training arm that offers specific training to members. Banks, insurance companies and many large multinational companies have their own training facilities. Businesses can win prestigious awards for demonstrating that their training is beneficial to employees and to the company. The Investors in People award allows a qualified business to display a Kitemark to say that they have been deemed an investor in people. There are also National Training Awards which are given for excellence in training.

The National Vocational Qualifications (NVQs) are very important in many businesses. These are qualifications that individuals can achieve by demonstrating that they are competent at certain tasks that are laid down in the specifications for the qualifications. There are five levels, from Level 1, which is a basic or foundation level, to Level 5, which is senior management level. Achieving an NVQ tells present and future employers that the individual has certain skills and attributes. There are other Government training schemes that help employees to develop the right skills for work, such as the Modern Apprenticeship Scheme, Youth Training and

Employment Training. These types of scheme help specific sectors of the community to find work and they help the employer to judge whether the employee has the relevant skills to do the job. Successive Governments change these schemes from time to time; they are given different names and different criteria. Whatever their name, they are an important tool in making sure that people have the skills for productive work.

Whatever method is used to ensure that the employee has the skills and knowledge to do the job, there needs to be a method by which it is recorded. It is also important that the training is assessed in order to make sure it is of value and that the employee has gained something from it.

The Human Resource Department or someone else in the business, possibly someone who is responsible for the training needs of the employees, needs to keep track of training for each individual in the business. In order to do this there should be a system which should include:

- A training needs analysis form.
- A record of training and development for each employee.
- An evaluation form that can be completed at the end of every training session.

Action Points

1 Explain why each of the different training record forms is important for:
   - The employee
   - The business
   - A future employer.

2 Look for training companies in a local trade directory in your area. Send a business letter to a selected training provider and ask for information about the kind of training they provide.

3 Investigate a job role that interests you.

4 Recreate the training needs analysis form on computer. Complete the form outlining the training you might need in order to be able to apply for the job of your choice.

TRAINING NEEDS ANALYSIS FORM

Department/Team	Area of Development	Proposed Activity	Success will be measured by	Cost	Person to take action

TRAINING RECORD

Monthly Learning Log

Name		Date		
Nature of Learning e.g. book, video, workshop seminar, etc	Cost to the Organisation	What benefits **to you** did you identify?	What benefits **to the organisation** did you identify?	Who else would benefit from the same learning activity?

Next month I will be undertaking the following learning:

EVALUATION FORM

Review Date

Activity No.	Activity	Costs To Date	Benefits To Date	Next Action	Reviewed By

TERMINATION OF EMPLOYMENT

As discussed earlier in this chapter, the Human Resource Department is responsible for the recruitment and selection of new employees, their induction, training and development. They will advertise the job, interview the candidates, ensure their induction was appropriate and then monitor their levels and method of training. This will all be done to ensure that the employee is motivated in their work and that the business receives value for the money they are paying the employee.

There is, however, another important function of the Human Resource Department which needs to be considered here. This Department is also responsible for dealing with employees who

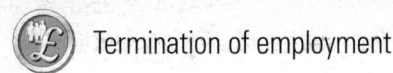

leave the business for one reason or another. The main reasons why an individual leaves an organisation are:

- Dismissal
- Redundancy
- Resignation
- Retirement.

We need look at each of these headings in some more detail.

Dismissal

Dismissal is the final stage of a disciplinary procedure that most large organisations have in place. Dismissal is the termination of the contract of employment between the employer and employee. There are a number of legal and **ethical** obligations that the employer has to take into account to ensure that fairness is maintained. If the employer puts the employee in a position that makes it impossible for him or her to stay in the business, then this is known as 'constructive dismissal'. This can be brought about by the employer:

- Changing the employee's wages without telling him or her.
- Changing the place the employee has to work without telling him or her.
- Changing the duties that the employee has to perform without telling him or her.
- Changing the job description without telling the employee.

An employer will nearly always have a reason for dismissing an employee, whether that reason is right or wrong in the eyes of the employee. There are, however, four major reasons for dismissal:

- If an employee has proved that he or she is not capable of doing the job. He or she may have shown serious errors of judgement.

- If an employee was given the job on the understanding that he or she achieve a certain level of qualification in a certain time, but failed to do so.

- **Misconduct** – there are several forms of misconduct, including:
  - absenteeism – when an employee is away from work too often;
  - lateness – where an employee constantly turns up late for work;
  - insubordination – where an employee refuses to carry out instructions from a supervisor or manager of the business;

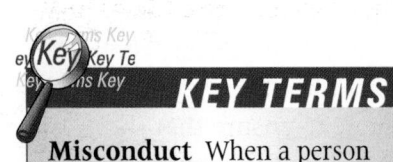

KEY TERMS

Ethical Socially responsible, honest, truthful and clear in all of its dealings

KEY TERMS

Misconduct When a person fails to adhere to the rules of the business he or she is employed by

- incompetence – where the employee shows on several occasions an inability to do the job;
- immorality – where the employee behaves in an unacceptable manner;
- breaking safety rules – where an employee endangers his or her life or the life of others by not taking notice of safety rules;
- theft – where the employee has stolen the property of the employer.

Redundancy

If the employer closes down the business, or a part of the business, he or she may no longer need the services of some or all of the employees. In such cases, the employer must consult the employees, having fairly selected those to be made redundant, and, if possible, offer them alternative employment. There is always a way around the problem of redundancy, particularly if the employer can freeze bringing in new employees and give existing employees new jobs within the business. An alternative to this is for the employer to reduce the number of hours worked by all employees rather than make some redundant.

Resignation

There are lots of different reasons that an employee might choose to resign from their job and go to a new one. Normally the contract of employment will state how many days' or weeks' notice has to be given to the employer before the employee will be allowed to leave the business. The employee will also be entitled to any remaining holiday pay or other payments which are due to them up to and including the day that they leave. In many cases, once an individual has resigned or, more commonly, 'handed in their notice', the employer may be keen for the person to leave immediately or to train someone else to do their job in the time before they leave.

Retirement

Currently the retirement age is 65 for men and 60 for women, although there is much talk about either making it 65 for both sexes or increasing both by five years to 65 and 70. Although there is no upper age limit for work, normally, depending on the length of time that someone has worked for a business or organisation, retirement can be taken by employees in their 50s.

Normally, it is considered to be perfectly acceptable to consider retirement once an individual has worked for a business for around 20 to 25 years. By then, the employee has been paying into a pension fund for a considerable number of years and, although they cannot collect a state pension until they have reached the national retirement age, they can draw from their employer's pension fund from the date of their retirement. Many businesses are reluctant to lose their older members of staff as these are the most experienced and often the most difficult people to replace.

REMUNERATION

The Finance Department, or Accounts Department, of a business is just as important to the employee as the Human Resource Department, but for different reasons. Although the employees would turn to the Human Resource Department for help with any problems relating to their wages or salaries, it is the finance section that actually pays them the money they earn. The payment received for the work done is called remuneration and there are a number of different ways in which an employee could be paid by an organisation. As we already know, people can be a business's most expensive resource, but there are many other expenses that have to be met if the business is to be successful.

Whatever the size and nature of the business, it is essential that there are records and accounts of all the different financial transactions that take place.

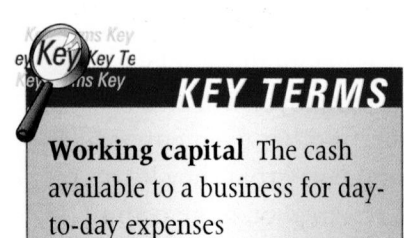

KEY TERMS

Working capital The cash available to a business for day-to-day expenses

A new business will need to find some money in order that it can set up and start trading. This is known as the business's **working capital**. It is a very lucky businessman or woman who can start the business without borrowing money from friends, the bank or another financial institution. A new business will need equipment, premises, insurance and something to make or sell.

Once a business is up and running there will be a need to buy new supplies (expenditure), and there must be systems in place that allow customers to pay for the products or services they buy (income), as well as systems to pay staff their wages or salaries (expenditure). All of these different systems need to have documents that keep track of the money coming into and going out of the business. Such documents record this income and

expenditure for the managers of the business and are known as the financial transactions of the business.

All of the different transactions that are recorded need to be collated at regular intervals so that it is possible to monitor how the business is performing. The business needs to ensure that there is more money coming into it from sales than money going out of it to pay for the different running costs. The information about the financial state of the business is gathered and turned into sets of accounts that show whether or not the organisation is trading successfully. The accounts show whether the business is making a **profit** or a **loss** and how many assets and liabilities the business has. Assets are things such as property, **stock** and money still owed from customers. Liabilities are things such as loans, debtors (people who owe the business money), and money owed by the business to suppliers.

Financial transactions

The survival of an organisation will depend upon its financial state. In order to monitor whether the organisation is spending more than it is earning, it is essential that the series of financial transactions are controlled in a strict way. There are both outward and inward transactions:

- Outward transactions pay for the costs that the business has to meet, such as wages, materials to make their products, lighting and heating. Often these payments are made by computerised systems, but some organisations still do so manually.
- Inward transactions are made to receive income, such as payments from customers.

When any financial transaction takes place, it is essential that a record is kept by the business. These records of transactions have to be stored safely and securely and it is important that they can be found easily and are kept up to date. Financial transactions are recorded for the following reasons:

- To provide evidence that the transactions have actually taken place – it would not be sensible to rely on memory.
- To provide the finance section with documents in order that they can pay the bills and collect any money which is owed to the business.
- To provide the finance section with a record of the transaction so that they can produce the **annual accounts**.

There are many different people who may be interested in the financial state of the business. These include:

- The managers, who will want to plan and control the business's activities.
- The Inland Revenue which takes tax from businesses. The business is required to complete documents for the Inland Revenue stating the profits (the amount of money made after expenses have been paid for). The Inland Revenue takes a percentage of the profits in the form of tax.
- Banks, financial institutions and shareholders who have provided some of the business's working capital will want to make sure the business is using their money wisely.
- Suppliers who may be owed money will want to know that the business is making enough money to pay them.
- Employees will want to be sure that they will receive their wages and salaries and that their jobs are not at risk.
- Anyone considering providing money for the business will want to know whether they are investing their money wisely in a healthy business.

Information has to be generated to produce final accounts that give a clear overview of how well the business is doing. Therefore, accurate systems must be in place to record each transaction and then information needs to be gathered together and kept somewhere safe until it is needed to create the accounts.

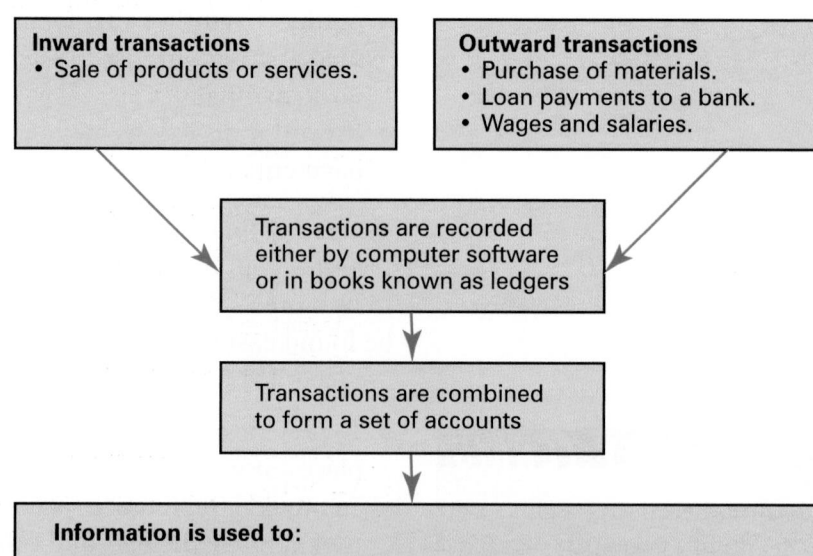

Inward transactions
- Sale of products or services.

Outward transactions
- Purchase of materials.
- Loan payments to a bank.
- Wages and salaries.

Transactions are recorded either by computer software or in books known as ledgers

Transactions are combined to form a set of accounts

Information is used to:
- Inform the bank about how well the business is doing.
- Tell the Inland Revenue how much money the business has made.
- Tell any shareholders how much money the business has made.
- Help the owners and managers of the business make decisions about the future.

Figure 3.1

KEY TERMS

Stock control A business procedure which aims to ensure efficient stock ordering, delivery and handling

Ledger A document used for recording different business transactions

At each stage of the process people are involved in recording and analysing the financial information generated by the business.

- Accounts clerks, checkout staff, sales staff, buyers of the business's material, and those who control the amount stored by a business (**stock control**) all complete documents or produce computer-generated documents that will record the income and expenditure of the business.
- Data (information) handling staff will put the information into different **ledgers**. These ledgers are the manual way of recording sales of products or services (sales ledger), the details of what the business has bought (purchase ledger) and the day-to-day costs of the business (nominal ledger). This somewhat old-fashioned way of recording documents is the job of a clerk or bookkeeper and the ledgers are in the form of a book with grids. It is more common nowadays to record financial transactions onto computerised ledgers designed as spreadsheets.
- Managers who need to help plan and control the future of the business will require the information contained in the ledgers or computerised records in order to produce a set of financial accounts.

Clear procedures need to be in place in all businesses, however large or small they may be, in order to make sure that every transaction is recorded accurately. There also needs to be a way to check that the recording is accurate, honest and clear.

Think about it!

Find a dictionary definition of the following accounting terms:

- Financial transactions
- Working capital
- Assets
- Liabilities
- Profit and loss accounts
- Balance sheet
- Sales ledger
- Purchase ledger
- Nominal ledger

Action Points **M**ost public limited companies (PLCs) publish their annual accounts on their websites.

1 Visit the websites of three businesses of your choice and print out their balance sheets and profit and loss statements.

2 Make some comparisons between the different documents and answer the following questions:
- Is there a standard way of laying out a set of final accounts?
- What features are the same for each of the documents?
- Describe the profit or loss for each business.
- What does each business spend on costs?
- What does each business spend on wages and salaries?

3 Now find out how your school keeps track of finances.

4 How does the school record money coming in, such as funding to run the school, and other money, such as payments for the use of the school hall or gym?

5 How does it record money that is spent running the school?

6 Produce a two-column table on your computer to show how the school records its financial transactions. Use the headings 'Money coming in' and 'Money going out'.

In all businesses there are some financial aspects that are the same, whatever the size and nature of that business. In many businesses all of the transactions will be input into a computer which will do much of the adding up and checking that used to be the job of the financial or accounts clerk. There are many accounts software packages on the market that take the strain out of recording financial transactions. We will look at these in more detail later in the book.

Action Points

1 Obtain a local newspaper and find an advertisement for an accounts clerk.

2 Find out from your Careers Department exactly what kind of experience and qualifications are necessary in order for someone to be considered for the post.

3 Write a job description and a person specification for the vacancy you have chosen. Use a word processor to produce these documents.

Larger organisations will have their own Finance Department which will deal with the financial transactions, but a sole trader may do his or her own accounts or employ a part-time, qualified individual to do this job for them. The accounts can be broken down into two main parts – the balance sheet and the profit and loss account. Before we look at these in a little more detail, there are some terms that need to be explained:

- Assets – these can be either cash, money in the bank, stock held by the business, or the business's buildings or equipment. Also, any money that the business is owed is an asset.
- Liabilities – this is the money which the business owes to other businesses or suppliers.
- Gross profit – this is the difference between the price of buying the raw materials needed to make the product or service and the price the business can charge its customers for its products or services.
- Net profit – this is the gross profit minus all the costs involved in making the product or service. Examples of such costs would include electricity, wages and salaries, and heating.

The profit and loss account includes a summary of all the financial transactions that the business has carried out during the year and it will show whether it has made a profit or a loss. The balance sheet will show the profit or loss made (this is transferred from the profit and loss account) as well as the business's assets and liabilities.

Wages and salaries

For an employee, the most important job of the finance section is the payment of wages or salaries. As we already know, the term for this payment is remuneration. Depending on the type of job, an employee will normally be paid either a wage or a salary. Wages tend to be based on the number of hours which have been worked in a particular week. Salaries, on the other hand, are one-twelfth of the yearly (annual) pay and are paid once a month. In both cases payment is nearly always made 'in arrears', which means that the employee will have worked for several days or even a few weeks before they get paid. Wages tend to be paid on a weekly basis and salaries tend to be paid on a monthly basis.

Action Points

1 Make a list of the jobs that you think are 'wage' earners and those you think are 'salaried'.

2 Discuss these with the rest of your group.

There are several different ways that an employer can pay an employee. The employer will choose the form of payment most suitable to them, but the following list gives the most common forms:

- Cash – in the past, payment by cash was, perhaps, the most common form of receiving a wage or salary from an employer. However, many employers do not wish to risk having a delivery of several thousands of pounds on, say, a Friday, and they do not want the extra work involved in splitting up that delivery into individual pay packets. Cash is often still paid to part-time or casual workers (those who work for the business from time to time).

- Cheque – this could arrive at the employee's home by post or be handed to them personally (as is usually the case for casual employees). This is not the most convenient way for an employee to be paid because they have to go to the bank to pay the cheque in. Also, they will have to wait for the bank to confirm that the business has enough money in their account to pay the money (this is known as 'clearing' a cheque, and it could take up to a week). Some large organisations have an arrangement with their own bank which allows their employees to go into that bank, show suitable identification and have the cheque cashed immediately.

- Credit transfer to bank – this form of payment is now the most common way of receiving a wage or salary. From the employer's point of view, they only need to complete a summary sheet which shows the details of the employee's account and the amount they are to be paid. Payment is guaranteed on a particular day of the week or month and the employee does not have to wait for the bank to clear the money. This is an electronic transfer of funds or electronic data interchange (EDI) from one bank account to another. Employees will still receive a document which gives them the details of the amount of money that has been paid into their account – this is known as a pay statement or payslip.

- Bankers Automated Clearing Services (BACS) – this is used by large organisations to pay their employees and it reduces the amount of paperwork involved. The details of the amount of money to be transferred from the business's bank account to that of the employee is supplied to the bank and processed by computer. Once the details have been processed the money is transferred automatically so the employee has access to their money immediately it reaches their own bank account.

Which system of payment (BACS, cheque or cash) do you believe is the most efficient:

- For the business?
- For the employee?

Give reasons for your answer.

Employees do not receive all of their wage or salary. Before the money is either given to them or transferred into their bank account, various common deductions are made by the finance section of the business. Some of these are required by law (compulsory), such as income tax, and others are voluntary deductions, such as pension contributions. The compulsory deductions include the following:

- Income tax – this is deducted by law by the employer on behalf of the Inland Revenue, which is a Government department. Income tax is deducted on a Pay As You Earn (PAYE) basis, which means that employees pay their income tax regularly and do not have to pay a large amount of money at the end of each year. The Government uses this money, or part of it, to help fund schools, the police, the fire brigade and ambulance service, and to build roads. The employer must make these deductions and pass the money on to the Inland Revenue by following this process:
  - the Inland Revenue works out what is known as the 'personal allowance' to which each employee is entitled. This amount of money will depend on each individual's circumstances, for instance whether or not they are married and how many children they have;
  - the employee is then taxed on all the money they have earned above this personal allowance. In other words, the more money earned, the more tax has to be paid;
  - the employee receives a statement of how much tax has been deducted from their pay each week or month;
  - the employee receives a statement (a P60) which tells them the total amount of tax paid in the past year.
- National Insurance contributions – as well as income tax, all employees also have to pay 'national insurance' and businesses have to make a contribution to this on behalf of each of their employees. Unlike income tax, there is no

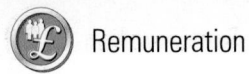

personal allowance and you have to pay National Insurance on everything earned. National Insurance contributions help the Government to pay for the National Health Service, sickness benefits, maternity pay and pensions being paid out to people. The employer is responsible for collecting the National Insurance on behalf of the Department for Work and Pensions and must pass on to that Department any money collected. The amount deducted for National Insurance will also appear on an employee's pay statement or payslip.

Voluntary deductions include:

- Union subscriptions – employees who belong to a trade union will pay a weekly, monthly or annual subscription as a membership fee and this can be deducted from their wage or salary.
- Pension contributions – although we all pay National Insurance which goes towards our state pension when we retire, many people believe that the state pension will not give them enough money to allow them to stop working, and they choose to have a certain amount of money deducted from their wage or salary in order to provide them with more money later in life.

To summarise:

- Wages and salaries are calculated using the PAYE system.
- The amount of money the employee earns before deductions is known as gross pay.
- The business takes income tax and National Insurance (NI) contributions from earnings (deductions).
- The money that employees receive after deductions is known as their net pay.
- The business sends the tax and NI contributions to the Inland Revenue.

There are few businesses that still use a manual system to calculate how much to pay their employees. This system uses a set of tables that can be obtained from the Inland Revenue. Most businesses now use computerised payroll software that calculates net pay and prints out a payslip that identifies all aspects of the payment, including:

- Hours worked during the week or month.
- Gross pay earned during the week or month.
- Total deductions during the week or month.
- Net pay earned after deductions.

- Total income tax paid so far throughout the year.
- Total National Insurance contributions paid so far throughout the year.

NAME			Week number		
DEPARTMENT			Tax week number		
Gross wages paid to date			Gross deductions made to date		
	£	P		£	P
Basic wage			Company pension		
Overtime hours @			PAYE Income tax		
hours @			National Insurance standard rate		
hours @			reduced rate		
Bonus/ holiday					
Sickpay					
Total wages			Total deductions		
			Gross wages		
			Gross deductions		
			Sub total		
5 029987 135821			Income tax refund		
adams MU3582 Made in USA			NET PAY £		

The Finance Department, or sometimes a special section of that department known as the payroll section, will need to find out from all other departments or functions in the business how much each employee is to receive in wages or salary. Employees can be paid in different ways depending on the type of work they are employed to do. However, in recent years the Government has passed laws which ensure that employees receive a **minimum wage**. This helps to ensure that individuals do not work for a very small amount of money. But there are other things to think about when discussing wages and salaries.

KEY TERMS

Minimum wage The lowest legal amount per hour that can be paid to employees; set by Government

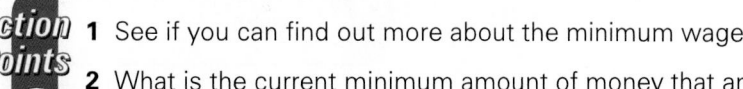

Action Points

1 See if you can find out more about the minimum wage.

2 What is the current minimum amount of money that an employer has to pay?

3 What does the Government law say about the minimum wage?

4 Discuss what you have found out with other members of your group and produce a leaflet that illustrates to a new employer what they have to consider when employing a new employee with regard to how much they should pay them. Remember that they have to stick to the law of the Government on this!

Hourly rate

Rather than pay an employee a fixed salary, many businesses choose to employ people on the basis of the number of hours they work. From an employer's point of view, paying an hourly rate is ideal for the employment of part-time or casual workers. However, a large number of full-time employees are paid on an hourly rate. If full-time employees' hours are always the same each week, then apart from the fact that they are paid weekly, their circumstances are almost exactly the same as those of a salaried worker. Part-time workers may be offered a minimum number of hours per week and then, if they are asked to do more hours, their wage will be amended accordingly. Casual workers, on the other hand, who cannot rely on a set number of hours per day or week, are often called in by the employer to help cope with busy periods.

Piece rate

Alternatively, an employee may be paid what is known as 'piece rate'. This is quite common in factories and in home-working or assembly work. For example, those working at home addressing envelopes may be paid on the piece-rate basis. Piece-rate workers tend to be paid on completion of a batch of work. This means the employee is paid for each item produced or sold. An employee might put together the different parts of 10 televisions a day and be paid £10.00 per television; this would mean gross pay of £100.00 per day.

Action Points

1 In groups discuss the advantages and disadvantages of both piece rate and hourly rate.

2 Write down three advantages and three disadvantages of each.

Overtime

The term 'overtime' relates to the extra time that the employee has worked over and above the amount of time they are supposed to work. For most employees this will mean that they are paid more for that hour or those hours than they would normally be paid on their hourly rate. Sometimes this can be one-and-a-half times their hourly rate or double their hourly rate. Employers do this to encourage their employees to do overtime rather than having to go to the expense of employing casual or extra workers. Sometimes employees are given time off as an alternative to an overtime payment. This means that they will be allowed to take off the same number of hours or days as they have worked overtime.

Bonuses

Bonus payments are often paid to employees for one of the following two reasons:

- If an employee has achieved a particular goal or objective set by his or her supervisor or manager.
- If the business itself has achieved a particular goal or objective set by the owners or managers of the business.

Sometimes all members of a department or team receive the same amount of bonus for achieving a goal. This encourages the department or team to work together. Alternatively, all members of a business receive what is known as a 'company bonus' at a particular time of the year, often at Christmas, provided the business has made a good profit.

Some businesses, rather than giving a cash bonus, will offer prizes to their employees for meeting goals and objectives, and these can include holidays or one of the business's products.

Commission

Commission is usually paid to employees in addition to their basic pay. Commission is a percentage of the value of sales made by an individual. In other words, an employee may receive 1 per cent of all sales he or she has made, so that selling £100-worth of products or services would be worth £1 commission to the employee.

Performance related pay

Performance related pay is an additional payment made to employees provided they achieve certain goals that have been agreed. Employees may be paid extra money for their efficiency, helpfulness or good attendance. Normally employees who achieve their goals and improve upon them will receive a higher pay rise than those who have only just met their goals and considerably more than those who did not reach their goals at all.

Fringe benefits

Rather than offering extra pay, or higher rates of pay, some employers offer a series of fringe benefits to attract employees or to keep the staff they already have. Fringe benefits are also known as 'non-financial incentives' which are aimed at providing employees with a little extra that cannot be taxed. In this way, they receive the full effect of the fringe benefit.

- Subsidised meals and drinks – if the employee works for an organisation which is involved in the catering (food) industry, then subsidised, or even free, meals and drinks are often commonplace. Many larger organisations, which may have no association with food, offer their staff reduced rate (sometimes known as 'at cost') food and refreshment. Whilst the promise of a three-course lunch for under £1 may be attractive, it is rarely the only reason for someone to choose to work for that particular employer. As an alternative to food and drink offered on the premises of an organisation, some employers give lunch vouchers. These can be exchanged for food and drink at a number of places, including supermarkets in most High Streets or town centres.

- Travel – another **incentive** to employees is free or subsidised travel. The nature of this type of incentive will differ from organisation to organisation, but could take one of the following forms:
  - free pick up and drop off – for employees who live in remote areas and would otherwise find it difficult to get to work;
  - free travel passes – offered by some larger organisations to enable their employees to travel on public transport, either in the course of work, or during their leisure time;
  - travel loan schemes – employers pay for the employee's season ticket in order to take advantage of discounts available. The employee pays back the employer with regular monthly payments which are **interest free**;
  - company cars – key employees or those that have to travel considerable distances in the course of their work are often provided with a company car and a company credit card to pay for petrol;
  - essential car users' allowance – organisations that do not offer company cars give some of their key employees a credit card or a charge account at specific petrol stations to help towards the running costs of their own cars being used for company business;
  - overseas travel – for employees who have to make regular

trips abroad, the organisation provides them with the means to purchase tickets as and when they need to. This may be done through a recommended travel agency, or by giving the employees a credit card to buy the tickets. The organisation will be able to monitor the use of the credit card and it will be useful to the employee for other business expenses as well as travel;

- reimbursement – for occasional travel undertaken by employees, or other expenses met in the course of their work, organisations tend to use 'expenses claims forms' to pay back to employees any money they have spent in the course of their work for the organisation.

- Discount on purchases – some businesses, particularly those involved in retailing, offer their employees a discount on purchases from the organisation. This not only serves as a useful incentive to employees, but also ensures that they use the company's products and, by doing so, they find it easier to sell them to other customers. It would not do for the employees of a retail organisation to purchase products from a competitor; this is not a very good advertisement for their employer. The procedures used when employees purchase from their employer are often monitored very carefully to avoid misuse of the incentive. Some employers restrict the amount that employees can purchase in order to stop them from selling the products on to other people. For larger purchases, the employee may be able to obtain not only a discount, but also a reduced rate or an interest-free loan.

- Loans – banks and building societies in particular offer their employees loans or mortgages at reduced rates and these are a very valuable incentive. Whilst the employee works for the organisation he or she can enjoy loans and mortgages at considerably lower rates of interest than the normal rate. Other organisations give advances on wages and salaries which are, in effect, loans, and are paid off gradually by the employee. Employees need to be aware that any loans and mortgages given to them by their current employer will have to be paid off if they leave the company.

- Health insurance – key members of staff may be offered health insurance as part of their overall wage or salary package. This private health insurance often covers their families too. The employer, by ensuring that key employees are covered by private health insurance, can be assured that the minimum

amount of time is lost if the employee falls ill or needs medical attention. From an employee's point of view, he or she can feel secure in the knowledge that any serious medical problem can be dealt with as quickly as possible and that valuable time will not be lost by having to wait for medical attention on the National Health Service.

- Pensions – there are two different types of pension in addition to the state pension which employees receive as a result of paying National Insurance. These are:
  - contributory pensions – where the employee and employer both pay into the pension scheme;
  - non-contributory pensions – where only the employer pays into the pension scheme on behalf of the employee.

Bearing in mind that an employee could pay up to around 17.5 per cent of his or her total income to a pension scheme tax free, this can prove to be quite an incentive to both the employer and to the employee. The Government is very keen for employees to be able to support themselves financially when they retire and has made it relatively easy to set up a pension scheme and monitor the payments. Organisations may offer one of the following:

- company pension schemes – where a specific pension fund has been set up to pay the pension of retired employees. All employees pay into this scheme and the benefits from this joint 'saving' is passed on to the retired members of staff;
- personal pension schemes – where the pension scheme is a more general one and is not company based but is related to the employee as an individual. One of the advantages here is that the personal pension scheme is movable from one employer to another. It has the additional benefit of being part of a much larger overall pension fund.

In the past, planning for retirement was not something that many people necessarily considered at a young age. However, nowadays it is rare to find an employer who does not encourage staff to join a company pension scheme.

- Sports and social clubs – some organisations, particularly those who value team work and team building, offer their employees a range of sports and social activities to engage in either free of charge or at heavily subsidised rates. Many banks and other large organisations have their own sports and social clubs with a variety of different activities on offer.

Other smaller organisations have entered into agreements with local leisure and sports clubs and have paid a lump sum for the membership of a large number of employees. Some organisations take this even further and positively encourage inter-departmental competitions or organise day trips or visits for their employees.

● Clothing – even though many company uniforms are not exactly to the taste of most employees, the fact that they are provided by the employer can be seen as something of an incentive. By having a company uniform to wear, employees do not have to wear their own clothes to work and can save money as they do not have to buy clothes for that purpose. Sometimes employers give their employees a clothing allowance which allows them to buy their own work clothes, but with certain restrictions laid down by the business.

Action Points

1 Put the information detailed in the following Table into a spreadsheet.

2 Calculate the total wages due for each employee.

3 When you have done that, find out what the total cost of wages will be for the business and the total hours worked by all employees.

Name of employee	Hours worked	Pay rate	Wages due
Paula Davies	24	5.50	
Gillian Wilson	35	6.50	
Angela Jones	35	7.00	
Baljit Singh	6	6.50	
Ty Malik	45	4.50	
Karl Flynn	23	5.60	
Bob Baker	12	7.60	
Total			

Action Points **M**ake the following changes to the data in the Table on page 125.

1 Paula Davies has had an increase of £1.50 an hour.

2 Baljit Singh has worked another six hours.

3 Bob Baker did six hours overtime at double time.

4 Recalculate the total hours worked, the total wages due for each employee and the total wages bill for the business.

INFORMATION COMMUNICATION TECHNOLOGY (ICT) AND HUMAN RESOURCES

Over the past few years, organisations and their employees have had to make changes to their normal way of working. The introduction of new technological advances has forced them to adopt new procedures. Organisations which fail to appreciate the need to constantly monitor their use of technology risk failure. Equally, if employees are unwilling or unable to adopt new working practices that are necessary because of the introduction of some new technology, the business may fail.

Although we will be looking at information and communication technology in greater detail throughout the remainder of the book, and you will also be studying this as a separate topic during your course, it is necessary to consider its impact on business and employees in general. It is sufficient to say here that its impact has had the following effects which the management of the business, often through the Human Resource Department, has had to address:

● Redundancy – the introduction of ICT has had a gradual and dramatic effect on not only the types of jobs which employees do, but also the numbers of employees in a business. There comes a point when it is not possible to retrain individuals to do new jobs using ICT. Simply their jobs have been replaced by ICT and the old-fashioned ways of working are no longer needed. In these cases employees are made redundant by their employers. This means that the employer does not have a job for them any more and they cannot be moved to an alternative job within the business.

● Job change – as ICT develops and new ways of working are created, it is often necessary for employees to gradually or sometimes dramatically change the way in which they work. Retraining and updating is necessary to ensure that the employees are able to use the new technology and learn new ways of carrying out their jobs.

- Resistance to change – it is not always the older members of staff who are reluctant to change the ways in which they work. Many employees believe that the way they have been working is perfectly adequate and efficient. Employers who are introducing ICT or changes in ICT need to explain the benefits both to the business and to the employee in order to overcome any reluctance to accept changes in working.

- Training systems – one of the main ways to include employees in any changes in ICT is to ensure that they are given regular training updates and to have an efficient system which identifies which employees need to be trained or retrained as ICT develops. This task will usually fall to the manager of the employee or directly to the Human Resource Department. Time will be set aside and expert trainers will be made available to ensure that the most up-to-date techniques are passed on to the employees.

- Demotivation – if an employee feels anxious or insecure about their job, then they will not be as motivated. They may view the introduction of ICT as a threat to their job security, and they may feel that each change brings redundancy ever closer.

- Information flow – in organisations which use modern ICT, all employees at every level will be able to have all of the information that they need at their fingertips (access to certain information may be restricted to those with authorisation). If information such as newsletters, bulletins and emails to all employees are accessible, then news and vital information can be passed on to everyone who needs it to carry out their duties.

- Working conditions – the introduction of ICT has had a huge impact on working conditions. Offices are now organised differently, and it is no longer necessary to have all employees working in one large complex. ICT allows employees to work flexible hours and work from home or in a smaller office near their home. Managers can monitor exactly what employees are doing through a **network**. ICT allows businesses to use their employees in order to carry out work that needs to be done 24 hours a day, seven days a week, as many businesses now operate worldwide. It is not uncommon for **call centres,** sales offices or administration departments to be based in different countries. They can communicate with one another easily and work during normal office hours in their own countries, thus covering the needs of the business for 24 hours a day.

KEY TERMS

Network A computer system which allows remote computers to be linked together

Call centres A central office, often in a remote location, used to deal with all enquiries and sales for a business, using the latest ICT

The above considerations about the impact of ICT are both positive and negative.

1 Create a three-column table using a word-processing package.

2 Key in all those reasons given above in either the column headed 'Advantage' or that headed 'Disadvantage'.

3 Add any other impacts you can think of or have been told about.

4 Now, in the third column headed 'Reasons', state why you think each is an advantage or disadvantage.

Communication

IN THIS CHAPTER YOU WILL INVESTIGATE ...

- The purposes of business communications
- The communication process
- Effective internal and external communication
- Effects of poor internal and external communication
- Barriers to communication
- Verbal communication
- Written communication (documentation)
- Developments in communication technology
- The internet
- E-commerce and customers

THE PURPOSES OF BUSINESS COMMUNICATIONS

However large or small the business, it relies on its customers for success. Looking after the external customer is vital. Without customers a business cannot function and will not survive.

People who work inside the business are also customers of the business and are called internal customers. They are employees, and the business provides them with an income, with self-esteem and identity. In many cases these people rely on the business to provide them with opportunities to gain new skills and to develop and progress in their working life.

In a small business where there may be only a few employees, or internal customers, it is not difficult to communicate the information necessary to keep the business on the right tracks for success. For example, a small, local estate agent might have four or five people who all work in the same office. Each answers the telephone and takes details of houses or answers questions about houses already for sale. The business will have systems to record details of customers who want to sell houses and those who want to buy. There will be systems for recording telephone calls, incoming and outgoing post, and details of all financial transactions, such as payments made by customers or items bought by the business. It is likely that this team of four or five people will know just by being there whether a house has sold or whether someone is unhappy with the service they have been given. This form of communication is known as 'word of mouth' and might well be the most common method simply because the team all work in the same room, or in the same small block of offices.

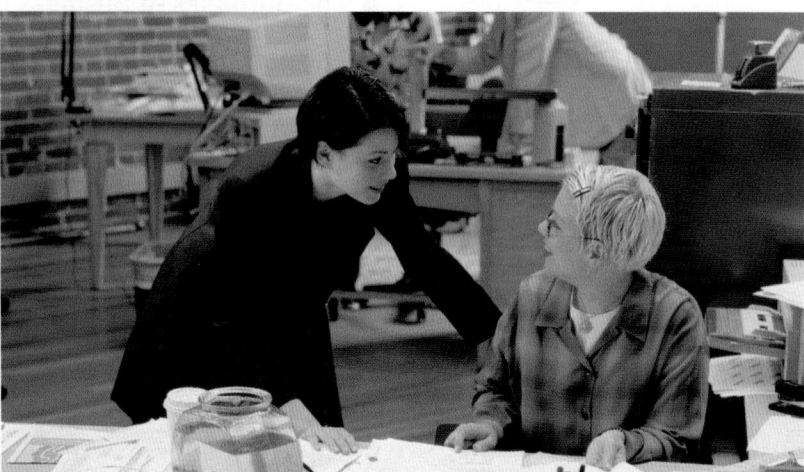

In a larger business, communication can be more complicated. The business may be divided into different functions or departments and these may be located on different floors of a building, or even in different buildings. People who work in the Finance Department may never see people from the Human Resource Department. In some large businesses different functions might be carried out in different buildings, different parts of the country or even in other parts of the world. In large businesses it is impossible to rely on the informal methods of communication that might be used in a small business situation.

Whether the methods of communication are informal in a small office or more formal because people are not in close contact, it is vital that the message is communicated effectively and accurately. One inaccurate, lost or misused piece of information can have serious effects on the success of a business or the impression a customer has of it.

Think about it!

Before we go into more detail about communication, look at the different mistakes listed below. Explain the consequences of these mistakes made by staff in different businesses:

- A house is advertised in the local newspaper at £35,000 less than it should have been.

- One of the employees has taken a call from an unhappy customer. He has promised to find a manager who will phone the customer back. The telephone number has been written down incorrectly.
- An order has been placed for 60 boxes of cat food when it should have been for 60 tins.
- A large document to be presented at an urgent meeting has been lost on the computer. There is no backup copy.
- A new customer has placed a large order. The person who took the call has written the details on a scrap of paper. This has been lost.
- A new member of staff is upset because she has found a copy of her curriculum vitae on an email that anyone can read.

It is essential that all those who work in a business communicate messages accurately, however small or large the issue. After all, the main purpose of communication is to select the right message and transmit it accurately so that the correct information is received.

Communication inside the business can be formal or informal depending on the message. Some formal methods of communication are:

- Business letters
- Reports
- Invoices and accounts
- Contracts of employment.

Some informal methods of communication are:

- Face-to-face conversations
- Rumours and gossip (through the 'grapevine')
- Telephone conversations
- Notes left on desks.

There is a place for both formal and informal communications in any business. It is vital that a member of staff is given a formal letter of appointment and a contract of employment. However, where one member of staff is aware that another is unhappy about a particular situation, it may be that one of the employee's managers will have an informal conversation with the colleague to try to sort the situation out.

THE COMMUNICATION PROCESS

All forms of communication are about sending and receiving messages. The sender of the message must be clear, and the message must be sent using the most appropriate method of communication if it is to be received accurately. For example, it is not a good idea to send a junior member of staff to inform someone verbally that their services are no longer required. Equally it would not be a good idea to write a memo in order to simply ask someone if they would kindly make a cup of coffee.

The way a message is transmitted is known as the medium. Different mediums include:

- A conversation
- A telephone call
- A letter
- A memo
- A report
- A newsletter
- A message on a notice board
- A meeting
- A fax message
- An email.

Choosing the right medium is, therefore, essential and the person who wishes to send information should think carefully about the medium they intend to use. This might be a formal means of communication where the business already has set procedures in place, or it may be an informal communication simply requiring a note to be left on a colleague's desk.

The message is communicated along different routes or channels in the organisation. These channels of communication can be between a manager and one of the employees for whom they are responsible (vertical communication) or between two different areas of the business (known as a horizontal channel of communication).

The message passes information along a channel by way of a particular medium and is communicated to the receiver.

When we talk about the different methods of communication, we are considering the following:

- Conversation (informal) – this method of communication might be very useful if two people have some gossip and want to pass it on to others. This is known as 'grapevine communication' and is not a good method of communication if the conversation is about a confidential business matter.

- Telephone call (informal) – this is a very quick and efficient method of communication. It is useful if you want an immediate answer to a question or you wish to make arrangements with another person, although it does have some disadvantages, for example:
  - the person you wish to speak to may not be available just when you want to talk to them;
  - a message may get into the wrong hands;
  - sometimes you can spend a long time talking on the telephone about other issues as well as the main one that you telephoned about;
  - you do not have a written statement of what has been said.

- Letter – a letter has two purposes:
  - a letter to a friend is an informal method of communication and is not as widely used as it once was since people often prefer to stay in touch by means of telephone or email;
  - a business letter is a formal method of communication. It can formalise arrangements, inform someone of another's intention, give information or ideas, or confirm an agreement.

- Memorandum (or memo) (formal) – this is a widely used form of internal communication in business. It is less formal than a letter and is used inside the organisation to pass on information or to inform others of a meeting or an event.

- Report (formal) – this document can provide details of research or activities that have taken place within the business or outside the business. A report is generally an extended document and will be written for a specific purpose and have a specific audience.

- Newsletter (formal) – many businesses have newsletters that are produced for their employees as a means of communicating different events and issues that have occurred in the business over a period of time. The newsletter may inform all employees of any new members of staff, those who have left, major changes that have taken place in the business and issues outside the business that have an effect on the running or activities of the business.

- Notice board – this method of communication has its limitations. It is not easy to guarantee that everyone will read the notice board. The notice may be removed before everyone reads it. Therefore, it is only really useful for imparting general information that is not crucial.

- Meeting – this is an essential form of face-to-face communication. A meeting might be called to discuss issues that relate to a team of people working on a similar project or a group of people who need collectively to make a decision. Meetings can be informal or formal, and good communication

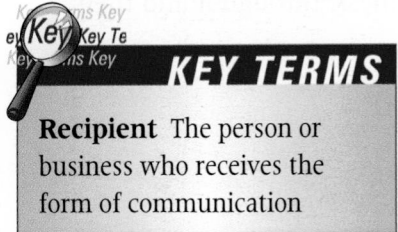

KEY TERMS

Recipient The person or business who receives the form of communication

within the meeting itself is vital if the business is to be run effectively. Later in this chapter the various documents that are issued as a result of a meeting taking place are discussed.

- Fax message (formal) – this method of communication is used when it is necessary to pass on information that is part of a document or a set of documents; for example, sending a map to give directions, giving a quote for a spare part or for a new product, sending a set of drawings or pictures. The sender of the message receives a transmission report which confirms that the correct number of pages have been sent to the correct fax number.

- Email (formal and informal) – this is a widely used method of communication because of its speed and efficiency. The message can be sent directly to the person it is intended for. The message can include attachments which can be very large documents, diagrams, or charts and photographs. The **recipient** is the only person who should see the correspondence (many businesses include a statement to this effect at the end of each email). The disadvantage of this method of communication is that the recipient may not have access to their computer and therefore may not read the material for a few days. So it is not the best method of communication to use if the message is urgent, unless the person can be contacted and asked to make sure that they check their email inbox.

These are just a few of the different methods of communication and, as we will discover later in this chapter, they all have their own uses, advantages and disadvantages.

Think about it!

What method of communication would you use in each of these different scenarios?

- To invite a colleague at another branch to meet you for lunch.
- To provide information for the owners of the business on some research that has been undertaken about moving into new premises.
- To inform all employees that there will be a mobile blood donor unit in the business's car park the following Wednesday.
- To tell someone they have a pay rise.
- To explain to someone that they are the subject of disciplinary action.
- To inform everyone about the Christmas party.

EFFECTIVE INTERNAL AND EXTERNAL COMMUNICATION

Communication flows into, through and then back out of the business in a number of different ways:

- From the top to the bottom of a business.
- Across the different functions or departments within a business.
- To and from those outside the business who are affected by the organisation's activities.

At every stage there can be factors that influence how well the message is received. The following diagram shows how communication flows into the business, through it and then out again.

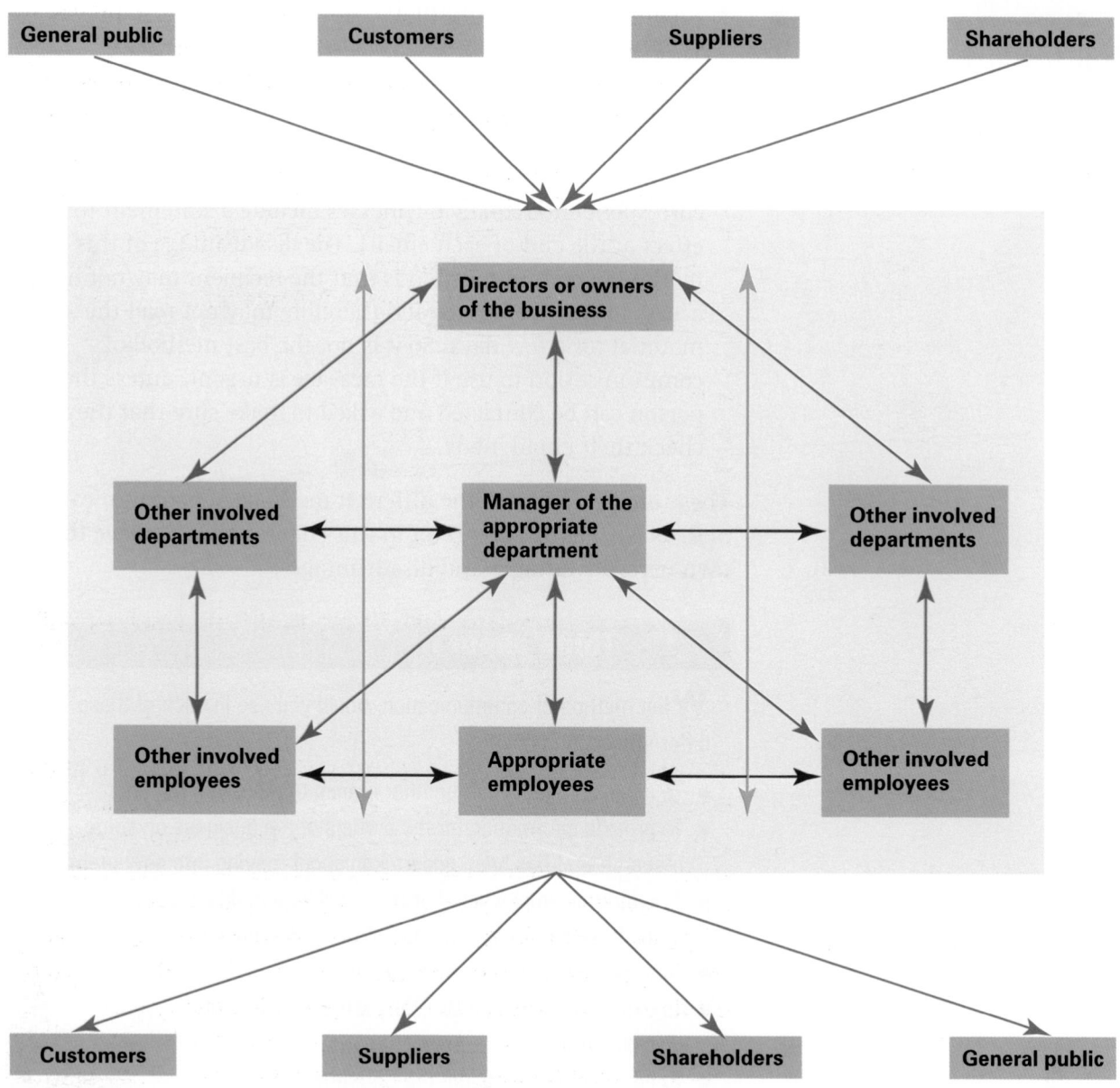

Figure 4.1

Effective communication is all about making sure the message is given in the most appropriate way, is passed on accurately and is given to the right person at the right time. In order for the message to be received accurately it is important that:

- The correct method of communication is used.
- The person that the message is intended for wants or needs to receive it.
- The right person receives the message at the right time.
- The person it is intended for can understand the message. The message should not be too complicated or have too many unnecessary stages that could confuse the recipient.

The need to have effective internal and external communication touches almost every part and function of an organisation. A business will attempt to maintain effective internal and external communication in order to:

- Ensure employees are aware of organisational procedures.
- Maintain effective customer relationships.
- Ensure coordination and clarification of information.
- Receive feedback of information.
- Ensure accessibility to up-to-date information.
- Be cost effective.
- Motivate employees.
- Ensure efficient working.
- Provide customer satisfaction.
- Ensure a good company image.
- Increase profitability.
- Ensure effective marketing.
- Maintain customer interest.

Because these points are so important to all businesses, we will discuss them in more detail.

Organisational procedures

Most businesses have favourite ways of working and each of the different departments within the business will communicate using set procedures. They may even produce a manual which states how employees should carry out their work. This may mean that there is a set procedure for doing every task. Employees will have these procedures explained to them when they begin work with the business. They will have the manual to hand to remind them, and if the organisation changes its procedures then replacement pages for the manual will be issued and additional training will be provided if necessary. Setting clear organisational procedures is very important as it ensures that all of the necessary processes, including the completion of all documents, are carried out.

Effective customer relationships

Increasingly, customers expect to be fully informed of developments and news from businesses. Most organisations which provide products and services to customers now have **call centres** and websites through which customers can contact the business. Customers want more information and faster responses to **complaints** or problems. In order to maintain a good relationship with customers, businesses know that they need to respond quickly and effectively. Helplines and customer query lines are common for even the most ordinary products, such as jars of coffee or bags of crisps.

KEY TERMS

Call centre A central contact point set up by a business to allow customers to contact the business from anywhere in the world, often 24 hours a day, seven days a week

Complaints Those negative comments, often received from customers, about the service provided by a business

Think about it!

An article in *Winning Business Strategies* (ICAEW, 2000) started by saying, 'Call centres are springing up across the nation at breathtaking speed. It's one of the true boom areas for business – and it's a success story that is driven by technology.'

The advantages of call centres as opposed to a one-person helpline are as follows:

- Customers may feel embarrassed ringing the same human helper for advice several times a week.

- The automatic voice response is a recorded message and therefore it is anonymous.
- The employee does not spend a lot of time dealing with routine enquiries.
- Customer Service Departments can now call up on-screen documentation immediately to verify the caller's details.
- This is seen as a better deal for business, providing greater efficiency, lower costs, better time management and new opportunities.

What do you think about call centre technology?

The above list states the advantages and disadvantages for a business. Now you state the advantages and disadvantages to the customer of a call centre system.

Coordination and clarification

Even the smallest business needs to make sure that all parts of the business are cooperating and working for each other's benefit. For example, a shop which is low on stock of a particular product needs to be able to tell the person who is responsible for buying in new stock that a re-order needs to be placed. The buyer needs to be able to tell the shop when it can expect new deliveries so that the shop, when it runs out of that product, can tell the customers when a new delivery is expected.

The larger the organisation, the more complicated coordination becomes. A business which makes products from raw materials may have to plan months in advance in order to make sure sufficient raw materials are available. This means effective communication with its suppliers, the managers and employees responsible for making the product, the delivery and transportation team, and the customers who will eventually buy the finished product. Each group of people involved needs to be told exactly what is expected of them and by when. This is what is meant by clarification. Each group will then know when they become part of the process and how much time they may need to devote to it. All this can be done by ensuring that the right information reaches the right person at the right time.

Feedback of information

Many forms of communication require someone to give an answer. Many of the communications, both internal and external, ask questions which need clear answers. Feeding back information is very important as that information may change plans and action may need to be taken as a result of comments made. Once the feedback has been received, it is also important to communicate with all those who will be affected by the news.

Feedback can be received from suppliers, customers, or even other businesses, and it needs to be taken into account and considered carefully.

Accessibility of up-to-date information

Once communications have been received or sent it is important that they are not simply ignored, and a system must be set up so that it is easy to find the information. There are a number of different ways in which up-to-date information can be filed, either manually (as paperwork) or electronically (as files saved on a computer).

Most businesses will either place a number, date or code on paperwork that they receive. For example, it may be the responsibility of a receptionist to manually date stamp each letter that arrives in the morning's post before it is passed on.

There are many occasions when a business needs to find information quickly. If memos and letters etc. are simply stored in a heap it is unlikely that the relevant piece of information is going to be on the top of the pile. Therefore, it is essential that any information system is organised in such a way that the relevant information is easily retrievable. This requires a well-organised storage system. There are a number of different ways in which paperwork might be stored. These are:

- Alphabetically
- Numerically
- Alphanumerically
- Chronologically.

Data can be filed alphabetically by name, by subject or by location, depending on which is the most important factor. The phone book is a good example of alphabetical filing by name. Filing by location might be useful if you had information for different branches of the same organisation. Filing by subject might be useful if you wished to keep records of certain products. The Yellow Pages uses subject classification as a means of organising data.

There are rules that apply to alphabetical filing. These are important so that everyone knows exactly where information is stored. Some of the rules for alphabetical filing are listed below.

The rule	An example
People	
Surname first	Smith Allan
Identical names – surname followed by first name or initial	Smith Jane
	Smith Jane
	Smith Mary
Short names come before longer names	Field Lucy
	Fielding Graham
Nothing always comes before something	Duval M
	Duval Malcolm
	Duval Malcolm K
	Duval Malcolm Kenneth
Mac and Mc are both treated as Mac and come before M	McAbe M
	McAlpine W
	MacPherson P
	Mohammed B
	Ogden G
Apostrophes are ignored	O'Maddy C
	Ownsdale G

Action Points

1 Find out from your school library about the Dewey classification system that is used to catalogue library books.

2 Find out what systems are used in school to keep information about pupils.

3 Make an alphabetical list of all your classmates using a spreadsheet.

The rule	An example
Organisations	
Ignore the word 'The'	(The) Post Office
If the names are the same, the street or town is then used	(The) Granary Restaurant
	Pickfords Gallery Brentford
	Pickfords Gallery Matlock
Initials are placed before full names but ignore the use of and or &	J L Clarkson
	J & L Motors
	JTR Systems
	Stanton's Transport
The word Saint and the abbreviation St are treated as being the same	St Benedict's Church
	Saint Jude's School
File public bodies under the town or city, or by the name of the department	Barnsley District Council
	Birmingham City Council
	Bridgnorth Town Council
	Employment Office, Corby
	Environmental Health Office, Derby
	Social Security Office, Dudley
Numbers change into words, for example '13' would be filed under 'T' for thirteen	Seven Spices
	Four Seasons Chinese Restaurant

Action Points

Complete the exercise by rearranging the following files into alphabetical order by name:

5 Live	7 Stars Public House
JTH Footwear	Paul & Dobey
Cartwrights & Son	BJP Windows
John Shakespeare	Bewise Limited
Mathew O'Donnell	MacVitie & Co
Jones Brothers	Department of Health
The Charity Shop	McTavish Lee & Naylor
Thomas Blyth	GH Davis
Wild Heart Boutique	GH Davies

Where there are many files it is easier to have a system where they are organised using numbers. For example, a solicitor may have 20 clients all with the surname Smith. Giving each Smith a number is the simplest way to file the data. A numbering system might be used to describe a supplier, a customer or an employee. A numerical system might simply give each new file the next available number. This is known as sequential numbering. Earlier numbers that become available because a file becomes **obsolete** can be used again. Alternatively a business might use an alphanumeric system where files are given a letter and a number, so each Smith client would be allocated an S and a number, e.g. S1, S2, S3, etc.

A numerical system can only work if there is also an index that clearly shows which number is allocated to which client, customer, supplier or employee. There are a number of different types of index system that you might find in use:

- Index cards – these are stored in a small cabinet or box. The main information is stored at the top of the card. These are usually stored in alphabetical order with a front card indicating the letter.
- Strip index cards – much smaller strips which fit into special holders. Different colours are available which help to differentiate particular kinds of files.
- Visible edge cards – these fit into plastic wallets which are stacked one upon the other with the key information visible at the bottom edge of each card. These cards are large enough to contain quite a lot of information.
- Rotary index cards – these are put into a small drum in a metal cabinet. The drum rotates to reveal the relevant card.

Think about it!

Which system would you use in each of these different situations?
- Patient records in a doctors' or dental surgery.
- Employee records in a large firm.
- Information on different branches of the same firm.

1 What might happen if a customer's file is lost forever?
2 Why is it important to put files away as soon as you have finished with them?
3 Why is it important never to leave confidential documents lying on a desk?
4 Why is it important to have everyone use the same system of filing?

Cost effectiveness

Communications need to be efficient and cost effective. Businesses will hope to find the cheapest means of ensuring effective communications. Information communication technology (ICT) has helped to make communications cost effective, particularly by the use of email, which is fast and cheap, or fax machines, which are reliable and quite inexpensive.

ICT also allows businesses to store information on computers so that it can be accessed when needed. This avoids the need for mountains of paperwork occupying miles of shelving and filing cabinets in expensive office premises.

Motivation

One of the many things that can affect the way that employees view their jobs is a lack of information about what is going on. Employees may feel very demotivated if they think that information is being kept from them. When there is no news or information about the business, employees will often think the worst, and rumours and gossip may make them insecure or anxious about their work and their jobs. By using ICT to pass on information about the business's progress, employees can be kept up to date and will feel far more valued and much more motivated.

Efficient working

Employees who do not have access to information that they need to do their jobs or to make decisions, cannot be expected to work efficiently. Organisations that do not make sure that information is shared may often find that employees are repeating work that has already been done. Even simple tasks, such as informing a customer that a product that they have ordered has arrived, can end up being done very inefficiently if it is not noted that the customer has already been informed. The customer may be informed by more than one employee, and this is not cost effective to the business due to the cost in the employees' time and/or the cost of the telephone calls.

By using ICT the latest data can be at employees' fingertips and they can use this information in order to make more effective use of their working day.

Customer satisfaction

As well as ensuring that a business has good customer relationships, customers also need to be happy with the products and services supplied by the business. Many businesses have Customer Service Departments that routinely contact customers who have made purchases and ask them how the product has performed and whether they are happy with it. Sometimes businesses do this by telephone, or alternatively they may email the customer or send them a **questionnaire** by post. By finding out customers' views and whether or not they are satisfied, a business may be able to avoid mistakes or problems in the future.

Company image

The company's image, as opposed to the corporate image (which is usually taken to mean a business's logo), is of vital importance. The company image is how customers and the general public view the business. In other words, this is the business's reputation. Making sure that the company's image is favourable is very important and this may be affected by the way that the business deals with its customers and how satisfied the customers are with their dealings with the business. So a company's image may be affected by poor communications.

Increased profitability

Effective and cost-effective communication means that a business is not wasting money. If a business can identify the best way of communicating with either suppliers or customers, or, indeed within the organisation itself, then it will find that necessary information reaches the right people. Each time a business has to resend information as a result of choosing the wrong communication method, it costs money. If the business has too many of these rising costs, then it will cut into the profits. A business will experiment with ways of communication and eventually it will find the best way to get messages across and get information to the right people when it is needed. A business will regularly review the way in which it sends information out and will look for cheaper ways of achieving the same results. ICT helps in this, particularly through email, which can inform customers about the business and new products offered. Email is also a simple way for customers to contact the business to place orders or ask for more information.

KEY TERMS

Questionnaire A document containing a series of questions that are designed to discover information required for research purposes

Effective marketing

ICT has had an enormous impact on the way in which businesses can market their products and services. In the past, Marketing Departments would have placed advertisements in newspapers and magazines, on the television or radio, or they would have paid to have posters or billboards displayed. Now it is possible to buy the email addresses of potential customers and to send emails offering products and services, not just to people in their own immediate area or country, but across the world.

Many people who have email accounts receive dozens of emails every day. Although some businesses send 'junk' emails or 'spam' emails to thousands of people every day and abuse the system, some businesses have found that by finding out more about the person who has an email account, they can target their emails towards people who would be interested in their products and services.

Websites are also very useful in terms of marketing, provided people know where the website is and have its address. This can be achieved by sending emails to the right people.

Maintaining customer interest

A major part of maintaining good relationships with customers and ensuring that they are satisfied is keeping them up to date. As the business develops new products and services, existing customers or customers who have bought from the business in the past should be told of these developments. By regularly updating customers (particularly in the case of computer software, where, for example, a business could offer a free update to **download**), a customer might be tempted to purchase something new when they visit the website to download the update.

Businesses will also send printed catalogues, newsletters and sales letters by post to existing customers to tell them about new products and services. These communications, if they are sent to the right people, may well encourage customers to make another purchase.

KEY TERMS

Download Transfer a file from the internet onto a personal computer

EFFECTS OF POOR INTERNAL AND EXTERNAL COMMUNICATION

Having considered the importance of effective communication, many businesses may find that their communications are not good enough and that this causes them problems. If poor internal and external communications are allowed to continue, then many of the following will affect the overall performance of the business:

- Poor working relationships – if information is not passed on to all of the employees who need it, some employees may feel that they are being disadvantaged and that they have to work harder in order to achieve the same as someone who had that information. It is the responsibility of managers and supervisors to make sure that information that will affect the way in which their employees work is passed on and not kept to themselves. Employees may become suspicious of their managers or supervisors if they think they are keeping secrets.

- Poor company image – if a business gets a reputation for being an inefficient communicator with suppliers or customers, this will probably affect its overall image. Businesses that do not respond to queries or do not fulfil promises may find that the damage to their business is enormous and that it is very difficult to regain their reputation.

- Loss of business, customers or opportunities – businesses which do not handle their communications properly may find that potential customers will avoid them. If customers request information or find that a business is reluctant to communicate with them effectively, they will look for an alternative when they make their next purchase. When a customer is dissatisfied with the way that a business has communicated with them, that customer will probably be lost and they are likely to tell others of their bad experience. Suppliers may also be reluctant to deal with a business that does not have effective communications. That may mean that the business has to look for new suppliers.

- Demotivation of staff – if a business does not share information with its employees then the employees may have to work harder to carry out their jobs. Employees often need clear instructions and information from their managers or supervisors in order to do their work. If their boss is a poor communicator, then the employees may feel let down and become demotivated. This has a bad effect on the business because their staff are not working to their full potential.

- Misinformation and misinterpretation – if a business fails to pass on information to its employees, customers or suppliers, or it does not send all of the relevant information, it is easy to

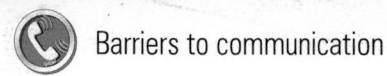
misunderstand or misinterpret what is being said. Without clear information, mistakes will be made which could cause a business to lose profits and potential sales, as well as causing problems for the person that required the information.

BARRIERS TO COMMUNICATION

There are a number of reasons why businesses fail to communicate effectively. They may be unaware of these failures or they may not understand them until a problem occurs. Some of the problems are avoidable if the communication methods are thought through properly. In other cases the problem will remain until something dramatic is done to improve it. Barriers to communication mean problems between the sender and the receiver of the information. In other words, there is a block of some sort between the two parties which stops the message getting through or stops it getting through in the intended way. Some common barriers to communication are:

- Lack of training – if employees are not effectively trained to use different types of communication then they will either make mistakes or will not be able to use that form of communication at all. Training in the use of equipment and, more basically, in the ways that communications should be written or spoken is essential. This training will often be part of organisational procedures.

- Lack of information – one of the most common barriers to communication is not having all of the information that you need to make a decision or to help someone make a decision. If, for example, a customer phoned a business and asked for the price and availability of a product and was told that it was out of stock, a sale would be lost. If the employee who had taken the call had known that the **warehouse** had just received a delivery of that product, then the sale would have been made. Information that affects an employee's job or role in the business must be passed on in order to make sure that they can work in an effective manner.

- Personal relationships – one of the most common reasons why communications are ineffective within an organisation is that individuals either do not like one another or do not understand one another. Personal likes or dislikes may mean that employees avoid each other, even if this means that information is not passed on between them and has a bad effect on both their own work and the business itself. This is a very difficult barrier to deal with, but the solution may involve getting to the root of the problem between the two individuals

Warehouse The large section of the business, often not attached to the business itself, where products or raw materials are stored until used or sold

KEY TERMS

Team building A series of activities that help members of a team to get to know one another and to feel comfortable together in order that they can work well together

or changing the job role of one of them so that they do not have direct contact with one another as often. An alternative to this is for the business to try and help them get along better by giving them some **team-building** training.

● Faulty systems – although ICT has offered cheaper and more effective methods of communication, not all systems are used in the best way. Often ICT systems are not linked together. Sometimes different software is used. This can contribute to the problem of information not passing from one part of an organisation to another. Faulty systems may also affect the ways in which organisations handle information. In other words, there may be a problem with the organisational procedures, which causes a communication difficulty. Perhaps one part of the whole process of dealing with an order has not been considered and this causes a delay in the customer receiving the product or service.

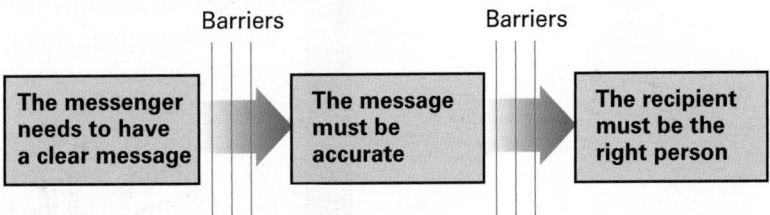

Figure 4.2

Barriers to good communication with customers might include:

● Writing something down incorrectly.
● Not hearing the customer's request.
● Losing important notes or documents.
● Not telling the right person about a problem.
● Having too many other things to do.
● Not realising the importance of the query.

Action Points

1 Gather some examples of customer service questionnaires. You can find these in many different places; for example, the local council often ask the public to tell them about their service and how good it is, local supermarkets may have leaflets, and restaurants and hotels also often ask for the opinion of their customers.

2 Find out the difference between open and closed questions.

3 Look at the questionnaires and how the questions are phrased and see how effective the use of questioning is in providing the business with answers.

Action Points

Every year the Railway Wanderers Football team met for a meal. There were 14 of them altogether. They had all played football as a team for some years and although many of them were no longer part of the team they liked to meet up for an annual reunion.

Most of the friends still lived in the same town, although a few had travelled a fair distance to be there. The restaurant that had been chosen was part of a large chain, but this branch was new and none of the friends had visited it before.

The starter was fine, in fact it was very enjoyable, and the friends began to think this was a very good choice. The waiters began to bring out the main course and served nine out of the 14 friends. There was a wait of about ten minutes before the rest of the food was served; politely the others waited and did not start to eat until everyone had been served. No apology for the delay was offered. There were some mutterings that this was not really good enough, but nobody actually complained. One of the party bit into his steak and realised that it was frozen in the middle. He politely called the waiter over to the table. He explained that he did not want the steak taken away because the meal had already been disrupted by the delay in bringing out all of the food. However, he did want the fact that he was dissatisfied to be reflected in his share of the bill at the end of the meal.

When it came to paying the bill there was no reference to the fact that at least one member of the party was unhappy. When this was mentioned the manager was called. She refused to make allowances for the steak and would not offer any recompense by reducing the bill. In fact, she was very rude and suggested that there was nothing wrong and that the person who had complained was not in any way justified. After all, he had not asked for another steak. In fact, she suggested that they would not be welcome in the restaurant again.

The friends left the restaurant feeling that the whole evening had been a bit of a disappointment. All of them have relayed the story of their dissatisfaction with the restaurant at least a dozen times!

Answer the following questions:

1 What might have caused the delay in bringing all of the food out to the friends at the same time?

2 What should the waiter have said to the friends when it was clear there would be a delay?

3 Do you believe the manager was justified in refusing to recognise that the steak was unsatisfactory?

4 In your opinion, how should the manager have acted in order for the friends to leave the restaurant in a better frame of mind?

5 What implications might an incident like this have on the future of:
- this branch of the business?
- the business as a whole?

Action Points Visit www.johnlewis.com-customerservice and see what John Lewis, the department store chain, has to offer its customers.

We need to look more closely at the ways in which businesses communicate with their customers.

Function	Methods used
Researching the market	Producing questionnaires to find out about customers wants and needs. Analysing national data in order to look at consumer habits. Producing data about their product or service sales.
Advertising the product or service	Creating a corporate image using a logo, colours and style. Having special company literature such as letterheads, brochures or leaflets, a website or catalogues.
Having a database of all their suppliers and customers	Keeping accurate records of all customers and suppliers and making sure the records are always up to date.
Continually seeking new markets and new customers	Encouraging new customers through sales and promotion techniques. Selling directly to new customers who have not been targeted before.
Keeping track of the way the business collects money	Having efficient systems, such as till procedures, good debt collection, electronic money transfer systems.
Communicating directly with the customer	Writing letters, answering queries, talking on the telephone, speaking directly, using email and fax, sending out literature, collecting cash and debts.

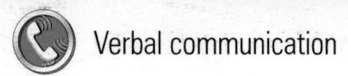
The above Table illustrates the direct link between the external customer who will receive the communication in all its different forms and the internal customer who works closely with others in the business to create an effective communication link to the customer outside.

The quality of communication will be the measure of how the external customer views the business. It is therefore essential that the business keeps a very close eye on the way it presents itself to the external customer at all times.

The larger the business the more difficult it is to keep track of the different methods of communication. Good systems need to be adapted to make sure that nothing can go wrong. These might include:

- Regular meetings between a manager and his or her team to discuss customer service and how it might be improved.
- Strategies for acting upon questionnaires given to customers in order to find out their needs and expectations and to ask where there are problems.
- A system to check on the quality of the product or service before it is marketed to the customer.
- Regular briefings of staff to train, retrain and reinforce **strategies** for good customer service.
- Having a system that makes sure all communications with customers are carefully recorded.
- Having strategies to ensure that all requests from customers are acted upon within a reasonable time frame.
- A set of financial documents that record the process of buying, from working out how much to charge for an item, ordering goods and services, to methods of requesting payment.
- Good filing systems so that information can be found easily.

KEY TERMS

Strategies Plans on how to achieve objectives

However good the systems are that the business puts in place, they will never be perfect and things will go wrong. Good businesses constantly strive to improve their service. Knowing what can happen to spoil the relationship between the business and its customers will help to ensure that the business avoids the pitfalls and maintains good customer relations.

VERBAL COMMUNICATION

Verbal communication is communication that involves speech. Because this form of communication is involved in most aspects of business activities, it is necessary for us to look in some detail at each of the ways of communicating verbally.

Face-to-face communications are conversations, talks or discussions within a work situation. ICT and telecommunications have improved the ways in which people can talk with one another, but it is still necessary to have face-to-face communications. There are a wide variety of situations within an office or a business that involve verbal communication:

- Private or social discussions within a business.
- Chats with people in corridors or during lunch breaks.
- Formal and informal meetings – as we will see, formal meetings have their own sets of documents and strict procedures. Informal meetings can be as simple as a group of employees gathering around a desk to discuss a problem and look for solutions. It has also become common, particularly when a new team of employees has been established, for the business to give them team-building training. This training helps the employees to understand a little more about the people they will be working with and how they can best work as an effective team, pooling their skills and using one another's strengths and offsetting others' weaknesses. When these teams are brought together for training, obviously they do not know each another and it is common for there to be an ice-breaker activity. These activities aim to get people talking so that they are not shy or embarrassed.
- Talking to customers.
- Giving and receiving instructions.
- Attending an interview.
- Giving a presentation to a group of colleagues or customers – sometimes employees may be expected to give presentations to customers or other employees. ICT has helped to make this a much less frightening prospect. Microsoft® PowerPoint® presentations can be used on large screens and notes can be created for each slide. Printouts of the slides, including space for notes, can also be created.

ICT and telecommunications now allow individuals to have a meeting or a discussion regardless of where they are in the world. Videoconferencing requires a camera and screen in front of each person in the meeting, and these are linked by a network or via the internet with appropriate software, so that each person can see and hear all of the other people taking part in the discussion. The costs of videoconferencing have dropped, and expensive and complicated equipment is no longer required. The more expensive equipment usually has better sound quality and pictures.

Teleconferencing is very similar except that you can only hear the voices of those involved in the discussion or the meeting. Typically, all of those taking part in the discussion will call a central switchboard which will then manage the conversation by allowing everyone on the telephone lines to speak to and hear one another. The advantage that videoconferencing has over teleconferencing is that you can both hear and see, and it is often easier to detect when someone is directing a question to you.

For most businesses, the telephone is the commonest and cheapest form of verbal communication, although this is not a face-to-face communication. Telephones are used for both internal and external communication and, despite the fact that we use telephones frequently in our homes, there are lots of things that can go wrong when using this as a way of communicating. Telephone conversations are different to face-to-face communications in three main ways:

- Everything has to be explained in words.
- Your attitude has to come across in your voice.
- Voices can sound very different on the telephone.

Many businesses now have digital switchboards which allow each employee who has a telephone to leave what is, in effect, a personal answerphone message. Voice mail, as it is known, allows a caller to leave a message that can be dealt with when the recipient returns to their office.

If you have ever been to an airport, railway station, large department store or supermarket, you will have heard messages being broadcast via loudspeakers or Tannoy systems. These public messaging systems not only allow communication between employees but can also pass on information to customers or visitors to the business. In a supermarket, for example, they could inform customers of a price reduction to clear overstocked products, or in an airport they may announce the fact that a flight is boarding and that all passengers (customers) should head for the departure gate. Public messaging systems are effective in informing large numbers of people, provided that:

- The message is clear.
- The loudspeakers are well placed.
- There is little other background noise.
- The person broadcasting the message has a clear voice.

WRITTEN COMMUNICATION (DOCUMENTATION)

The term 'documentation' refers to traditional paperwork, typically in the form of letters, business cards, newsletters, questionnaires and business stationery related to buying and selling. Although some of the paper documents can be replaced with electronic documents, it is often the case that businesses actually prefer to have a hard copy for their records. There are a number of documents which need further explanation.

Corporate image

Although corporate image is not, in itself a document, it can be found on almost every document, as we will see, in the form of the logos and fonts used, house styles of writing or formatting documents, and even the colours used. A corporate image needs to be the same throughout all forms of documentation sent out by the business so that customers and suppliers know automatically that the document has come from that particular business.

Business letters and letterheads

A business letter is a communication sent outside an organisation, typically either to suppliers or customers. These letters need to be neat, accurate and well presented. Businesses will use headed paper as part of their corporate image, giving the person who receives the letter the following details:

- The name and address of the business.
- The telephone number, fax number, email address and website of the business.
- The registered address of the business (this may be different from the postal address).
- The company registration number (in effect, the number on the company's 'birth certificate').
- The names of the directors or owners of the business.
- The names of any other companies or organisations which the business has a relationship with (such as membership of a professional organisation).

nelson
thornes

Delta Place
27 Bath Road
Cheltenham GL53 7TH
United Kingdom

t +44 (0) 1242 267100
f +44 (0) 1242 221914
e mail@nelsonthornes.com
w www.nelsonthornes.com

Ref: 270902/DEC
27 September 2002
URGENT
Jonathan Sutherland
Blackfriars Close
Northumberland
NB21 5DC

Dear Mr Sutherland

GCSE Business and Communication Book
xxxxxxxxxxxxxxxxxxxxxxxxxxxxxxxxxxxxxxxxxxxxxxxx
xxxxxxxxxxxxxxxxxxxxxxxxxxxxxxxxxxxxxxxxxxxxxxx
xxxxxxxxxxxxxxxxxxxxxxxxxxxxxxxxxxxxxxxxxxxxxxx
xxxxxxxxxxxxxx
xxxxxxxxxxxxxxxxxxxxxxxxxxxxxxxxxxxxxxxxxxxxxxx
xxxxxxxxxxxxxxxxxxxxxxxxxxxxxxxxxxxxxxxxxxxxxxx
xxxxxxxxxxxxxxxxxxxxxxxxxxxxxxxxxxxxxxxxxxxxxxx
xxxxxxxxxxxxxxxxxxxxxxxxxxxxxxxxxxxx
xxxxxxxxxxxxxxxxxxxxxxxxxxxxxxxxxxxxxxxxxxxxxxx
xxxxxxxxxxxxxxxxxxxxxxxxxxxxxxxx

Yours sincerely

Brian Forbes

BRIAN FORBES
cc Nelson Thornes Publishing
Enc

Nelson Thornes Ltd
A member company of Wolters Kluwer
Registered in England No 108 3699
VAT Reg. No. GB 302 3194 07
Registered Office:
Croner House, 145 London Road,
Kingston-upon-Thames, Surrey KT2 6SR

The layout or format of a business letter will also be part of a business's corporate image and different businesses will have different rules about the way their letters are displayed. It is common to use a fully blocked method of display, which means that each part of the letter starts at the left-hand margin. A business letter will be ordered in a certain way so that it contains all the necessary information, as can be seen in the example given above. In addition to the information contained on the letterhead, there will be a date, a reference number and often a subject heading or a statement which says the letter is urgent or confidential. The letter will also include the name and address of the person to whom it was sent. If the name of the person is not known, then 'Dear Sir' or 'Dear Madam' will be used, which means that the letter will end with 'Yours faithfully'. When the name of the person is known it will say 'Dear Mr, Mrs, Miss, Ms' and end with 'Yours sincerely'. After the 'Yours sincerely' or 'Yours faithfully', the sender will sign the letter and their name will be printed underneath the signature. If the letter is being sent to a number of different people it will have the letters 'cc' on it together with details. If other documents are included with the letter it will have 'Enc' at the bottom of the page.

Logos and house styles

Most businesses will have their own logo, which may be a simple drawing or symbol or the fact that their name is always displayed in the same font and in a particular colour. Many businesses will have a logo and a catch-phrase placed on each of their printed documents, always in the same place, perhaps in the top right-hand corner, or at the bottom, in the middle of each document. This is an easy way of maintaining corporate image and making it absolutely clear where the document has come from.

Action Points

1 Design your own logo to use on all your own work. Use a graphics package or some clipart to develop your logo.

2 Reshape the design until you feel it is right for you.

3 Keep all your drafts to show how the logo developed.

A compliment slip can look very much like the top of a business letter as it has all of the information usually found on a letterhead. But it is a different size (around one-third of the size of a letter) and it has 'With compliments' preprinted on it. Compliments slips are usually used instead of a letter and are included in an envelope along with other information requested by a customer.

A business card is another version of a document which has elements found on a letterhead. Business cards have the name of a person who works for the business printed on them and they are used to help potential customers or suppliers to contact that person by referring to the business card for their telephone or email details. They are usually printed on stiffer card so that they do not bend or tear. A modern development in business cards has been to print them on plastic (rather like a credit card) or even to produce a mini CD which can then be put into a computer and by clicking on an email address or name a communication can be sent directly to the person who gave the digital business card.

Meetings documentation

As we have seen, meetings can be formal or informal. Informal meetings do not tend to use the documents below, whereas formal meetings may use all or some of these documents which are specifically designed for meetings.

- Notice of a meeting – this is a communication which calls for everyone who should attend a meeting to make themselves available at a particular time and place. The notice should include where the meeting is, the date and time, the type of meeting, the name of the person calling the meeting and brief headlines of what will be discussed.

1 August 2003

NOTICE OF MEETING

There will be a meeting of Walpole Safety Representatives in the Conference Centre on Friday, 22 August 2003 at 11.30am. All members are requested to attend as a vote will be taken on the question of the new safety regulations.

MICHELLE HARDING

Secretary

Agenda – this document is also sent out before the meeting to those who will attend, so that they can prepare themselves for what needs to be discussed. The agenda will detail exactly what will be discussed and who, at the last meeting, was made responsible for bringing information to this meeting.

Walpole Safety Representatives Meeting

A meeting of Safety Representatives will be held in the Conference Centre on

Friday, 22 August 2003 at 11.30am

Agenda

1 Apologies for absence.

2 Minutes of the last meeting.

3 Matters arising from the minutes.

4 Report from the Chief Safety Officer on recent legislation received on Health and Safety at Work procedures.

5 Consider implication of possible new extension to the office block.

6 Feedback report from those who recently attended the training session at Head Office.

7 Any other business.

8 Date of next meeting.

MICHELLE HARDING
Secretary

- Minutes – these are a written record of what happened at a particular meeting and the decisions which were made. Minutes record the following:
  - who was present;
  - what discussions took place;
  - tasks allocated to individuals (action points);
  - reports received from individuals;
  - decisions made.

- Normally, one person attending the meeting will be made responsible for taking the notes of what has happened at that meeting (the Minutes Secretary).

Memorandums (memos)

Memos are internal communications used to pass information from one department or function of a business to another. They are usually shorter than a business letter, but they can be compared in the following ways:

- Both should always be dated.
- Both will often include a reference number. This will indicate where it should be filed after having been dealt with, and often the reference number will be used in all communications about the subject of the memo.
- Both will often include the words 'confidential', 'private and confidential', 'personal' or 'urgent'.
- Both will often include the letters 'Enc' to show that other documents have been included, or 'Att' if they have been attached (stapled).
- Although a memo is not always signed, it does sometimes include the initials of the sender.

Action Points Your employer has asked you to write a memo to all staff in your department. There is concern about wastage of paper.

Create a memo and word process it to all your colleagues. Make it clear that the wastage of A4 paper has meant that the stationery bill for your department has increased by 12 per cent in the last three months and that they need to be more careful about checking work before printing off hard copies.

Reports

As we discussed earlier in this chapter, reports can be produced as the result of some research that has taken place. Reports can be either informal or very formal, but both types contain certain common items. The Research and Development Department of a business might carry out report writing in order to:

- Identify any problems associated with the machinery or equipment.
- Obtain up-to-date information on sales of products or services.
- Receive progress reports on a certain project being undertaken.
- Identify the need to change policies and procedures.

A formal report will contain the following:

- Title page.
- Terms of reference – this will state what has been asked for, for example research on a particular topic.
- Procedure – this will say how the information has been gathered, for example interviews or visits.
- Findings – this will state what has been found out.
- Conclusion – this would give a general statement about the findings of the research.
- Recommendations – on the basis of the findings and the conclusions, this is where the researcher would make recommendations for future research or projects.
- Appendices – these are additional documents that would be attached to the report.

An informal report is less complicated and the format would include these headings:

- Introduction
- Conclusions
- Information
- Action required
- Findings

Notices

When a business needs to send information to a number of its employees, a notice may be put on the staff notice board. Such a method of communication may be formal or informal. It could be that it tells staff about a change in procedures, or it may be an informal social event that is being planned. Notices allow for quick and easy communication with a large number of people, although they are not always regarded as such a significant form of communication as reports and memos. However, they can be used to inform all employees of:

- Social events
- Job vacancies
- Planned leaving parties
- Items for sale at discount to employees
- Items for sale by employees.

Electronic notice boards can similarly pass on information to a large number of people. A good example of an electronic notice board can be found on motorways and major roads. Information is highlighted by flashing lights and it is possible for the police to notify all those driving along the road of any enforced speed restriction or a hold-up ahead which is causing a delay.

ICT has made it possible for a business to contact a large number of employees by using email. We consider the ways that computer technology has made this possible in the next two chapters of this book.

Itineraries and schedules

Another important form of written communication which requires precise accuracy and checking is what is known either as an **itinerary** or a **schedule**. This document will be written by the Administration Department for people from within the organisation who are making a journey in order to visit a customer or a supplier. Alternatively, it may be written for a group of individuals who are visiting the business itself. Naturally, the nature of the schedule may vary depending on what is involved, but it could be that the person responsible for organising the visit would have to:

- Book travel arrangements (for example provide maps; book train, boat or air tickets).
- Book accommodation (hotel rooms, possibly for a large number of employees or visitors).
- Book resources and equipment (book other people to give presentations, book computers or projection equipment).

When planning a schedule, it is important that the people taking part in the visit have all the information they will need. Being thorough in the planning and preparation stages will help to ensure that the visit is successful. Visitors should be aware of each of the following before the visit:

- The name and address of the organisation they are visiting.
- The place the meeting is being held (this may be different from the above).
- The person or persons they are to meet on arrival.
- The arrival time and meeting point.
- How their time will be spent during the visit. This will be detailed as much as possible, giving exact times throughout the visit for each of the activities planned.
- Whether they can expect refreshments during the visit and if so at what times.
- The likely time they will be free to depart from the visit.
- Any travel information.
- Any accommodation information.

ICT has made the production of itineraries and schedules much less complicated and time consuming than it used to be.

Bookings services have removed the need to make many telephone calls to hotels and **route planners** make it possible to estimate the length of time that a journey could take.

Flow charts

A flow chart is a way of communicating a complicated piece of information. Very often individuals can understand something better if they see it in the form of a graphic image rather than a lot of words. In presentations, an individual might choose to produce a flow chart to explain something that involves a number of different stages. This would be the case if someone from the Production Department of a business was presenting the different stages involved in the making of a new product. Additionally, someone from the Marketing Department might present the stages of a new product promotion this way.

Other ways of presenting complicated data in a clear way include:

- Graphs
- Pie charts
- Bar charts
- Tables
- Pictograms.

In other words, anything that breaks down the information either into an image form or into stages helps to ensure the communication will be understood by the audience.

An organisation chart is a way of explaining who has the authority and responsibility in a business. It is a much simpler way of explaining where all the different job roles fit into the business as a whole.

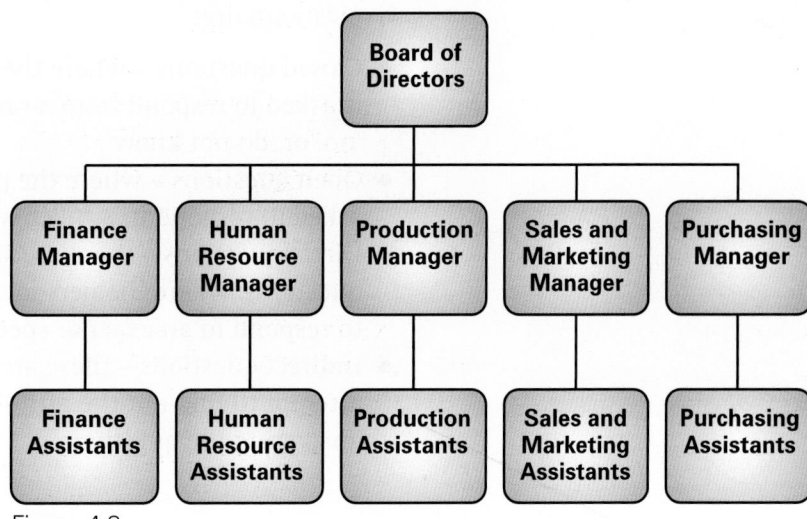

Figure 4.3

Action Points

1 Using Figure 4.3 as your outline, complete a chart of your own for your school's organisation.

2 Decide first who will be at the top with the most authority and responsibility, who will come on the second level and third and so on.

3 Where do you fit into the structure?

4 Where do the teachers fit in?

5 You can complete an organisational structure using your computer. In a Microsoft® Word document select the following:
  ● Insert
  ● Picture
  ● Organization Chart.

KEY TERMS

Wants Products or services desired by customers

Needs Essential products and services required by customers

Competitors Other businesses or organisations offering similar products or services

Questionnaires and surveys

In order to carry out market research the Marketing Department of a business will design some suitable questionnaires. Market research is the collection of information that is relevant to the product or service. An organisation needs to know what the intended buyers of their product or service require from it. In other words, they have to find out what their customers' **wants** or **needs** are, as well as finding out what their **competitors** already offer.

Because questionnaires are such an important part of finding out this information, it is important that this written communication is designed in a well-constructed way. There are a number of different types of questions that can be included on a questionnaire:

● Closed questions – where the person answering the questions is asked to respond from a range of set answers, usually 'yes', 'no' or 'do not know'.

● Open questions – where the person answering the questions is asked to respond in a fuller way using their own words.

● Direct questions – these are similar in some ways to closed questions, where the person answering the questions is asked to respond in an exact or specific way.

● Indirect questions – these are very general questions and attempt to find out the attitudes or behaviour of the person answering the questions.

A structured questionnaire is one that relies mainly on closed questions with the occasional open question. An unstructured questionnaire is one that makes use of direct and indirect questions.

Once a suitable questionnaire has been developed, the researcher will then either ask the questions of a number of different people, or ask those people to complete the questionnaires and return them by post. When the required number of questionnaires have been completed, the researcher will look at the range of answers and work out which answers are the most common.

Survey research is one of the most common ways for a business to collect information as it can provide data on their customers':

- Attitudes
- Beliefs
- Feelings
- Behaviour
- Knowledge
- Personal characteristics
- What they already own or wish to own.

There are several ways that a survey can be carried out, including:

- Direct surveys – where the researcher or team of researchers personally ask the questions on the questionnaire.
- Indirect surveys – where the questionnaire is mailed to the individuals for completion. The questionnaire would be accompanied by a letter explaining the purpose of the questions and the importance of completion and return to the business.

A market is where goods and services are sold. A market trader selling cheap goods from a stall is using the market to sell his wares. A car producer, such as Renault or Ford, sells to a much wider market by advertising on the television, producing brochures and creating a brand image that we can all recognise.

Marketing is simply the term used to describe all activities that help to promote and sell products and services to satisfy the needs and wants of people in all walks of life.

The marketing function in any business has to look to building relationships with customers. A business, however large or small, depends on its customers to buy goods and services in order that the business can make a profit and succeed. The business needs to be in touch with what the customer wants and be able to adapt when change takes place.

Marketing becomes ever more crucial when the business has fierce competition and its competitors try to build a bigger and better relationship with the same group of customers. The marketing function needs to look carefully at the activities of competitors, studying what they produce and sell, and then make changes where necessary.

The marketing team will need to work closely together to best assess:

- The needs and wants of the customer.
- The best ways of satisfying those needs.
- The most effective way of advertising goods and services.
- How to persuade the customer not to go elsewhere.

In order to make this happen the marketing team need to have a strategy or a plan of what to do. The marketing team will have to develop a strategy that includes the following.

Figure 4.4

Action Points

Your class is considering setting up a school shop to stock items that pupils in the school might buy in the time leading up to Christmas. You want to find out some information to decide:

- What products to sell.
- Where the shop should be situated.
- How much money your customers (the pupils) have to spend (this is known as their 'disposable income').
- Which school year each pupil who responds to your questions is from.
- Where else pupils will shop before Christmas.
- Any other comments those answering the questions may wish to make.

1 Design a questionnaire to gather the information you need. Remember to include open and closed questions. Include the date of each interview.

2 Collate your information onto a spreadsheet. Produce graphs to show:
- The most popular products.
- Ideas about where the shop should be situated.
- How many pupils responded from each different year group.
- The average amount that can be classed as a pupil's disposable income.
- The most popular places where pupils might shop this Christmas.

3 Now write a report to the Head stating your case for opening a Christmas shop. State what goods might be sold in the shop, where it should be situated and how popular the idea was with pupils in general. Put some of your graphs into the report as appendices to illustrate your findings.

Action Points

Mervyn has just left college. He has trained as a carpenter. He is thinking about setting up his own business. His dad has agreed to lend him some money as long as Mervyn does some market research. His dad wants him to prove that there are people who would like to use his skills and also to show him that there are not too many other carpenters operating in the same area and doing the same kind of work. Mervyn has also decided that he will need to find out how much other carpenters charge for their services.

1 Advise Mervyn how he might find out who else provides a carpentry service in his local area.

2 What might he do to find out about his competitors?

3 What are the different ways that Mervyn might use to find out if his service would be popular?

4 Design a questionnaire that Mervyn might give to some local people to find out if there is a demand for carpentry.

5 Design Mervyn a logo to put on all his business stationery.

6 Design a leaflet for Mervyn to use to advertise his carpentry service.

A tally sheet is a simple data collection form used to note down how often something happens. It is an easy and efficient way to collect and organise information, particularly when analysing the market research information gathered.

Events	Day one	Day two	Total
A	|||||||	|||||	12
B	||||||||||||||	||||||||||	28
C	||||||||||	|||||||||||||	25

An example of a typical data capture sheet is an application form for a store card or a subscription to a magazine. In addition to basic questions, such as name, address and telephone number, other questions are asked which will be useful to the business. The information contained on the sheets can then either be read by a computer, using optical character recognition (OCR) or keyed in by hand by a computer operator. This information can then form the basis of a database and customers can be sent emails or postal offers based on the information given on the data capture sheet. The use of database software is discussed in the next two chapters of this book.

Action Points

1 From the activity given earlier, when you designed a questionnaire to find out about the popularity of a shop in your school, now design a suitable data capture sheet which will obtain the required information.

2 You should gather all the information you need, on your capture sheet, and keep this information in a safe place as it will be required for an ongoing activity using a computerised database in Chapter 6 of this book.

Catalogues, leaflets, brochures and price lists

These different items together are known as the business's sales literature and they play a vital role in the ongoing marketing effort of the organisation. They aim to communicate to the customer the vital information about the business's products or services that will help them to decide to buy. In order to ensure that the sales literature helps the customer to make the right decision, this communication needs to be professional looking and have a strong company image. It must be easy for the customer to understand and it should contain as much information as possible so that the customer is not left with outstanding questions.

Sales literature can be used to send out responses to enquiries or it can be given to sales representatives of the business to hand to current customers personally. Although such a communication with customers can be quite cheap to produce, it is important that sales literature:

- Is of reasonably good quality and does not look cheap.
- Follows any organisational conventions, such as the use of the logo or catch-phrases and slogans.
- Is designed to communicate quickly and clearly and is not packed with too much technical or complicated information.

Action Points

1 Produce a leaflet to inform your fellow students about the opening of your new shop.

2 Use the logo you designed earlier, although you may need to amend this slightly to make it more appropriate.

3 Give them all the information they need to attract or encourage them to visit the shop.

Preprinted forms

There are a number of forms used in businesses that are what is known as preprinted. This means that they are a **template** and all the headings are already provided, so only the specific information has to be input onto the computer or written or keyed in each time. These preprinted forms are mainly used in the buying and selling activities of the business, for instance when goods are ordered from a supplier or products or services are sold to a customer.

Quotations are often sought from different suppliers to find the best price. Other considerations when requesting quotations from suppliers are their delivery times and the length of time that they allow before the buyer has to pay for the goods received. Sometimes a supplier will give the business a **discount** for buying large amounts of goods or for simply using them as their only supplier. Naturally the Finance Department of the business will need copies of the orders placed.

Buying goods and services for a business is the job of the buyer or the purchasing or procurement officer. Different organisations operate different systems when they buy goods or services. In some businesses there may be a system whereby each purchase has to have its own order number. Someone in the business will have the authority to issue this order number to another

KEY TERMS

Template The basic essentials of a form or document which can be set out so that there is no need to type them time and time again

Discount This is a deduction from or a reduction in the actual price of a product employee wishing to buy from a supplier on behalf of the business. The order number will only be issued if the person who is buying has the authority to do so. Other businesses may have less sophisticated systems.

The order number, if this applies, will be quoted on an order form that will be sent to the supplier. The supplier will process the order and send the items to the buyer with a delivery note that will detail exactly what is being included in the parcel. When the items arrive at the business they will be checked against the delivery note to ensure that all of the items ordered are present.

The supplier will then send an invoice to the business, asking for payment. The invoice usually states the date by which the invoice should be paid. These are often known as the 'terms of payment' and can be from seven to 30 days after the date of the invoice. A copy of the invoice will arrive in the Finance Department of the business.

After a period of time the supplier will send a statement of account to the Finance Department listing all the invoices that are still not paid. The statement will show invoices that are current and therefore do not necessarily need paying immediately, invoices that are 30 days old (these need paying), 60 days old (these certainly need paying), and 90 days old (these most definitely need paying). If the business does not pay after a certain amount of time the supplier may not be prepared to sell them any more goods or services.

The Finance Department will send a cheque or pay through the Bankers Automated Clearing Service (BACS) to settle the outstanding amount. If the manual method of paying by cheque is used, the Finance Department will have the cheque stub as evidence of the cheque payment and a bank statement that confirms the money has come out of their bank account. In this case, and in the case of the electronic payment of the amount, the Finance Department will also send to the supplier a remittance advice. This informs the supplying organisation that the money has been sent to settle the outstanding amount.

Action Points Create your own flow chart which identifies the different stages in the buying and selling process discussed above.

Having received the goods ordered, and, hopefully, checked them against the delivery note, it could be that a problem occurs. If, for instance, some of the goods are damaged or not in a state fit for the business to use, then the business will contact the supplier and complain about the fact that they have been charged for goods that are unacceptable. In such cases, in order to stay on good terms with the business, the supplier may issue a credit note which is a form of **refund** and would mean that the business can use this to buy replacement goods, or an amount could be taken off the sum they owe the supplier on the statement of account.

Action Points

1 Using spreadsheet software and a document wizard, create a set of documents for buying goods and services, including an order form, a delivery note, an invoice and a statement of account.

2 Complete the documents with the following details, i.e. the businesses where the items are bought from, what is purchased and who purchased it:
   - Paws Animal Foods, High Street, Dawley TF6 5TH; 12 boxes of cat food @ £12.50 a box bought two months ago; 25 bags of chewits @ £19.00 a bag bought a month ago.16 boxes of dog food @ £14.50 a box bought last week. Bought by The Pet Palace, Whitburn Street, Bridgnorth WV16 3RF.
   - The Steel Company, Cranley Way, Hanley, T12 3TF; 100 steel tubes @ £150.00 per tube bought yesterday; 250 steel bolts @ £25.00 a bolt bought two months ago. 120 sheets of steel @ £35.00 a sheet bought three months ago. Bought by Leppington Steels Ltd, Brierley Street, Dudley DY2 4WS.

3 You will need to add VAT of 17.5 per cent to the invoices and you should number the orders in sequence, beginning with 7593 for the first one.

4 Make up your own mind when to pay the invoices. Take a 10 per cent discount if you pay within 30 days.

5 The Pet Palace has not paid for cat food bought two months ago; write a letter asking for immediate payment. You will need to be firm but polite; the debt is not too old as yet.

Consider the following problems:

- You work in the bakery section of your local supermarket. It is 8.30am and the bread has not arrived from the suppliers. You have already turned six customers away.
- You have ordered some toner cartridges for a new laser printer. When they arrive they are the wrong ones. You have a large print run to do. The supplier says sorry but the correct ones are out of stock.
- A large order for computers is delayed because the supplier of the keyboards has not delivered the order placed six weeks ago. It was promised by the end of last week and there are still no keyboards. You have tried phoning but there is no answer.
- A lorry carrying fresh strawberries that you ordered has broken down. The strawberries are to use in your restaurant that evening for a special buffet.

1 In small groups role-play how you might deal with each of the situations described above. You may have other similar examples that you could use instead.

2 Appoint one of the group to take notes of the role-play, video or tape the proceedings and discuss other ways that it might be possible to tackle such situations.

3 Discuss how such disasters might be avoided.

Goods need to be moved from place to place in the most efficient and cost effective way possible. Good communication is essential if this is to happen. The business in need of supplies or stock needs to tell their suppliers exactly what they need and be clear as to when it will be delivered.

Goods can be sold in a variety of different ways:

- Directly to the customer.
- Through a shop or other retail outlet.
- Through a wholesaler or agent.

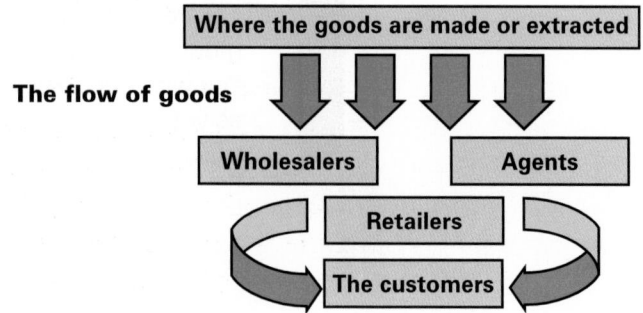

Figure 4.5

At each stage of the process there needs to be a clear system in place that records the transactions and allows for the accurate and efficient movement of goods and services. Computerised or manual systems are only as good as those who input the information in the first place. The system must:

- Record clearly the order for goods or services.
- Record clearly when the items are removed from the factory or the wholesale or retail outlet.
- Complete the paperwork for obtaining payment for the goods or services.
- Check that the right items have arrived at their destination.
- Check that all items have arrived in one piece.
- Stack or store items safely.
- Have a system for recording goods that are sold or removed.

Action Points

1 Find out what kind of procedures are in place in your school for ordering:
   - Stationery.
   - Food items for the kitchen.
   - Computer equipment.

2 Obtain an office supplies catalogue or look at the website of a company that allows you to order on line.

3 Choose some stationery or some computer items that you think would be useful in the computer room. Complete the order form.

4 Draw a flow chart to demonstrate the different steps in the ordering process of one of the items above.

DEVELOPMENTS IN COMMUNICATION TECHNOLOGY

Even as you are reading this, someone somewhere in the world is creating a new form of ICT, or at least developing an existing form. The pace of technology is moving so fast that new forms of ICT are being developed every day. Whether some of them will become as popular as the ones detailed below is something we will all have to wait to find out.

Mobile telephones

Most people now have their own mobile telephones but, in terms of business, the mobile phone has made cost effective and easy communication a reality. Sales of mobile telephones have exceeded all expectations, and a mobile telephone is used by many people in their everyday life.

Most mobile telephones use one of two different technologies. The old system is the analogue system, which works using a continuous signal. But the analogue mobile telephones will soon be a thing of the past. In many European countries, the analogue networks are expected to be shut down within the next few years. Digital mobile telephones are more modern. The digital telephone system has many advantages; it increases flexibility by giving the user more options, for example voice mail, texts, etc.

Pagers

Pagers or 'beepers' are a portable communication messenger device. The person sending the message uses a touch-tone phone and calls the pager's number, then the person enters their number or voice message and within moments the pager carrier is notified by an audible 'beep' or a silent vibration. The number or voice message can be read on the pager's screen. The pager's secret is that inside that little case is a simple, yet sophisticated receiver.

A pager is a dedicated device that allows the user to receive messages broadcast on a specific frequency over a special network of radio base stations. The first pager-like system was used in 1921 by the Detroit Police Department. In 1949 the very first telephone pager device was **patented** by Al Gross. The term 'pager' was first used in 1959, referring to a Motorola radio communications product: a small receiver that delivered a radio message individually to those carrying the device.

By 1980 there were 3.2 million pager users worldwide. Pagers had a limited range, and were used in on-site situations, e.g. employers within a hospital. By 1990 wide-area paging had been invented and over 22 million pagers were in use. By 1994 there were over 61 million pagers in use and pagers became popular for personal use.

Faxes

A facsimile machine (fax machine) is a device that can send or receive pictures and text over a telephone line. Fax machines work by digitising an image by dividing it into a grid of black and white dots. On the receiving side, a fax machine reads the incoming data, translates the zeros and ones back into dots, and reprints the picture.

While the idea of fax machines has existed since the 1800s, fax machines did not become popular until the mid 1980s. Now

KEY TERMS

Patented The inventor has obtained the right to be the only producer of his or her invention by obtaining legal protection that prevents others copying the idea

faxes are commonplace in offices of all sizes. They provide an inexpensive, fast, and reliable method for transmitting correspondence, contracts, handwritten notes and illustrations. A fax machine consists of an optical scanner for digitising images on paper, a printer for printing incoming fax messages, and a telephone for making the connection. Some printers on fax machines are thermal, which means they require a special kind of paper.

Some of the features that differentiate one fax machine from another include the following:

- Speed – fax machines transmit data at different rates. A 9,600 bytes per second fax machine typically requires 10–20 seconds to transmit one page.
- Printer type – most have printers that can print on regular paper.
- Paper size – some machines accept only narrow-sized paper.
- Paper cutter – most fax machines include a paper cutter because the thermal paper that many machines use comes in rolls. The least expensive models and portable faxes, however, may not include a paper cutter.
- Paper feed – most fax machines have paper feeds so that you can send multiple-page documents without manually feeding each page into the machine.
- Auto dialling – fax machines come with a variety of dialling features. Some enable you to program the fax to send a document at a future time so that you can take advantage of the lowest telephone rates.

As an alternative to stand-alone fax machines, you can also put together a fax system by purchasing separately a fax modem and an optical scanner. You may not even need the optical scanner if the documents you want to send are already in electronic form. More recently fax machines have become part of a multifunction printer that allows the user to print, scan, copy and fax all from the same machine.

ISP

This is short for internet service provider, a business which provides access to the internet. For a monthly fee, the service provider supplies a software package, username, password and access phone number. The customer needs a modem in order to log on to the internet and browse the world wide web and to send and receive email.

In addition to serving individuals, ISPs also serve large companies, providing a direct connection from the company's networks to the internet. ISPs themselves are connected to one another through network access points (NAPs). ISPs are also called IAPs (internet access providers).

Internet

The internet is a global network connecting millions of computers. More than 100 countries are linked into exchanges of data, news and opinions. Unlike online services, which are centrally controlled, the internet is not centrally controlled. Each internet computer, called a host, is separate and independent.

Each user of a computer can choose which internet services to use and what information held on the computer should be made available to the global internet community. There are a variety of ways to access the internet. Most online services, such as America Online (AOL), offer access to some internet services. It is also possible to gain access through a commercial ISP, which is usually the preferred method for businesses with larger websites.

As can be seen in the chart below, the main language on the internet is English.

**Online Language Populations
Total: 619 million
(September 2002)**

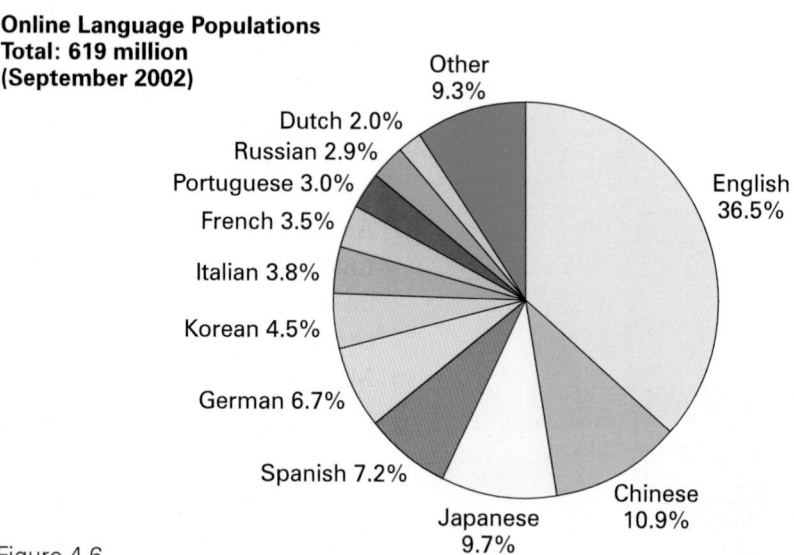

Figure 4.6

Action Points Convert the information in the pie chart into a bar chart using an Excel spreadsheet.

Intranet

An intranet is a network that belongs to an organisation which is only accessible by the organisation's members, employees, or others with authorisation. An intranet's websites look and act just like any other websites, but the firewall surrounding an intranet stops others from making unauthorised access.

Like the internet itself, intranets are used to share information. Secure intranets are now the fastest growing part of the internet because they are much less expensive to build and manage.

Web phones

The newest generation of cellular phones have matchbox sized screens and built-in internet browsers that let users access the web. Industry analysts expect that most cellular phones will be web-ready by 2004. Users can check email, make travel arrangements and even make a phone call. Unlike personal digital assistants, interactive pagers or other wireless devices, the wireless web phone lets the user do all this without having to buy other devices.

The ability to receive information on devices that you carry around with you all day is claimed to be the next wave of technology. The development has been slow and not many websites are set up to allow connection via a web phone. Emails can be sent, mainly at present using Yahoo Mail or Microsoft's Hotmail. New generation web phones are also more easy to use with a separate keypad or three to four buttons to access the web, and are much more user friendly. The biggest problem now is that the tiny telephone screen is not big enough for most people who are used to a 17-inch colour monitor.

Wireless application protocol (WAP)

Wireless application protocol (WAP) is a new, advanced, intelligent messaging service for digital mobile phones and other mobile terminals that will allow you to see internet content in special text format on special WAP-enabled GSM (global system for mobile communications) mobile phones. The main points regarding WAP are:

- It uses wireless markup language, a distant cousin of HTML, to format web data for the tiny screens used in WAP-enabled devices.
- Wireless devices receive and transmit data at 9.6 kbps (kilobytes per second), which makes for long waits while surfing.

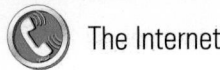

- Currently, only a small percentage of mobile phones support WAP, and few websites serve up WAP content.
- When you connect to a wireless network and request access to a website that supports WAP, your mobile phone sends the request via radio waves to the nearest cell, where it is routed through the internet to a gateway server.

THE INTERNET

KEY TERMS

Global Worldwide

The internet (also called the net or the web) is a **global** system that links small networks of computers together. The internet is the collection of computers, software and cables that allows any computer in the world to communicate with any other computer in the world.

The internet began as a project of the US Defence Department in the late 1960s designed to link scientists working on defence and research projects around the country. During the 1980s the National Science Foundation took over responsibility for the project and expanded the network to include the major universities and research sites in the US. Links were then established to similar networks in other countries. Today, the majority of countries in the world are linked in some way to the internet. More connections are being made every day.

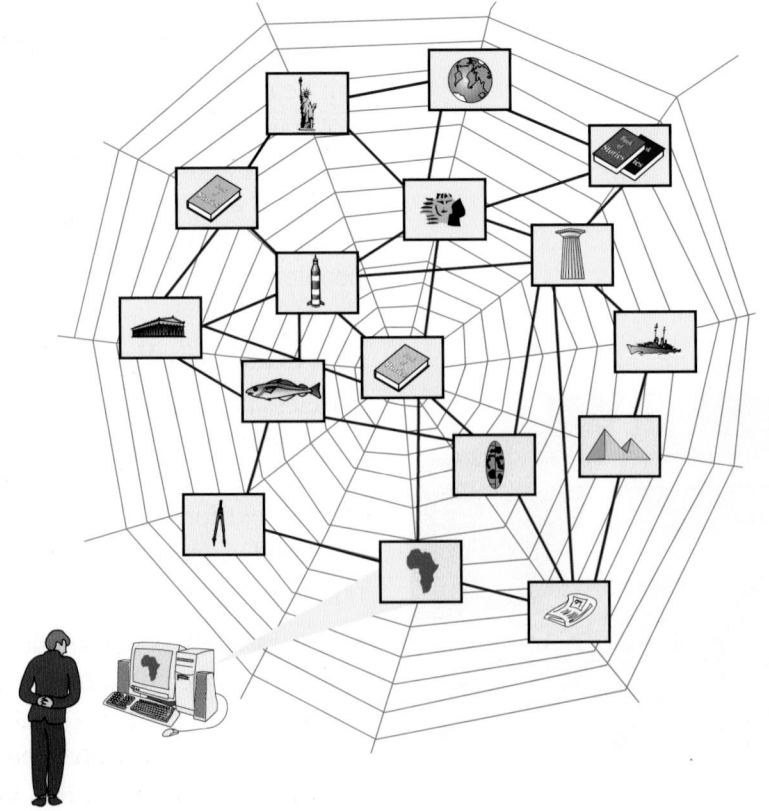

Figure 4.7

It is important to understand that the internet is not a single entity. Each separate network is managed by its own network administration staff. The internet is made up of many separate networks which are able to communicate with each other. The internet works because all the different networks follow internet standards. There is no single governing body in charge of all the networks connected to the internet.

Internet and business

E-commerce, or electronic **commerce**, is a general term for any type of business, or commercial transaction, which involves the transfer of information across the internet. This covers a range of different types of businesses, from retail sites like Amazon.com, through auction and music sites like eBay or MP3.com, to businesses exchanging or trading goods or services between different organisations.

Electronic commerce has expanded rapidly since the late 1990s and this growth is expected to continue or even get faster. Like most computer or internet related things, there is plenty of jargon that you need to wrestle with. Let us begin with the basics:

- B2B stands for business-to-business and refers to electronic commerce between businesses rather than between a business and a customer.
- B2C is e-commerce with customers other than businesses.
- Electronic transactions have been around for a while in the form of EDI (electronic data interchange). However, EDI generally requires each supplier and customer to set up a data link between them. E-commerce using the internet provides an easy and cheap method for companies to set up multiple links. E-commerce has also led to the development of electronic marketplaces where suppliers and potential customers are brought together.

The first thing a business needs is a product or service to sell, then it needs a website. This can either be an existing website to which you can add e-commerce capabilities, or you can build the site from scratch.

The next step is to have some way of accepting online payments. This normally means accepting payment by credit cards, although there are other options. Lastly, but most importantly, you need to have a strategy for marketing your site and attracting customers. This is far harder than you might think.

KEY TERMS

Commerce Exchange of goods or services by businesses; buying and selling of goods and services

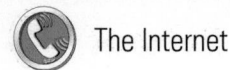

Internet as a source of information

The internet is packed with countless billions of pages and information on nearly every subject. The main problem is finding that information and figuring out whether it is relevant or up to date. The best way to start to find information is to use one of the search engines (such as yahoo.com or google.com).

Search engines use software robots to survey the web and build their **databases**. Web documents are found and indexed. When you enter a query (a word or series of words) at a search engine website, what you type is checked against the search engine's keyword. The best matches are then returned to you as hits (pages which contain the words you typed).

There are two main methods of text searching:

- Keyword searching – this is the most common form of text search on the web. Most search engines use keywords. Words that are mentioned towards the top of a document (web page) and words that are repeated several times throughout the document are more likely to be important. Some sites index every word on every page. Others index only part of the document.
- Concept-based searching – unlike keyword search systems, concept-based search systems try to determine what you mean, not just what you say.

Most sites offer two different types of searches, either 'basic' or 'refined.' In a 'basic' search, you just enter a keyword without sifting through any pull-down menus of additional options. Depending on the engine, 'basic' searches can be quite complex. 'Refined searches' differ from one search engine to another; you might be able to search for proper names or for phrases. All the search engines have different methods of refining queries. The best way to learn them is to read the help files on the search engine sites and practise.

KEY TERMS

Database A collection of information stored on a computer for a specific reason. It can be quickly accessed, added to and edited

The internet as a means of communication

Email is not the only way that a business can communicate with customers or suppliers using the internet; there have been many new developments over the past few years to make communications simpler and cheaper. These include:

- IP telephony. This is also known as voice over IP or internet telephony and it represents the technology which uses data networks to transmit telephone calls. It works by taking the voice or data from the source where it is then digitised, **compressed** and sent across the network where the process is reversed. When the idea of using the internet to make telephone calls first became reality, a handful of businesses offered services with poor voice quality and disorganised dialling directories for tracking the handful of people who could receive calls.
- Web cameras. Over half a million web cameras are being sold each year, and the United States accounts for half that business. When the first web cameras were developed they sold at extremely high prices, but recently the prices of the cameras have dropped drastically. The most popular cameras sell for under £100. Web cameras can be used in videoconferencing or simply to have a direct and live connection with another office in the organisation.

Action Points

More than 40 per cent of the leading UK and US public companies are failing to take the web seriously as a communication channel and are not using it as a direct communication medium with customers, investors and other target audiences. Some are even in the position of failing to deliver on basic promises they make on their sites to customers and investors.

This is the conclusion of the second Rainier Web-Index™ study into the use of the web by the FTSE 100 and the top 100 Fortune companies, conducted over 100 days between 4 March and 1 July 2000 by Rainier, the international technology marketing communications consultancy. The results demonstrate a clear requirement for large organisations to adjust their global internet strategies to ensure that their public web response capabilities are at the very least as effective as telephoning, faxing or writing to their national or international headquarters.

The Rainier Web-Index™ study found that in Britain only 71 of the FTSE 100 companies could be contacted by email via their website and of these more than 20 per cent including National Grid, P&O and Telewest failed to respond to multiple requests for basic investor information after a wait of three months.

A total of 29 of the FTSE 100 companies including Bass, Marks & Spencer and Thames Water could not be reached by email via their website or did not have a website.

Of the 56 FTSE 100 companies that responded to queries via their website in this year's Rainier Web-Index™ study, the ten least responsive companies were Colt Telecom (27 days 17 mins); Abbey National (14 days 1 hr 37 mins); Old Mutual (12 days 42 mins); Wolseley (8 days 4 hrs 34 mins); BG Group (6 days 2 hours); Unilever (5 days 4 hrs 21 mins); British Telecom (5 days 4 hrs 12 mins); BAA (5 days 3 hrs 27 mins); Sainsbury (5 days 1 hr 49 mins); and Logica (4 days 11 hrs 51 mins).

Why might top businesses in the UK and the USA not be using the internet to its full potential?

Try using an internet search engine to find some of the top companies in the UK and find their email addresses. Ask them a simple question about ICT and see how long it takes for them to respond.

Source: www.rainierco.com/survey_2000

Try carrying out this exercise with the rest of the class.

1 You can easily find out the top 100 companies in the UK by looking in the business section of a newspaper.

2 Divide the 100 amongst the whole of the group to make contact.

3 Then collect your data and see which was the quickest and which was the slowest.

4 To make sure your findings are correct, find out how you can tell when an email was sent and received.

The internet as a tool for marketing and selling (e-commerce)

E-commerce (electronic-commerce) refers to business over the internet. Websites such as Amazon.com, Outpost.com, and eBay are all e-commerce sites. The two major forms of e-commerce are business-to-consumer (B2C) and business-to-business (B2B).

While companies like Amazon.com cater mostly to customers, other companies provide goods and services exclusively to other businesses. The terms 'e-business' and 'e-tailing' are often used with e-commerce, but they refer to the same idea.

If a business is planning a large website or has no previous experience of website design, hiring a professional may well save them a lot of time and money. If they do build the site themselves, the trick is to keep things simple and concentrate on the priorities, i.e. keeping the site easy to use, secure and reliable.

Credit cards are the most secure method of collecting payment from customers and most storefront services or shopping cart software offers this facility. The business can process these details manually, or using an online credit card authorisation system to process the payments. Finally, the business will normally require a Merchant Account with a bank or other financial institution in which their payments can be deposited.

Website design can cost from virtually nothing to several hundred pounds per month because, as well as the cost of running the site, there is the additional expense of processing payments. If you intend to accept credit cards you will pay transaction fees to your bank and credit card processing companies as well as fixed monthly fees. Credit card payments account for around 95 per cent of online customer transactions.

Marketing is the hardest but most important part of selling online. Businesses can use search engines, banner ads or advertising mail shots to attract customers. Normal paper-based, television or radio advertising can also help to attract customers. Many online businesses are doing very well, but as with any business, care and planning are essential in order to succeed.

Email

Short for electronic mail, email consists of messages, often just text, sent from one user to another via a network. Email can also be sent automatically to a number of addresses. An email address is a computer mailing address to which electronic mail may be sent. Each computer system handles email addressing differently, but relies on various **protocols** for exchanging mail with other, not similar systems.

KEY TERMS

Credit cards Card holders can obtain goods and services using these but do not have to pay the organisation lending them the money until they receive a statement. This is known as buying on credit

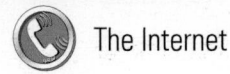

Website

When exploring a website you will usually begin with the home page, which may lead you to more information about that site. A single server may support multiple websites. A web page is a document created with HTML (hypertext markup language) that is part of a group of hypertext documents or resources available on the world wide web. HTML uses tags that describe the general structure of various kinds of documents linked together on the world wide web. Collectively, these documents and resources form what is known as a website.

You can read HTML documents that live somewhere on the internet or on your local hard drive with a software program called a web browser. Web browsers read HTML documents and display them as formatted presentations, with any associated graphics, sound and video, on a computer screen. Web pages can contain hypertext links, or hot links, which when clicked take you to:

- Other places within the same document.
- Other documents at the same website.
- Documents at other websites.

They can also contain fill-in forms, photos, large clickable images, sounds and videos for downloading.

A website can be run by an individual like yourself, or an organisation, whether it be a company or another kind of establishment.

Online catalogues

Thousands of businesses publish their catalogues of products and services on the internet. These allow customers to browse the catalogues online or print them as a hard copy. Not only does this mean that customers can see the catalogue immediately, it also means that the business does not waste valuable money printing catalogues and sending them out by post to people who may not end up buying anything from the business.

Think about it!

Visit www.catalogs.google.com and see if you can find a catalogue of a business that you have heard of and may have bought from in the past.

- What do you think of the catalogue?
- Is it up to date?
- Does it contain all the information you need?
- If you wanted to buy something from it, how would you do that: online, telephone, post? What options are there?

Booking services

Booking services are usually available for services such as flights, hotels, taxis or car hire. Some booking services allow the customer to search for the cheapest flight available to a particular destination on a particular day. Other booking services actually offer deals on the internet that are not available to other customers who book by telephone or call in to travel agents.

The best way of learning about booking services is to try it yourself (be careful not to actually book anything though!).

Action Points

1 Find the cheapest flight to Brisbane, Australia – flight only, leaving in ten days, and you want to stay in Australia for one month.

2 Find the closest hotel to Stamford Bridge Football Stadium in London. How much would it cost to stay for two nights, next Friday and Saturday?

3 Find out how to book a car from Heathrow Airport. The car needs to be available at around 11.00am next Wednesday and be available for hire for one week. What is the cheapest available car that could seat the driver and four adult passengers?

E-COMMERCE AND CUSTOMERS

The growth of the internet has resulted in two major developments:

- Businesses are now willing to trade online.
- Customers are happy to buy online.

It seems that each year, as the systems become more reliable and customers become more willing to pay bills, make purchases and find information, the internet is becoming *the* place to trade. E-commerce is moving on rapidly and there seems no reason why it will not become the most important way of trading in the future.

The impact of e-commerce

Research predicts that by 2004 online commerce will be worth $6.8 trillion. This huge amount covers both business-to-business and business-to-consumer transactions online.

The latest e-commerce figures for the UK (excluding the financial sector) show that there has been a 42 per cent increase in online sales, up from £12 billion in 2000 to £17 billion in 2001. Business-to-consumer in 2002 was worth £6.1 billion, up 53 per cent, and business-to-business was worth £10.9 billion, up 36 per cent.

Revenues generated by commercial websites				
Internet commerce in the UK will exceed £800 billion by 2003				
Consumer spending online (in $ millions)				
	1998	1999	2000	2002 (projected)
UK	60	190	450	1,940
Germany	160	350	720	1,940
European Union	298	770	1,970	4,978

Source: Datamonitor

Below is a news report about e-commerce, produced on the internet in October 2001.

Britain and Sweden have the highest proportion of businesses connected to the internet. In the last year, the number of businesses trading online in the UK has increased by 20 per cent, growing from 450,000 to 540,000. But this figure must increase by half a million within the next year to meet the Government target of having one million businesses trading online by 2002. The significance of the finding is also called into question by a recent report from the Office of National Statistics, which revealed that only 600 UK businesses were conducting more than 50 per cent of their trading online in 2000.

The UK Online for Business International Benchmarking Study 2001, [was] commissioned by the Department of Trade and Industry … E-commerce minister Douglas Alexander said: 'the study confirms we are making progress towards our primary aim of making the UK the best place in the world to do e-business. We have set demanding targets and we must continue the e-revolution and help UK businesses to get to the future first.'

The report measures the UK's performance in e-commerce against ten other countries – including the US, Canada and Germany. According to the study, the proportion of businesses with access to the internet is above 90 per cent in nearly all countries studied, with the figure reaching 94 per cent for the UK. Eighty per cent of British companies also have websites – a 14 per cent increase from last year.

The UK Government has already exceeded its target to have 1.5 million small and medium-sized businesses (SMEs) online by 2002. Last year, 1.7 million SMEs were online – that is having a website, using email frequently and using electronic data interchange – and this figure has now risen to 1.9 million.

Among the countries studied, the UK ranks second in terms of the proportion of connected businesses admitting that the internet has transformed sales and marketing, logistics and delivery, operations, processing and assembly. Britain ranks third for the use [of] the

> internet to improve purchasing and after sales service, and fifth for finance.
>
> 'UK business is feeling the benefits of using technology to improve its communications, efficiency and productivity,' said Alexander. 'The UK continues to be among the world leaders in making more sophisticated use of technology to transform their business process.'
>
> Source: www.news.zdnet.co.uk/story/0,,t269-s2097128,00.html.
> © Crown copyright

1 Think about the names of the businesses in your local High Street and write down a list of at least ten (try to choose ones that you think are national businesses).

2 Now try to find their websites on the internet. Can you buy products and services from the websites? Does the website list all of the branches of the business with addresses and contact numbers?

3 Rate the websites for ease of use, information and design from one to 10.

4 Put all of your findings on a table with your highest-rated business first and your lowest-rated one last.

Web stores, online banking and shopping

A web store is another term used to describe a business's website which offers e-commerce. Typically, it will have information about products and services and means by which customers can purchase them over the internet using a secure system.

Between 1999 and 2001 online banking saw European banks investing €13 billion to expand not only their presence on the internet but also their call centres. Banks in the UK, Germany and France closed down 11 per cent of their branches between 1995 and 2000. Despite this, European banks said that the internet had not been the main reason for the closing of branches. Almost 50 per cent of the banks have already started to connect their branches to online banking applications and 24 per cent are planning to do so in the near future.

Current research suggests that 39 per cent of the European banks believe they will manage to reduce costs by 15 per cent by improving the quality of their customer service. In the US around 33 per cent of households now pay their bills online, and this trend is expected to be followed in Europe.

Advantages of online banking are:

- Convenience – unlike your corner bank, online banking sites never close.
- Transaction speed – online bank sites generally execute and confirm transactions quicker.
- Efficiency – you can access and manage all of your bank accounts from one secure site.
- Effectiveness – many online banking sites now offer sophisticated tools. Most are also compatible with money managing programs such as Quicken and Microsoft® Money.

Disadvantages of online banking are:

- Start-up may take time – in order to register for your bank's online program, you will probably have to provide ID and sign a form at a bank branch.
- Learning – banking sites can be difficult to navigate at first.
- Bank site changes – even the largest banks upgrade their online programs, adding new features in unfamiliar places.
- Trust – for many people, the biggest hurdle to online banking is learning to trust it.

E-procurement

E-procurement is the business-to-business purchase and sale of supplies and services over the internet. An important part of many B2B sites, e-procurement is also sometimes referred to by other terms, such as supplier exchange. Typically, e-procurement websites allow registered users to look for buyers or sellers of goods and services. E-procurement software may make it possible to automate some buying and selling. Businesses expect to be able to control the process more effectively, reducing costs and improving their stock control.

E-commerce security

Here are some facts and figures about e-commerce and security which show that people have different views on the issue:

- Only 37 per cent of small to medium-sized businesses in the UK have a policy of reporting computer-related crime to the police.
- 92.6 per cent of the UK's smaller firms have been the victim of a virus attack, while only 8.7 per cent have suffered from credit card fraud.
- 86 per cent of UK consumers believe online retailers should do more to demonstrate that it is as safe to shop on the internet as it is on the High Street.

- 79 per cent of UK consumers would feel more confident about shopping online if they could 'sign' for the transactions.
- 42 per cent of UK internet users shop online, 58 per cent do not.
- 59 per cent of UK consumers who do not currently shop online would consider it if it was regarded as safer.
- Only one in three internet users believes online security is better today than it was a year ago.
- Only 2 per cent of all credit card fraud is now committed over the internet; 98 per cent is not.
- 66 per cent of online shoppers around the world are wary about purchasing goods from overseas websites.
- 58 per cent of international online purchasers plan to increase the amount they spend on online goods in the next year.
- 89 per cent of international e-commerce users determine their buying decisions based on transaction security, while 59 per cent base initial decisions on price.
- 30 per cent of internet users who do not shop online abstain because they do not want to give out their credit card details. This is up from 5 per cent in 2002.
- Denmark has the highest level of internet penetration in the world, with 63 per cent of adults online.
- The US has the highest proportion of online shoppers in the world with 32 per cent of internet users purchasing goods.
- Germany is the nation most reluctant to divulge credit card details over the internet, with 73 per cent of internet users refusing to do so.
- 28 per cent of global internet users have either shopped online or plan to do so in the next six months.
- There was a 3 per cent rise in internet users around the world between 2001 and 2002 to 34 per cent. However, there was no increase in the number of online shoppers.
- 72 per cent of e-commerce sites operated by small and medium-sized businesses in the UK are profitable.
- 26 per cent of smaller UK firms have e-commerce sites.
- 90 per cent of UK businesses offer online access to information.
- Almost 60 per cent of UK companies believe that e-business will reduce their costs by up to 10 per cent.
- 61 per cent of UK businesses claim to have experienced one or more computer-related crimes in 2002.

It is confusing, but read the following horror story about e-commerce security.

Think about it!

Many people don't think twice about handing over their credit cards or bank details in a shop, or over the telephone to a 'real' person. Millions more type in their credit or debit card details on to websites every day; the trouble is that no one can really be sure that this information doesn't get into the wrong hands. If the website's security is not using the most up-to-date and sophisticated technology to keep unauthorised people away from the information given to the site, then there is always a chance that customer's details may be used for fraud.

Nearly every major website or e-tailer has had problems like this and they continually update and change the ways that they protect the information given to them by their customers. The fear for customers and the credit card companies is that the smaller the site, the less security they have and the easier it is for criminals to break into their systems and steal customer information which they can use to make purchases online themselves.

For most credit card holders, the credit card companies cover them for unauthorised use of their credit cards, but this doesn't deal with the situation, it just makes it less painful for the customers. In the end, everyone pays in higher insurance and higher costs to borrow money.

Because of this, many people who buy online are now only using the biggest companies who have spent millions defending their payment systems from attempts to steal customer credit card details. Internet security companies and the e-tailers are quick to point out that handing your credit card to a salesperson in a shop or buying over the telephone is no less risky and there are millions of cases of fraud taking place like this every year.

The biggest problem for customers is trust – can you really trust that a website has done everything it can to stop this kind of fraud? After all, how does a customer know that the website is not under attack at the very moment they type in their credit card details? Hackers are determined people and it is very difficult to catch them; added to which there is a vast amount of information on the internet including customer's names, addresses, email account details, telephone numbers, credit card details, passwords and a host of other information. Although a website might include a statement on their web pages telling customers that it is safe to place orders with confidence and that everything is in place to stop hackers, who can ever be sure?

The biggest security risk is not when the customer clicks the icon to transmit the credit card details to the website – e-tailers have made sure that this transaction is encrypted and is very difficult for hackers to interfere with or steal. The major problem is the security of the site, as the majority of hacker attacks take place against the e-tailer's databases. Here they will find a record of all the e-tailer's past transactions with customers, thousands of credit card details and huge opportunities for fraud. E-tailers need to check the credit card details of their customers as a security measure and this means that the customer's information is passed to another database that could be attacked by hackers. Even companies that handle online payments for smaller e-tailers have not escaped the attentions of hackers and on one occasion at least, a hacker posted over 50,000 sets of credit card details on to the internet.

In the UK, the total cost of credit card and personal banking fraud has been estimated to be over £400 million per year. The most common fraud is by card 'skimming'. Skimming involves copying the data from a card's magnetic strip on to another card. This usually takes place in restaurants, shops and petrol stations. When the customer walks away, the fraudster has the customer's details which they can put on to a copy of their card or they could sell the details to someone else on the other side of the world! As long as the customer still has their original card, the credit card companies cover the costs of the fraudulent transactions. In the UK, skimming cards is said to bring in around £160 million to fraudsters every year. Increasingly though, frauds are being carried out over the telephone, by mail order and the internet. It is less common in the UK, but still worth around £100 million per year. In April 2002, the police and the banks launched a £5.6 million scheme to try and deal with personal banking and credit fraud, but only 23 police officers are permanently assigned to the task. The scheme is known as the Dedicated Cheque and Plastic Crime Unit and will initially run for two years.

In the USA, the fight against internet fraud is more sophisticated, with the Federal Bureau of Investigations (FBI) taking the lead with a dedicated taskforce aimed to beat internet fraud. The US Federal Trade Commission publishes a list of the 10 most popular 'dot cons' which are the internet version of the FBI's 'most wanted' list. Recently, the Cardwatch site was set up by the Association for Payment Clearing Services (APACS) to help make customers more aware of card fraud. It advises customers never to let their cards out of sight in a shop and to check receipts and their credit card and bank statements. In February 2002, APACS announced that by 2005 all UK face-to-face credit and debit card transactions will be authorised by the customer keying in their personal identification number (PIN) rather than by signing a receipt.

In February 2003, a computer hacker managed to gain access to more than 5 million Visa and Mastercard credit card accounts in the US. The hacker broke into the security system of a company that processes credit card transactions for shops and e-tailers. With more than 560 million Visa and Mastercard cards in the US alone, the credit card companies immediately contacted their customers. Mastercard had to tell 2 million of its customers that their accounts had been hacked and Visa another 3.4 million.

Visit three sites: www.amazon.co.uk, www.kelkoo.co.uk and www.ebuyer.com/customer/home/index.html. Find their security statement and decide whether you consider what they have stated is reassuring for people who might make a purchase using their sites.

Sale of Goods Act (1979 and 1994)

The Sale of Goods Act 1979, amended in 1994, states that when you buy goods from a trader they must fit the description, be of satisfactory quality – which includes lasting a reasonable length of time as well as being fit for their purpose. If goods are not of satisfactory quality you are entitled to compensation, which is normally the cost of repairs. The retailer, not the manufacturer, is legally obliged to sort out a problem if the goods do not meet these requirements.

A manufacturer's one-year guarantee is in addition to these rights – many offer free repair or replacement without quibble. Extended warranties are an extension of this.

Data Protection Acts 1984 and 1998

Since 1984 the Data Protection Act has offered some protection for the individual whose details may be held on the computer of any organisation. In 1998 the Act was revised to incorporate the European Union Directive which stated: 'any person, organisation or business wishing to hold personal information about people, must register with the Office of the Data Protection Commissioner'.

The amount of information held on computers about each individual person is growing because of the increasing use of computers to store that information. Under the Data Protection Acts any individual has a right to see information that an organisation holds on their databases about them.

Those companies that keep information about individuals must register with the Data Protection Commissioner. It is possible to see a list, in any major public library, of all those companies who have registered.

The register will have information on:

- The type of information they hold.
- The purpose for which it is used.
- Where the information came from.
- Who might be able to see this information.

All sorts of businesses might hold information about people, including the following:

- An insurance company may have information about people's health and lifestyle.
- A motor insurance company will have information about drivers' records in relation to accidents, traffic offences and the kind of car that each individual drives.
- A supermarket that has a loyalty scheme may have a great deal of information about individuals' buying habits and how much is being spent in a given period of time.
- A credit card company will also have a lot of information about people's buying habits and their attitude to credit.

- A health centre will have a great deal of information about its patients' health and lifestyle.

The information contained could be very valuable to some businesses. It could also seriously damage the reputation of an individual if the information is inaccurate or if some information falls into the wrong hands.

It is possible to find out what data is being held. In order to do this it would be necessary to:

- Ask the Data Protection Commissioner for a list of businesses that hold data about individuals.
- Write directly to the business to ask them to send details of the information that is held.
- Wait to receive a copy of any information held.

The Data Protection Act gives the individual the right to know what information is held about them. It also provides those businesses that hold information with a set of data protection principles that control how information can be stored and used. These principles are:

- Obtain and process the information fairly and lawfully and for clearly specified purposes.
- Hold only the information that is adequate, relevant and not excessive for the purpose for which it is held.
- All information held must be accurate and up to date.
- Only keep the information as long as it is required.
- Do not use or disclose the information in any way that is different from its original purpose.
- Give individuals access to information about themselves and, where appropriate, correct or erase the information.
- Take appropriate measures to ensure data is secure against loss, damage or unauthorised and unlawful processing.
- Do not transfer data to countries that are outside the jurisdiction of the European Union.

If a company is found to be in breach of these principles action can be taken against them.

However data can be used in certain circumstances such as:

- Preventing or detecting crime and catching or prosecuting criminals.

- For the assessment and collection of taxes due to the Government.
- Health education and social security matters.
- Household, personal and family matters.

Action Points

Visit the website of the Data Protection Commission at www.dataprotection.gov.uk and find out what kind of information can be obtained.

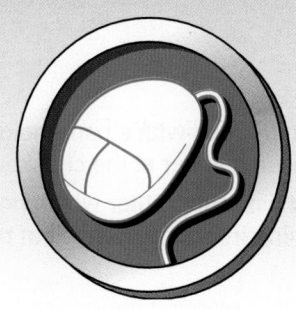

ICT in the business environment

IN THIS CHAPTER YOU WILL INVESTIGATE ...

- Introducing ICT – the considerations
- Data input devices
- Data storage devices
- Data output devices
- Applications software
- Payment systems and documentation
- Communication technology developments

INTRODUCING ICT – THE CONSIDERATIONS

The use of ICT touches every part of an organisation; our day-to-day contacts with businesses reveal just how much ICT is used. Take a normal supermarket, for example, to see the scope of ICT and how it touches all of their operations:

Checkout till	• Supermarket tills use scanners to read bar codes.
	• They are connected to the store's computer.
	• A till is now called a point of sale (POS) terminal.
	• Each checkout connected to a computer with a bar-code scanner is called an electronic point of sale (EPOS) terminal.
	• Each checkout connected to a computer with a bar-code scanner that can also transfer money from a customer's account using the customer's credit or debit card is called an electronic funds transfer point of sale (EFTPOS) terminal.
Scanners and bar codes	• All products have bar codes, which are a series of black lines representing a 13-digit number which is also printed under the lines. The bar code identifies the type of product.
	• The number identifies the country of manufacture, the maker and the product number, and a check digit, which is the last digit, validates the code as being correct.

	• The bar code can be read with a hand-held scanner or the laser scanner at the checkout.
	• The supermarket has a computer which holds a database containing information on all of the products sold.
	• When the product is scanned the bar-code number is passed to the computer and a search is made of the database; the number is matched with the data and the description and price is sent back to the checkout where the customer's itemised receipt is printed.
Stock control	• When the product is scanned, the bar code is sent to the database in the supermarket's computer.
	• The database holds a record of the number of those products held in stock; the database now reduces the number held in stock by one each time a product is scanned.
	• The supermarket now knows that the stock level has been reduced and when it was reduced, giving the manager of the supermarket an up-to-date record of the stock levels.
	• This allows the supermarket's database to create an order to replace the stock when the stock level reaches a minimum (set by the supermarket).
	• When the stock level reaches this minimum level an order to the supplier is created and sent either to the supermarket's own main warehouse or the supplier themselves.
	• The database is able to identify the supplier from the bar code and an order to replace the product is then sent electronically via a network.
Computer networks	• The supermarket's computer and each of the checkouts are linked together in what is known as a local area network (LAN). The main computer in the supermarket is located somewhere within the store where only the employees have access.
	• The main computer itself is connected to another network, a wide area network (WAN), which allows data to be passed to the head office, warehouse, suppliers and banks.

Loyalty cards	• Most supermarkets offer loyalty cards to their customers; these are plastic cards with magnetic strips. • The strips hold customer data as well as a number for that customer. • When the customer presents their card at the checkout, the supermarket is able to give them points based on the purchases made. When the points reach a certain total, the customer is rewarded with either money off their bill or gifts. • Each time the customer uses the card, the supermarket is able to capture the information about what they have purchased and when the purchases were made as well as the payment methods used. • This information helps the supermarket to decide what to stock in the store and to work out what other products the customer might buy in the future.
Self scanning	• Rather than carry out all of the scanning at the checkout, some supermarkets now allow customers to scan their own purchases as they walk around the store. • The customer puts their loyalty card into a reader and then takes a scanner from the slot. They can then go around the store and scan as they choose the products they need. • In this way, the products can be packed straight into boxes or bags in the trolley without the need to unpack them at the checkout and then repack them as they come off the conveyor belt. • The customer goes to a special checkout and hands the scanner to the employee. The employee connects the scanner to the till and the data is captured on the till and then passed to the supermarket's computer where the database carries out its usual procedures. The customer is then given an itemised bill.
Internet shopping	• Increasingly, the larger supermarket chains offer internet shopping. This allows the customer to make purchases via the supermarket's website. • The customer keys in their customer loyalty card number and then starts making choices from a series of menus which detail all of products available.

- A 'shopping basket' details all of the choices made by the customer. It is possible to add to this basket or take items out of it.
- Once the customer has completed their shopping, they click on the 'proceed to checkout' option and they are asked to choose the method of payment. Obviously only credit or debit cards can be used.
- The customer can then choose from the options regarding the delivery of the order to their home.
- Once the order has been placed the list is sent electronically to the nearest supermarket branch and an employee does the shopping for the customer and packs the products ready for a van to deliver at the time that the customer has chosen.

Action Points Find out the differences between a 'credit card' and a 'debit card'. You could do this by visiting a number of different banks or building societies and collecting their customer information leaflets.

Cost of installation

Obviously, one of the most important considerations for a business is how much the installation of a computer network and associated ICT devices will cost. The main points will be:

- What does the business want the system to be able to do? It may be necessary to ask a specialist to visit the business to discuss the options available.
- What are the options in terms of equipment and suppliers? There are hundreds of different brands of devices, from monitors to modems, across the whole range of ICT. Choosing the right device from the right manufacturer is difficult and plenty of reading and research is needed in order to make the right choice. It is often a good idea to visit a business that has already installed a system and ask them about the performance and reliability of what they chose and whether they have any advice.
- Do it yourself or get in the professionals? Many businesses choose to select and install their equipment themselves, which is often a mistake. Whilst it might be easy enough to buy a desktop computer and set it up yourself, a more complex

network needs an expert to make sure that everything is compatible and works.

- How complex is the system? This is an important consideration as the business may lack the skills and expertise to train staff on how to use and maintain the equipment. Training programmes may be needed to make sure that the business gets the full benefits of the system and that the employees can use it.

- What are the benefits of installation? The business needs to decide whether the installation will benefit the operations. Can savings be made? Is the business going to be more efficient? How is the installation going to affect the overall running of the business?

Action Points

1 Write a list of advantages for a business in installing ICT.

2 Now consider the disadvantages.

3 Present your considerations in the form of a word-processed two-column table headed ADVANTAGES and DISADVANTAGES.

Maintenance

The business must ensure that routine maintenance is performed on any system that is being used. This will include:

- Checking that the software and hardware are working properly.
- Making sure that vital data is backed up.
- Ensuring that there is sufficient storage space available on the system and deleting files that are no longer required.
- Checking all connections, cleaning machinery and running checks for viruses, illegal software and out-of-date **drivers** and other programs.

Upgrades and replacements

No matter how up to date the software and the **hardware** being used, it will always be necessary to consider replacing them with more modern versions. This means that machinery (hardware) needs to be checked for performance and efficiency in case there is better equipment on the market. There may be some compatibility issues here as simply replacing older equipment may actually mean having to make further upgrades (especially with software which runs the devices).

KEY TERMS

Drivers Software that enables printers and other hardware to operate

Hardware The physical shell or componants of a computer, such as the monitor, keyboard and mouse

Most **software** that is purchased and registered has upgrades available at the website of the manufacturer. Either an employee of the business or an outside professional needs to be made responsible for checking for upgrades and making sure that current versions of the software are downloaded onto the system. Most of these forms of upgrade amend the current software and delete files and sub-programs that are no longer being used. In most cases, older files are automatically overwritten (replaced) by the download.

Profitability

As with any form of purchase made by a business, the cost of the new equipment or software needs to be assessed in terms of what it will bring to the business. Obviously, machinery in particular will wear out and once the guarantee period has passed, it may not be cost-effective to repair some machinery and it will be cheaper to replace it. Most hardware and software have a guarantee period during which the cost of repairs and replacement is covered by the manufacturer or the supplier.

Given the fact that ICT is developing so fast, replacement is often the easier option as it is inevitable that a device which cost £100 two years ago can now be purchased for less than half that price. In all probability, the replacement device will be of better quality in terms of efficiency and performance.

All purchases represent expenditure for the business and this means that each one will reduce the overall profitability of the business, strictly speaking. The truth is that replacements can often speed things up and make the business more efficient (for example, replacing a 56K modem with a faster one would mean that internet connection is quicker, pages load faster and the overall telephone charges will decrease).

Security

The main threat to a business network tends to be from outside the organisation itself. Local area networks (LANs) tend to be less vulnerable than wide area networks (WANs) as LANs have no point of contact with the wider community.

Any system that is connected to the internet or has access to a telephone line is potentially at risk from hackers, viruses and the downloading of unauthorised software and programs.

The most common methods used by intruders to gain control of computers are described briefly below. Some of it is very technical and you will not have to remember all of the details. It is useful to know what some people are actually capable of doing to your computer if you give them the chance.

- Trojan horse programs – Trojan horse programs are a common way for intruders to trick you into installing 'back door' programs. These can allow intruders easy access to your computer without your knowledge; they can change your system configurations or infect your computer with a computer virus.
- Back door and remote administration programs – on Windows® computers, three tools commonly used by intruders to gain remote access to your computer are BackOrifice, Netbus and SubSeven. These programs, once installed, allow other people to access and control your computer.
- Denial of service – another form of attack is called a denial-of-service (DoS) attack. This type of attack causes your computer to crash or to become so busy processing data that you are unable to use it. In most cases, the latest **patches** will prevent the attack.
- Being an intermediary for another attack – intruders will frequently use compromised computers as launching pads to attack other systems. An example of this is how distributed denial-of-service (DDoS) tools are used. The intruders install an 'agent' (frequently through a Trojan horse program) that runs on the compromised computer awaiting further instructions. Then, when a number of agents are running on different computers, a single 'handler' can instruct all of them to launch a denial-of-service attack on another system. Thus, the end target of the attack is not your own computer, but someone else's – your computer is just a convenient tool in a larger attack.
- Unprotected Windows shares – unprotected Windows networking shares can be exploited by intruders in an automated way to place tools on large numbers of Windows-based computers attached to the internet. Because site security on the internet is interdependent, a compromised computer not only creates problems for the computer's owner, but is also a threat to other sites on the internet.
- Mobile code (Java/JavaScript/ActiveX) – there have been reports of problems with 'mobile code' (e.g. Java, JavaScript and ActiveX). These are programming languages that let web

KEY TERMS

Patches Updates of a program that improve it or repair faults and that allow the user to take advantage of the latest version of the software

developers write code that is executed by your web browser. Although the code is generally useful, it can be used by intruders to gather information (such as which websites you visit) or to run malicious code on your computer. It is possible to disable Java, JavaScript, and ActiveX in your web browser.

- Cross-site scripting – a malicious web developer may attach a script to something sent to a website, such as a URL, an element in a form, or a database inquiry. Later, when the website responds to you, the malicious script is transferred to your browser. It is possible to expose the web browser to malicious scripts by following links in web pages, email messages, or newsgroup postings.

- Email spoofing – email spoofing is when an email message appears to have originated from one source when it was actually sent from another source. Email spoofing is often an attempt to trick the user into making a damaging statement or releasing sensitive information (such as passwords). Note that while service providers may occasionally request that you change your password, they will not usually specify what you should change it to. Also, most legitimate service providers would never ask you to send them any password information via email. If you suspect that you may have received a spoofed email from someone with malicious intent, you should contact your service provider's support personnel immediately.

- Email-borne viruses – viruses and other types of malicious code are often spread as attachments to email messages. Before opening any attachments, be sure you know and trust the sender. It is not enough that the mail originated from an address you recognise. The Melissa virus spread precisely because it originated from a familiar address. Never run a program unless you know it to be authored by a person or company that you trust. Also, do not send programs of unknown origin to your friends simply because they are funny – they might contain a Trojan horse program.

- Hidden file extensions – Windows operating systems contain an option to 'Hide file extensions for known file types'. The option is enabled by default, but a user may choose to disable this option in order to have file extensions displayed by Windows. Multiple email-borne viruses are known to exploit hidden file extensions. The first major attack that took advantage of a hidden file extension was the VBS/LoveLetter worm which contained an email attachment named 'Love-letter-for-you.txt.vbs'. Other malicious programs have since incorporated similar naming schemes. Examples include:

Downloader (MySis.avi.exe or QuickFlick.mpg.exe) and VBS/Timofonica (Timofonica.txt.vbs). The files attached to the email messages sent by these viruses may appear to be harmless text (.txt), MPEG (.mpg), AVI (.avi) or other file types, when in fact the file is a malicious script or executable (.vbs or .exe, for example).

- Chat clients – internet chat applications, such as instant messaging applications and internet relay chat (IRC) networks, provide a mechanism for information to be transmitted bi-directionally between computers on the internet. Chat clients provide groups of individuals with the means to exchange dialog, web URLs and in many cases files of any type.

- Packet sniffing – a packet sniffer is a program that captures data from information packets as they travel over the network. That data may include user names, passwords and proprietary information that travels over the network in clear text. With perhaps hundreds or thousands of passwords captured by the packet sniffer, intruders can launch widespread attacks on systems. Installing a packet sniffer does not necessarily require administrator-level access.

 Think about it!

Below is part of a report produced on the Symantec website about internet security.

Internet attacks reported on the rise

About 70 per cent of all power and energy companies worldwide were hit by at least one severe internet attack in the past six months – an increase of 13 per cent over the previous six months, according to a report released today.

The Internet Security Threat Report, written by Riptech Inc., an Alexandria-based internet-security firm, said some of the attacks originated in countries on the Department of Homeland Security's Cyber-terrorism Watch List, but it was not clear whether crucial services here or abroad were being targeted by terrorist groups.

More attacks originated in the United States than anywhere else. Overall, about 80 per cent of all attacks, including those not labelled as severe, came from 10 nations in North America, western Europe and the Far East.

The report indicated that some smaller nations with a low number of per capita internet users – including those on the watch list – were carrying out a significant number of internet attacks.

About 51 attacks per 10,000 internet users originated in Kuwait, and about 30 attacks per 10,000 users originated in Iran. But overall, attacks originating in countries on the watch list were less than 1 per cent of the total attacks.

The average company received between three and seven attacks per month from watch-list nations. But Elad Yoran, executive vice president of Riptech and co-author of the report, did not discount the possibility that terrorist groups were beginning to use the internet as a weapon.

'It's a little premature to reach that conclusion, but there are several observations that point in that direction', he said.

Riptech's report was derived from more than 400 companies in 30 countries. The company analyzed more than 1 million possible attacks and 180,000 confirmed attacks.

About 96 per cent of all attacks were considered non-severe, or nothing more than nuisances. An attack is considered severe if it requires some sort of action or intervention by the victim or security company assigned to protect the attacked system.

The overall number of attacks increased 28 per cent during the past six months, and observers said hackers are becoming more aggressive and potentially more damaging.

'There has been a rise in the amount of aggressive attacks over time, and they are more likely to result in a compromise', Mr Yoran said.

Overall, however, Riptech said the number of companies receiving severe attacks during the past six months decreased by nearly half, thanks to improved security measures.

The report indicated that most attacks come from viruses or worms, which are programs written by hackers to scan and exploit vulnerabilities in software. The vast majority of these viruses or worms do nothing more than scan company computer systems before being stopped by basic security measures such as firewalls. There were no reports in the past six months of security breaches considered serious enough to disrupt power or energy services.

Severe attacks were twice as likely to hit public companies than non-profit groups or government agencies. High-tech firms, power and energy companies and financial-service companies received more internet attacks than all nonprofits combined.

'Public companies tend to be more visible, and that doesn't help them', Mr Yoran said.

Larger companies were attacked the most. Firms with more than 1,000 employees got hit 40 per cent more often than companies with less than 1,000 employees.

The increase in overall attacks in the past six months has come despite the lack of any new big threats, such as the Nimda or Code Red worms that emerged in the summer and fall of last year and caused more than $2 billion in clean-up expense and lost productivity.

A worm called SQL Spida appeared in May, but it was merely a nuisance to most firms. Code Red and Nimda, which are still active, have done little damage this year because companies have installed the necessary security patches. Overall, less than 1 per cent of companies received severe attacks from these three worms this year.

Mr Yoran did not rule out the possibility of a new worm emerging this year.

'Because we haven't seen one in the last six months does not mean we won't see one', he said.

Source: www.symantec.com, 2003

What do you understand by the following terms used in the news article:

- Lost productivity
- Non-profit
- Clean-up expense
- Internet-security firm
- Security patches
- Worms?

DATA INPUT DEVICES

Data input devices include all hardware which allows you to communicate with the computer. The following types of data input devices are the most commonly used.

Keyboard, mouse

A keyboard is a set of keys for computer input, which resembles a typewriter keyboard but with a few extra keys for computer commands and usually also a numeric keypad. On a computer keyboard, hitting on a key sends an electrical signal to a microprocessor, which sends a scan code to the computer's basic input/output system. Keyboards no longer need to be fitted to the computer itself and can be connected by infrared.

A mouse is a pointing device that is used to move a cursor on the computer screen and make various operations possible such as typing, drawing, editing text and graphics, opening and closing files, and giving other commands. The wire connecting it to the computer or keyboard looks like a mouse's tail, hence its name. A mouse is moved over a flat surface, usually a rubber mouse mat, and its position is read by the computer. It is now possible to buy a mouse without a tail (connecting electronically to the computer) as well as a mouse that does not have a track ball but uses infrared instead. The Figure shows a cordless infra mouse.

Digital and web cam

A digital camera takes pictures without film and records the images in digital form. The camera stores the snapshots in its memory for transfer to a computer. A web camera or web cam is a digital camera that uploads images to a website for broadcast.

Scanners

A scanner is an input device that reads images or text and converts the data into digital signals. Graphical scanners read photos or other images into the computer and digitise them, producing graphics files. Text scanners use optical character recognition software to read pages of text and produce editable text files. Bar-code scanners, as used in stores, convert bar codes into digital information.

There are a number of different types of scanner:

- Flatbed scanners have a flat piece of glass on which the document is put to be scanned. One of the problems with a hand-held scanner is keeping the scanner steady; this problem

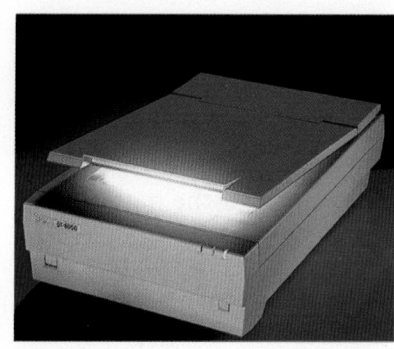

is eliminated with a flatbed scanner because the document is stationary and a mechanically-operated scanning head moves beneath the glass.

- Hand-held scanners are held in the hand and passed across the image to be scanned. Hand-held scanners are less expensive than desktop scanners, but they require a steady hand in order to get a clear image.
- Optical scanners use light to read patterns, and may then convert the patterns into digital or analogue signals. An optical scanner used as an input device for a computer can scan a picture or page of text and convert it into digital code as a graphics or text file on the computer.
- Sheet-fed scanners feed each sheet of paper across a non-moving scan head. This is different from the flatbed scanner in which the paper is laid on a sheet of glass and the scan head moves. Obviously, a sheet-fed scanner cannot be used to scan pages in books or magazines.

Voice recognition systems

Voice recognition allows a user to use his/her voice as an input device. Voice recognition may be used to dictate text into the computer or to give commands to the computer (such as opening application programs, pulling down menus, or saving work).

Older voice recognition applications require each word to be separated by a distinct space. This allows the machine to determine where one word begins and the next stops. This style of dictation is called discrete speech. Many people (especially those with learning difficulties) prefer these systems to the newer continuous speech.

Continuous speech voice recognition applications allow a user to dictate text fluently into the computer. These new applications can recognise speech at up to 160 words per minute. While these systems do give the user system control, they are not yet hands free.

Voice recognition software learns to recognise your voice. As you speak, the voice recognition software remembers the way you say each word. This customisation allows voice recognition, even though everyone speaks with varying accents and inflection.

In addition to learning how you pronounce words, voice recognition also uses grammatical context and frequency of use to predict the word you wish to input. These powerful statistical

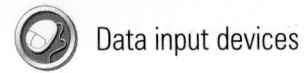

tools allow the software to cut down the massive language database before you even speak the next word.

While the accuracy of voice recognition has improved over the past few years some users still experience problems with accuracy either because of the way they speak or the nature of their voice.

The main points that a business may need to consider before purchasing voice recognition software are:

- Is it compatible with the computer?
- How difficult is it to learn to use the software?
- Does it work with existing word-processing software?
- Does it have its own microphone?
- Does it have macro compatibility (can you program simple commands that can be used to execute more complicated series of operations)?
- How fast is it?
- Do you need a remote model?
- Will you need a USB microphone (since it comes with its own sound card)?

OMR

Optical Mark Reader is a scanning device that can read marks such as pencil marks on a page. It is used to read forms and multiple-choice questionnaires.

OCR

Optical character recognition is the ability of a computer to recognise characters optically (basically by reading them). OCR programs are used with scanners to enter text into the computer when there is already a hard-copy version. A page of text scanned with OCR does not read as a graphics file as is the case with other scanned images. The text can then be edited and formatted just like any other text file. Text scanned with OCR will lose some of its formatting, and when a letter is blurred the program will guess, so mistakes are possible. Some OCR programs can recognise handwritten characters.

MICR

Magnetic ink character recognition is a character recognition system used on bank cheques; special ink and characters are used, which can be magnetised for automatic reading. The MICR reader can identify the bank account number, sort code and other common details, but the value of the cheque is added by the MICR reader as this was not known when the cheque was printed.

Pointing devices

A pointing device is an input device that is used to move the pointer on the computer screen. The most common examples are the mouse, stylus, trackball, pointing stick and touchpad.

Bar-code readers

A bar code is a pattern of bars of various widths and with varying spaces between them, printed on paper or similar material for recognition by a scanner that uses a laser beam or a light source and photocell. Bar codes are used by the Post Office to encode mail, in supermarkets and other retail shops to price items with the UPC (universal product code), and for many other purposes.

Magnetic strips

This is another method of storing computer data on an object (normally a card). Magnetic strips are used on credit and debit cards and also on 'smart cards' such as photocopying cards or loyalty cards where you collect points.

A magnetic strip is a short length of magnetic coating printed on the surface of a ticket or card. The strip usually contains data to identify the ticket or the card or its user (an account number and an expiry date.) To swipe a card with a magnetic strip means to move the card through a reader so that the strip can be read.

Here are some examples of how a magnetic strip is used:

- Tags attached to clothes in a shop.
- Railway, bus and underground tickets.
- Credit cards and bank cards.
- Phone cards.

The main advantages are:

- They are easy to make.
- They are not easy to damage.
- They store quite a lot of data (up to 72 characters).
- They cut down the amount of writing done during a transaction.

The main disadvantages are:

- The data can be changed or erased by magnetic fields.
- The strip can be damaged by scratching.

Smart cards are very similar, but the data in the magnetic strip can be changed easily by altering the contents of a very thin memory chip. They are used for photocopying cards and some loyalty cards where you collect points.

Magnetic strips are often used in credit cards. Here a shop or business will have a terminal where the card is checked and payment is authorised. The terminal is linked to the shop's own bank. The bank calls up the credit card company's own computer. This computer checks that the card is valid and has not been lost or stolen. A message is sent back to the shop which then goes ahead with the sale. Magnetic strips are also used in ATMs (automatic teller machines) which allow a customer to use a card to get money out of the bank when the branch is closed. The person goes to an ATM and it gives them money after they have put in the card and entered in a PIN (personal identification number).

EPOS

Electronic point of sale (EPOS) is a system used in retailing in which a bar code on a product is scanned at the cash till and the information is relayed to the store computer. The computer then relays back to the cash till the price of the item. In this way, the customer receives an itemised bill and the system removes that stock item from the figures. The EPOS system has revolutionised computer stock control in the following ways:

- It enables efficient, computerised stock control and reordering.
- It provides useful information about turnover and profitability.
- It eliminates incorrect charging of customers.
- It allows staff to work more flexibly and efficiently.
- It reduces the chance of orders being delivered incorrectly.
- It provides data for managers to assess the business.

EFTPOS

An electronic fund transfer point of sale (EFTPOS) is an electronic magnetic or chip reader system for credit or debit cards, for the completion of a transaction.

There are several benefits to the business of offering EFTPOS:

- It improves cash flow and provides opportunities for add-on purchases.
- Payment is assured on all 'Approved' response sales on the same day.

- It requires less cash to be kept on hand, therefore there is added security for staff.
- It is easy to operate.
- Reduced bank charges to the business.
- It saves time spent on administration.

Customers have become accustomed to using it and are more likely to revisit the business if they have the EFTPOS service.

EFTPOS has become a common feature of our society. There are few retail businesses without an EFTPOS facility; banks lease mobile EFTPOS units, which use technology that is similar to mobile phones. The EFTPOS telecommunications network is secure and reliable and organisations are using it to carry internet based transactions.

DATA STORAGE DEVICES

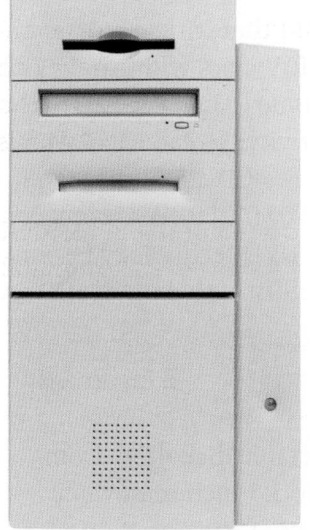

Data storage devices fall into two main categories – hardware and media. In many respects the hard drive of a computer is the most common place on which data is stored. With the exception of hard drives that can be removed from the computer or are external hard drives, the other forms of data storage are more flexible and allow the user the ability to insert the media (disk or similar) into any computer and access the data.

Hard drive

The hard drive (HD) or hard disk drive is a drive that reads from and writes to a hard disk.

Floppy disk drive

A floppy-disk drive is the disk drive where a floppy disk is inserted. A floppy disk (FD) is a removable, portable magnetic disk on which data and programs can be stored. They are also known as diskettes or floppies and are made of flexible plastic. The older 5½ inch disks are more flexible; the 3½ inch disks have a hard protective case around them and are the size normally used now.

CD

A CD is a compact disc. It is a format for storing audio data in digital form which can be played on a CD player or with a CD-ROM drive. A CD-ROM (compact disk read-only memory) is an optical disk that is physically the same as an audio CD, but it contains computer data. Storage capacity is about

680 megabytes. CD-ROMs are interchangeable between different types of computers.

CD-R

A CD-R (compact disk recordable) is a recordable CD-ROM which can be read by normal CD-ROM drives; data can only be recorded once onto a CD-R and it cannot be changed. CD-Rs were the first generation of 'writable' CDs, but they are gradually being replaced by CD-RW. A normal CD-ROM drive cannot record on CD-R; a writable drive is required.

KEY TERMS

Platform A standard system which allows developers to create software that works with that platform. Without platforms, developers would have to create much more complex software as the platform itself provides many of the basic processes required to run the software. Windows® is a platform, as are PlayStation and Game Cube

CD-RW

A CD-RW (CD rewritable) is a CD-ROM that can be written, erased and rewritten by the user. CD-RW discs will usually only play on multi-read CD-ROM drives; some CD players with exceptional speed may have the sensitivity to read CD-RW discs. A CD-RW drive (CD rewritable drive) is a CD-ROM drive that can write, erase and rewrite to a CD-ROM. CD-RW is considered to be the connection between CD and DVD technology because of its backward and forward compatibility with existing CD and future DVD **platforms**.

Zip drive

A Zip drive is a small, lightweight, portable disk drive from Iomega, which uses 100/500-megabyte 3.5 inch removable cartridges. They can be used just like a CD-RW.

KEY TERMS

Bandwidth How much information you can send through a connection; usually measured in bits per second

DVD

DVDs (digital versatile disks or digital video disks) are optical storage media which have greater capacity and **bandwidth** than a CD. DVDs can be used for multimedia and data storage. A DVD has the capacity to store a full-length film with up to 133 minutes of high-quality video in MPEG-2 format, plus audio. A major breakthrough recently has been the DVD+ReWritable which is a DVD-based storage format similar to CD rewritable (CD-RW) and it allows home or office recording. DVD-ROMs (digital video disc read only memory) are disks like CD-ROMs, but they have more storage (4.7 gigabytes) and can provide digital video. DVD-ROMs with 17 gigabyte storage will soon be available.

DATA OUTPUT DEVICES

A data output device is an piece of equipment that allows you to see data. The most common is the monitor and the printer which allow the user to view the data (a word-processed document or a picture). The monitor (with the exception of laptops and personal digital assistants (PDAs)) does not allow the user to view the data away from the desktop machine. Printers, of course, allow the data to be viewed at any time and in any place.

Monitor

A monitor is also called a display. This is a device that displays text and graphics generated by a computer. Desktop monitors are usually cathode-ray tubes, and laptop monitors are usually liquid crystal display. A monitor can be monochrome (black and white), which are increasingly rare, or colour. Colour monitors may show either digital or analogue colour.

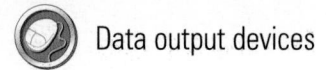

There are some other specific types of monitor:

- Low-radiation monitor – a computer monitor that is designed to minimise the radiation it emits. VLF (very low frequency) and ELF (extremely low frequency) radiation from computer screens are a health concern, but their effects are not known.
- Multimedia monitor – is the standard home version suitable for use with multimedia and has its own speakers.
- Multi-scan (multi-sync) monitor – these can scan at more than one speed, making it possible to work with various kinds of equipment and video modes.
- RGB monitor (red green blue) – this is a display screen in which separate red, green and blue signals are used to make up the different colours on the screen. It can be an analogue or digital display.

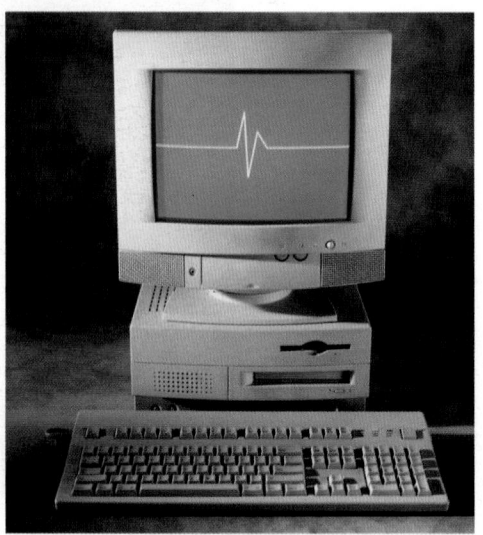

Printer (dot matrix, inkjet, laser, thermal and printer plotter)

There are a wide variety of different printers available. Some of the main types are as follows:

- Dot matrix is a kind of impact printer that uses small closely packed needles or 'pins' and an ink ribbon to make a pattern of tiny dots which form the letters on a page. Dot matrix printers are noisy and cannot print fine-quality type, but they are inexpensive and have many uses. Dot matrix printers are virtually obsolete.
- An inkjet printer produces an image by spraying tiny ink droplets from a nozzle onto a piece of paper. Inkjet printers can produce high-resolution colour or black-and-white images.

- A laser printer is a type of printer that uses a laser beam to produce an image on a drum. The light of the laser alters the electrical charge on the drum wherever it hits. The drum is then rolled through a reservoir of toner, which is picked up by the charged portions of the drum. Finally, the toner is transferred to the paper through a combination of heat and pressure. This is also the way copy machines work.

- A thermal printer (although many inkjets are now referred to as thermal inkjets) uses a thermo autochrome (TA) print process, which is considerably more complex than either inkjet or laser technology. This has emerged recently in printers marketed as companion devices for use with a digital camera. TA paper contains three layers of pigment – cyan, magenta and yellow – each of which is sensitive to a particular temperature. Of these pigments, yellow has the lowest temperature sensitivity, then magenta, followed by cyan. The printer is equipped with both thermal and ultraviolet heads and the paper is passed beneath these three times.

- A printer plotter is essentially a very large inkjet printer which can print pages up to around 36 inches wide. It is extensively used by designers, architects and artists.

Communication hardware (modem)

A modem is a peripheral device that connects computers to each other to send communications via the telephone lines. The modem modulates the digital data of computers into analogue signals to send over the telephone lines, then demodulates them back into digital signals to be read by the computer on the other end; hence the name 'modem' for modulator/demodulator. Modems are used to send and receive electronic mail, to connect to bulletin board systems, and to surf the internet.

APPLICATIONS SOFTWARE

As far as most computer users are concerned, applications software falls into the areas listed below. For each of the applications, a summary is given as to its uses, advantages and disadvantages. You will find detailed information on how to use each of these applications in the next chapter.

Word processing

The most used system is Microsoft® Word and this can be used for a wide variety of different tasks other than simply typing words onto a blank document.

Advantages of word processing	• Documents can be stored electronically and only printed when needed – this saves paper. • Text is stored in the computer's memory and can be edited at a later date. • Mistakes can be edited rather than retyping the document again. • Documents are produced to a professional standard. • Mistakes are corrected before printing. • Documents can be sent by email. • People can produce their own documents rather than give them to a typist to produce.
Checking spelling and grammar	• Internal dictionary. • Have to be careful as computer will not pick up every mistake (names, text with figures, word art, etc.).
Software	• Word-processing package either on its own or as part of a larger package, such as Microsoft® Office.
Hardware required	• Computer. • Printer (output device). • A mouse (input device). • A keyboard (input device).
Mail merge	• Combining a list of names and addresses with a typed letter so that a series of letters is produced, each addressed to a different person. • The list is created using the word processor importing data from a database or spreadsheet. • The letter is typed using the word processor and blanks are left where the data from the list is to be inserted. • The computer then inserts the data when the document is merged.

Presentation software

PowerPoint® is the industry standard, and this state-of-the-art presentation software is both easy to use and powerful. Users can create detailed slides that can be updated at a moment's notice. Highly mobile, PowerPoint documents are most often presented with a projector and laptop computer.

PowerPoint advantages include:

- Easy to update and customise for any use.
- Powerful enough to include customised graphics, images and sounds.
- Reduces paper storage and reprinting costs.
- Ideal for employee presentations, new employee training, client meetings, sales calls, etc.

Spreadsheets

Spreadsheets are commonly used for listings of data (particularly figures) as the software can be used to add, divide, subtract and make other mathematical calculations.

Spreadsheet capabilities	• Grid of cells into which text, numbers or formulae may be placed. • Useful for 'what if' calculations to test changes on business. • If the contents of one cell is changed then the contents of related cells will also change. • Cells can be formatted so that they automatically format data (currency, date, etc.).
Modelling	• Predicting changes to things by changing contents of cells in a spreadsheet.
Uses of modelling	• To predict changes to a business if the price charged for products is increased/decreased. • To predict changes to the economy if interest rates change. • To predict changes to weather patterns if temperatures rise/fall.
Advantages of modelling	• Changes can be tested before they are made for real. • Helps in the decision-making process for a business. • Helps to predict results.

Databases

Databases are electronic filing systems; in fact both Microsoft® Access and Excel are both specialised database software. Most organisations will need to maintain a database for some of the following reasons:

- To collect and store information about customers.
- To profile products or services sold and purchased.
- To collect and store personnel records of employees.

A database is a collection of records; each record is stored in a 'field' and each of these fields contains specific information. The overall structure and the range of records can be flexible and can be designed by the user. A record is a collection of facts about a specific product, supplier, customer or employee. The record could also hold a list of sub-records relating to stock, prices and the number of units sold or ordered.

In choosing the right database for the business, most will opt for the standard version of Access and design their own personalised versions of the database. It is possible to use existing templates, either those provided with the package or those that can be downloaded from the manufacturer's website. There are also database professionals who will design a specific database to match the needs of the business.

A database held on computer can have a massive effect on the business in the following ways:

- All information will be readily available to authorised individuals.
- Information can be tracked, updated and deleted as required.
- Data held here does not have to be stored in bulky, paper-based filing systems.
- Data, as long as it is backed up regularly, can be safe and easily transported or accessed from remote sites (via LANs and WANs).
- Databases form the backbone of order systems, stock control and other vital functions of the organisation.

Graphics

Graphics can be used in most word processing and desktop publishing software. There are, however, a number of different forms of graphics which you will encounter, particularly if you have downloaded images from the internet.

Types of graphics	• Line diagrams. • Bitmap images. • Photos. • Graphs. • Charts.
Features of graphics	• Produces professional-standard documents without the need for designers or printers. • Images can be scanned into graphics software using a scanner or digital camera. • Digital cameras do not need film for processing.
Clip art	• Difficult to produce high-quality images using a mouse. • Clip art images are copyright free. • Gives a professional look to documents. • Clip art gallery can be held separately or as part of an integrated software package.
Vector graphics details	• Stored as equations inside the computer. • Expressed as a vector format so each line has a start, end and a direction. • Easy to change without loss of resolution. • As the image is enlarged the number of pixels increases so the quality of the image stays the same. • CAD packages make use of vector graphics.
Bitmap images details	• Each pixel is a single piece of data. • Colour images require additional data. • Images are difficult to change as they have to be altered a pixel at a time. • When a bitmap image is enlarged the number of pixels stays the same so the resolution of the image is affected. • Clipart images are often bitmap images.
Graphics software	• Fills the images with colour. • Draws own shapes with freehand tools. • Changes font sizes and styles. • Inserts clip art images. • Uses preproduced shapes (AutoShapes).

DTP

A desktop publishing package, such as Microsoft® Publisher, allows users to produce professional documents such as newsletters and business stationery, without having to pay a designer to do the work for them. Modern desktop publishing packages are very powerful and flexible pieces of software which incorporate the features of a word-processing package with the advantage of being able to design a huge variety of layouts and styles.

Features of DTP	• Photos can be scanned in and resized or edited for a particular position on the page. • High-quality documents are produced without having to employ a designer. • Produces documents combining text and graphics. • Different fonts can be used with text flowing around pictures and clip art images. • Text and pictures can be placed in columns on the page. • The page is constructed using frames; each frame can be moved around the page. • Graphics can be embedded with text flowing around the images. • Clip art images can be inserted using the clip art gallery. • Different fonts can be selected. • Templates can be used to produce various documents (leaflet, postcard, invitation, etc.).
Equipment needed	• Large amount of **RAM** (DTP files consist of text and graphics and so take up a lot of space). • Mouse. • DTP software. • VDU, ideally a large one (17.5 inch to avoid eye strain). • High-quality printer (laser jet). • Scanner to add photographs. • Digital camera to add photos (no film and so no developing costs).
Advantages of DTP	• Control over the layout of the document. • Combine different types of file (text/graphic/clip art). • Professional-quality document. • Document can be edited and printed at a later date and saved.

KEY TERMS

RAM Also called memory, this is a temporary storage space on chips in the computer. RAM stands for random access memory

Computer-aided design

Computer-aided design (CAD) has had a huge impact on various professions including architects and technical illustrators. It is now possible to create complex (often three-dimensional) designs using CAD and to print them in large scale using a plotter.

Who uses CAD?	• Architects. • Engineers. • Producers of high-quality technical drawings.
What is produced using CAD?	• Plans of houses. • Circuit diagrams. • Technical drawings. • Engineering drawings.
Advantages of CAD	• Images can be viewed in 3D and rotated to be viewed at different angles. • Drawings can be edited and changed without starting all over again. • Accurate drawings are produced to scale. • Changes can be made to drawings on screen. • Images can be saved and edited before printing. • Drawings can be sent electronically via email. • Images are only printed when they are perfect.
Disadvantages of CAD	• CAD packages can be expensive. • Training to use packages is required. • If system crashes the document could be lost. • Images can be stolen easily as they are stored as a single file.

Project planning and diary systems

The main features of project planning software and systems are:

- It manages projects, tasks, clients and activities.
- Workflow capabilities for managing projects.
- It monitors project completion time and time to market.
- It monitors productivity for users, managers and departments.
- It monitors project cost on an incremental and completed basis.
- It monitors user communication.
- It provides detailed reports on status and project cost.
- It accurately measures project progress.

The benefits to the business are as follows:

- It increases productivity.
- It reduces cost.
- It improves horizontal and vertical communication.
- It eliminates project cost overrun.
- It minimises delays in project completion.
- It increases employee efficiency.
- It eliminates time-consuming paperwork.
- Evaluation of employee, group and division performance.
- Detailed and reliable reporting.

Microsoft Project is a project management computer program for the Windows **operating system**. Microsoft® Project provides knowledge workers with the flexibility to collaboratively plan and track projects and deliver the results that their business demands. It is the single planning tool needed in an organisation. Microsoft Project has a delegation feature that enables tasks to be delegated from leads to team members or from peer to peer. Users can create custom report formats and request and receive team member status updates that Microsoft Project Central automatically rolls into a group report.

Copyright, Designs and Patents Act 1988

Copying computer software, or software piracy, is now a criminal offence under this 1988 Act. The Act covers stealing software, using illegally copied software and manuals, and running purchased software on two or more machines at the same time without a suitable licence. Quite often organisations will purchase software licences to cover the number of stations on their network. They then neglect to purchase additional software licences as they buy more workstations. The legal penalties for breaking the copyright law include unlimited fines and up to two years in prison.

It has been estimated that half the software used is copied illegally and in some countries pirated software accounts for 90 per cent of the total. Two organisations fight to stop software being copied:

- FAST (Federation Against Software Theft) – founded in 1984, a non-profit organisation that promotes the legal use of software.
- BSA (Business Software Alliance) – exists to make organisations and their employees aware of the law and encourage its implementation.

KEY TERMS

Operating system Also known as 'OS', this is the software that actually communicates with the computer's hardware. Without an operating system all software programs would be useless. The OS is what allocates memory, processes tasks, accesses disks and peripherals, and acts as the user interface. With an operating system, like the Mac OS or Windows 98, developers can write to a common set of programming interfaces using the operating system to talk to the hardware

PAYMENT SYSTEMS AND DOCUMENTATION

ICT has had an enormous impact on the way in which banks and other financial institutions handle payments. The new systems touch every aspect of their operations as can be seen in the following table.

Paying for goods and services	<ul><li>Cash – obtained from a cash machine and used to pay for smaller items (food, drink, travel, etc.).</li><li>Plastic cards – convenient way to pay for goods; used for larger regular payments (weekly shopping, petrol, clothes and internet purchases).</li><li>Cheques – often used when paying bills by post or where shops cannot take plastic cards.</li><li>Direct debits/standing orders – used to make regular monthly or annual payments.</li></ul>
Cash machines	<ul><li>ATMs – automatic teller machines.</li><li>Bank card is inserted into the machine and the user is asked to input their PIN (personal identification number).</li><li>User is then offered a number of services (e.g. cash with receipt, cash without receipt, balance, order a statement, order cheque book).</li><li>The card is then returned with the cash, etc.</li><li>All ATMs are connected to their own banks through a wide area network.</li><li>The network reads the magnetic strip on the back of the user's card.</li><li>The user's details and choices made from the menu on the machine are communicated back to the bank's central database and records are updated automatically.</li><li>New ATMs are being tested at the moment that can allow the user to book airline tickets and theatre seats and even pay bills.</li><li>ATMs have reduced the number of staff required in banks, and many small village and town branches have closed as people can access their money 24 hours a day seven days a week through an ATM.</li></ul>
Plastic cards	<ul><li>Credit card – allows user to make purchases and draw cash up to a predetermined amount.</li><li>Each month the user receives a statement showing the purchases they have made using the card.</li><li>The user can then either pay off the full amount or pay in monthly instalments. If they choose to do the latter they are charged interest on the money they owe.</li></ul>

	• Debit card – this card is linked to a bank account. When a purchase is made, money is taken directly out of the user's bank account. Debit cards are also used to withdraw money from cash machines (ATMs). • Loyalty card – issued by shops to promote customer loyalty by awarding points that can be exchanged for discounts. • Store card – issued by stores and allows customers to make purchases on credit. At the end of each month the user is issued a statement showing the purchases made on the card. As with a credit card, the user can either clear the total balance or pay for the goods in instalments.
Using a plastic card	• Internet/telephone – customer's name and numbers on the card are used. The details asked for include the cardholder's name, the card number and the card expiry date. • Checkout/cash machine – details are processed electronically; on the back of the card is a magnetic strip. The card data is held in digital form. The data includes the cardholder's account number and PIN number, the bank's sort code, the cardholder's credit/withdrawal limit and the amount withdrawn that day. The data from the magnetic strip is communicated to the bank or credit company's main computer database where the money is transferred and records are updated.
Card fraud	• Three of the most common areas involving plastic card fraud include: cards being lost/stolen, cards being copied (counterfeiting), payments being made over the telephone or internet where the card is not present. • When a person realises their card is lost or stolen it is vital that they contact their bank or credit card company so that the details of their card can be electronically registered as lost. Then the card cannot be used. • Using a small hologram image on a card also makes it difficult to copy that card.
Plastic cards with chips	• Cards can be made more secure and also more versatile if they contain a tiny circuit. • The standard for this chip is ICC (also know as a smart card).

	• The silicon chip will eventually replace the magnetic strip on the back of cards and it contains a processor and memory facilities. • Storing data on chips makes it difficult for criminals to copy the card.
Cheques	• Blank cheques are issued to customers by banks. They are a legal document allowing the account holder to pay a specified sum of money to the person named on the cheque. • The method used to input data from cheques onto a bank's computer is called magnetic ink character recognition (MICR). • The cheque contains three groups of magnetic numbers: the cheque number; the sort code for the owner's branch; and the customer's bank account number.
Cheque clearance cycle	• It takes three days for a cheque to be cleared. • The cheque is paid into the bank and passed to the local clearing house. • The cheque is scanned and data is passed electronically to the paying bank clearing centre. • The cheque is taken to the central exchange centre. • It is decided whether to pay the money or not. • Money is deducted from the customer's bank account and the payee's bank is sent the money electronically.

Cheque

These are issued to customers with their name, account number and sort code already printed ready for MICR. The customer fills in the details on the cheque, including the name of the person or business that the cheque is made payable to, the amount to be paid (in words and figures), the date of payment and signature of account holder.

In many instances, businesses now have computer terminals which can print cheques ready for MICR with all of the payment details; the customer then simply has to sign the cheque after they have approved it.

BACS

The Bankers Automated Clearing Service is a system which allows businesses to transfer funds from their own accounts to another business or employee, for example. The full details of the business or individual are required (primarily the bank details including account name, number and sort code). When the transfer is made the funds leave the account and are automatically credited to the account into which they have been paid.

EDI

Electronic data interchange is a system which links businesses directly to their bank and allows them to make immediate payments automatically. It is much more efficient than the business writing cheques in order to make payments. The writing of cheques is time consuming, especially if there are a lot of transactions to be carried out, and there is a great deal of manual record keeping involved with checking bank statements and cheque stubs. Payment through EDI is instant. This is efficient but it may be a disadvantage to a business that might prefer to delay payment due to cash flow problems.

Credit transfer

Credit transfer is a payment transaction originated by the payer, who issues a payment order to his bank instructing it to transfer funds out of payer's account to the payee or to the payee's account.

Standing order

A standing order is a method of transferring a fixed amount of money out a bank or building society into another account. This system may be used to pay off a loan over a period of time or to pay for goods and services by way of a fixed amount each month. The account holder decides the amount of the payment to be made from his account. This system is similar to direct debit.

Direct debit

This system differs from the standing order in that a financial organisation receives an authority to directly debit an account. That organisation can change the amount to be debited without the direct permission of the owner of the account, although that person should be notified of the change before the transaction takes place. The account owner will have signed a document authorising this. Not all organisations are authorised to use direct debit. It is a system widely used to collect utility payments such as electricity, gas and telephone charges.

Telebanking

This system is being used increasingly by busy people who do not have time to go to the bank. Most banks now use central call centres to deal with the many enquiries and instructions to transfer money or to change standing order payments, etc. The internet is also used to carry out banking transactions. This will undoubtedly become more popular as time goes on.

Internet banking

The first internet sites of banks appeared on the world wide web around the middle of the 1990s. Before that, for many years banks had experimented with different forms of online access to accounts. They implemented 'closed' systems in which clients gained access to the bank by a committed telephone channel. Such systems limited the number of potential clients since they involved additional expense both from clients and from the bank. The development of the internet provided credit organisations with technology for remote access to bank accounts, which could possibly fuel further development and reinforcement of the banking business.

Not surprisingly, the first e-banking systems appeared in the United States. A customer moving from town to town was compelled to change banks unless there was a regional branch. This situation was inconvenient for the client and unprofitable for the bank. The systems for remote access to bank accounts, which arose in the middle of the 1990s, provided a solution to the problem. In addition, online services opened up new markets for banks providing virtually unlimited coverage in order to attract customers.

The advantages of internet banking seem obvious. Through the online services, customers save time because they do not have to personally visit their bank in order to carry out a transaction. Accounts are accessible 24 hours a day, and it is possible to check your account and carry out a transaction (for example paying a bill) almost instantly. Internet banking makes it very convenient for the customer to control his own operations with credit cards: any withdrawal from his account quickly appears in the **electronic abstract** of account.

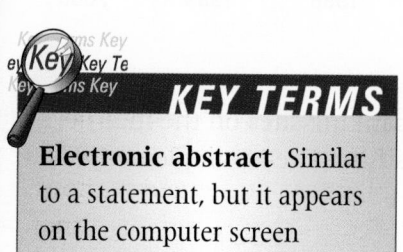

KEY TERMS

Electronic abstract Similar to a statement, but it appears on the computer screen

For a bank, transition to the internet means that expenses resulting from renting and servicing branches are considerably reduced. A good-looking office becomes worthless under online servicing. The number of staff and therefore the cost of wages decrease significantly due to automation of banking accounts. As a result, the cost of transactions goes down and even the small accounts of private customers with their negligible savings become attractive to the bank.

The development of internet banking services has led to the appearance of completely online banks (net-only banks) which have virtually no physical office. The first net-only bank, Security First Network Bank, opened in the web on 18 October 1995 in Chicago. The average growth of the bank capital amounted to 20 per cent per month, assets increased to $40 million by 2000 and 10,000 accounts were opened during the first year-and-a-half of its existence.

Net-only banks were expected to develop actively and to replace traditional banks because of their lower organisational costs, their virtually unlimited capacity for accounts and the competitive advantages due to efficiency of servicing. They have partly succeeded in this respect, but it is taking a long time to convince people to switch to internet banking.

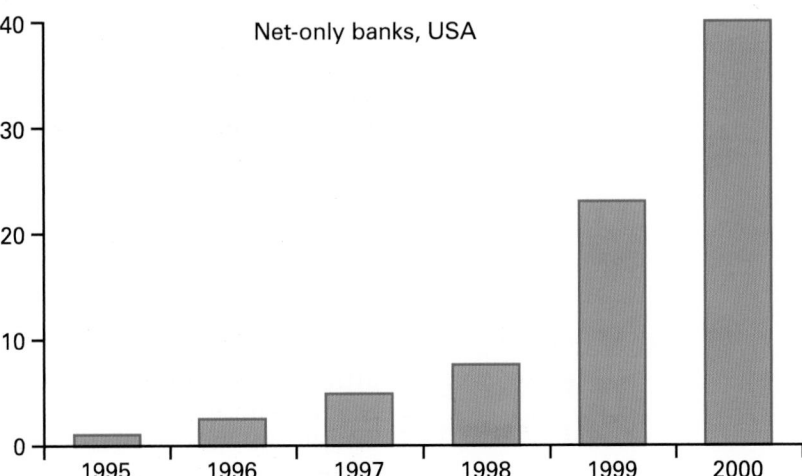

Figure 5.1

Today, there are more than 3,000 banking sites on the internet. More than half of European banks have already implemented systems of online banking.

E-commerce

E-commerce could not be easier for the customer:

- You select the items you wish to purchase and put them in your shopping cart.
- When you are ready to check out, you click on the checkout icon or symbol which takes you to a page where you are given the option to pay by debit or credit card. The website then processes your payment as it is connected to the store's bank processing network where the credit card is verified as valid.
- You are then given an electronic receipt and the transaction is complete.

E-commerce services are very similar to shopping in a normal store, only without a sales clerk and cash register. Just think of your computer as the sales staff.

E-mail receipts are sent after a transaction is processed, thus giving the customer an instantaneous online verification that the transaction was completed.

Action Points

1 Collect from a bank different forms that a customer will need to complete for each of the different payment systems described above.

2 Give one example of when each could be used to make a payment.

3 Using a graphics software package, produce an advice leaflet on the different methods of payment available to the customer.

COMMUNICATION TECHNOLOGY DEVELOPMENTS

The pace of change and development in ICT continues to offer new ways of working and new methods of production, retailing and providing services. Each time there is a new development, new opportunities to improve service and efficiency are offered to businesses. Gradually, ICT has made its presence felt in all areas of business and has touched nearly every organisation.

The National Health Service has been gradually introducing ICT and is beginning to see the benefits.

Patient records	• When a patient visits the doctor or hospital their details, along with details of any treatment they receive, are recorded in the person's medical record. • Until recently all of these notes were kept on paper. However, they are now being transferred to computerised databases.
Paper records	• Medical folders are very bulky and can get lost/destroyed easily. • Searching for information is time consuming and difficult. • Completion and management of records is also time consuming. • Clerical staff need to be employed to maintain paper records.
Computerised records	• Data can be entered quickly. • Records do not have to be fetched from storage but can be instantly retrieved from networked computers. • Hospitals can reduce their spending on wages by employing fewer clerical staff. • Patient details can be stored securely using access rights and passwords. • Information can be searched for quickly and easily.
Monitoring patients	• Intensive-care equipment has built-in microprocessors to help doctors and nurses monitor the vital body functions of patients. • The equipment uses special input sensors that collect data from the patient and pass it to the computer. • If this data falls below or above set limits that have been programmed into the computer, an alarm is triggered. • Intensive-care equipment constantly measures a patient's progress, detecting changes in the patient's condition as soon as they happen.

NHSnet	• NHSnet is a major project to connect all doctors' surgeries around the country to a private computer network linked with hospitals.
	• The project was started in 1996 and aims to provide a fast and secure method of transferring data between surgeries and hospitals.
NHS Direct	• A service that allows the public direct access to medical information.
	• The computer terminals are easy to use with touch-screen operation and are situated in schools, universities, health centres, supermarkets and holiday resorts around the UK.
	• You can also access NHS Direct by telephone or over the internet.
	• The NHS Direct website provides a lot of information on health and well being.
	• The service is backed up by trained nurses 24 hours a day.

Action Points

Since 1980 all of Britain's major utilities (electricity, gas, water, etc.) have been privatised, changing from public services with a focus on universal service to private companies with an obligation to provide shareholder returns.

Retail banking has also undergone major change, with over 25 per cent of local branches closing. Whilst affluent customers are being targeted with telebanking and online banking, an estimated 1.5 million households have no account at all.

Within the food retailing sector, over 70 per cent of all grocery shopping is now dominated by four major companies; their development of out-of-town supermarkets has resulted in the closure of many local neighbourhood shops.

1 How has ICT affected your local High Street? Ask someone who remembers what the High Street looked like 10 or 20 years ago.

2 What sort of shops or other services have disappeared? See if you can find some old photographs of the High Street 40 or 50 years ago.

3 What other things can you think of that might have affected the High Street in your area?

Computer networks (LAN, WAN, Bus, Star and Ring)

A network is a group of interconnected computers, including the hardware and software used to connect them. They can be connected in a number of different ways:

- A local area network (LAN) is a network that connects computers that are close to each other, usually in the same building, linked by a cable.
- A wide area network (WAN) is a network in which computers are connected to each other over a long distance, using telephone lines and satellite communications.
- A bus network is a network in which all nodes are connected to a single wire (known as the bus); it has two end points.
- A star network is a network configuration in which each node is connected to a separate line and all lines lead to the same central hub. From the central station any line can be connected to any other line.
- A ring (token) network is a type of computer network in which all the computers are arranged (schematically) in a circle. A token travels around the circle. To send a message, a computer catches the token, attaches a message to it, and then lets it continue to travel around the network.

Think about it!

Can you identify which the following diagrams are which type of network?

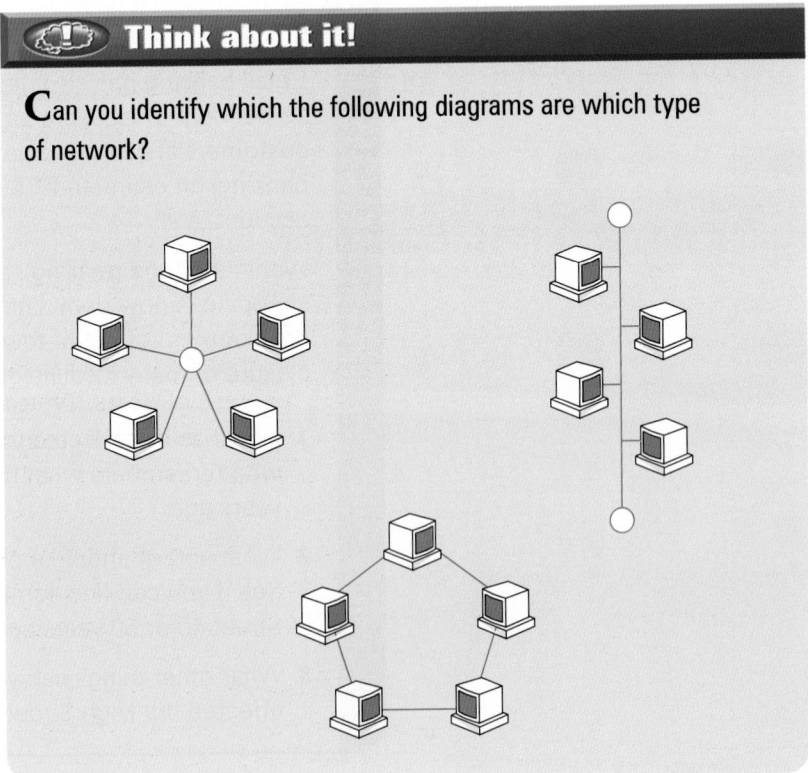

What is a network?	• A collection of computers. • Linked together using a cable or telecommunications equipment. • Every computer in the network can access the network server. • Every computer in the network can communicate with each other.
LAN (local area network)	• Computers are connected by cable and are often in the same location.
WAN (wide area network)	• Computers are connected by telecommunications and are not in the same location. • A good example of a WAN is the internet.
Advantages	• Data is shared between computers. • Computers can share hardware (printers, plotters, scanners). • Computers can share software. • Security is controlled from the network server. • The software that runs on a network is covered by a site licence; this is often cheaper than buying lots of different licences for different machines.
Disadvantages	• If the network breaks down none of the connected computers will work. • Many computers operating on the same network may make the network run slowly.

Storage area network (SAN)

A storage area network (SAN) is a high-speed, special-purpose network (or sub-network) that interconnects different kinds of data storage devices with associated data servers on behalf of a larger network of users. Typically, a storage area network is part of the overall network of computing resources for a business. A storage area network is usually close to other computing resources such as mainframes, but it may also extend to remote locations for backup and archival storage, usin̄g ʲ̄de area network carrier technologies such as asynchrơ   ̄ᶜᵃʳ mode or synchronous optical networks.

A storage area network can use existing cờ technology such as IBM's optical fibre ES newer Fibre Channel technology. Some ᶜ liken it to the common storage bus (flow of data) in a personal computer that is shared by different kinds of storage devices such as a hard disk or a CD-ROM player.

Desktops, laptops, palmtops and PDAs

A desktop computer is designed to fit comfortably on top of a desk, typically with the monitor sitting on top of the computer. Desktop computers are broad and low, whereas tower model computers are narrow and tall. Because of their shape, desktop computers are generally limited to three internal mass storage devices. Desktop models that are designed to be very small are sometimes referred to as slimline models.

A laptop or notebook is a portable personal computer that is small enough to fit in a person's lap and weighs less than eight pounds. Laptops usually have a flat screen and LCD display, and are powered by a rechargeable battery. They can be connected to a larger monitor or other peripherals when back at the office.

Palmtop computers are small computers that literally fit in your palm. Compared to full-size computers, palmtops are severely limited, but they are practical for certain functions such as phone books and calendars. Palmtops that use a pen rather than a keyboard for input are often called hand-held computers or PDAs. Because of their small size, most palmtop computers do not include disk drives. However, many contain **PCMCIA** slots in which you can insert disk drives, modems, memory and other devices. Palmtops are also called PDAs, hand-held computers and pocket computers.

PDA is short for personal digital assistant, a hand-held device that combines computing, telephone/fax, internet and networking features. A typical PDA can function as a cellular phone, fax sender, web browser and personal organiser. Unlike portable computers, most PDAs started out being pen based, using a stylus rather than a keyboard for input. This means that they also incorporated handwriting recognition features. Some PDAs can also react to voice input by using voice recognition technologies. Current PDAs are available in either a stylus or keyboard version. The PDA was pioneered by Apple Computers, which introduced the Newton MessagePad in 1993. Shortly after, several other manufacturers began offering similar products. Today, one of the most popular brands of PDA is the series of Palm Pilots from Palm, Inc.

KEY TERMS

PCMCIA Personal Computer Memory Card International Association (PCMCIA is pronounced as separate letters). This is an organisation consisting of some 500 companies that has developed a standard for small, credit-card-sized devices, called PC cards. They were originally designed for adding memory to portable computers

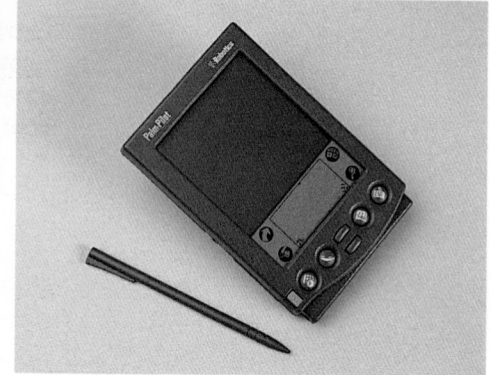

The internet

Experts are divided regarding the future development of the internet, but what is certain is that more businesses will hope to trade more efficiently via websites. This relies on increasing access to the internet by more people, by methods other than using computers to connect.

At present, the main features of the internet are as follows.

Benefits to the average user	• Homework can be researched on the internet. • Information is constantly updated and therefore always current. • Internet shopping and banking. • Implications for the disabled and their ability to shop/bank/socialise at home. • Social aspects of chat rooms. • Getting to know people in different countries and cultures. • Students have access to experts online and can ask questions.

Problems for individuals and businesses	• Sites that are unsuitable for young people. • Risk of contracting and spreading computer viruses. • Junk emails. • Large telephone bills. • Antisocial behaviour. • Health problems due to spending too much time at the computer. • Expensive equipment is needed and training is required. • Lots of people using the system can slow it down.
Extra features related to email and conferencing	• Ability to communicate online. • Need a computer with internet access. • Need a web cam to transmit pictures of people in conference. • No travelling expenses to get people to conference. • People can take part whilst at home or in the office.

The European Union is moving gradually towards increasing internet access for all citizens across Europe. eEurope 2005, the European Union's new information society action plan designed to improve electronic services across Europe, was presented to Heads of State and Government at their Summit meeting in Seville on 21–22 June 2002. The new eEurope 2005 action plan replaces eEurope 2002, the first EU plan, which focused primarily on improving internet connections.

This time, the European Commission proposes more targeted action, geared towards:

- Establishing a legal framework to guarantee competition between the various technologies.
- Greater use of broadband infrastructure.
- Incentives for regions to use best practice.
- The development of electronic services by national authorities, particularly in the areas of education and health.

Over the period to 2005, the EU should stimulate services, applications and content, covering both online public services and e-business, and develop a widespread availability of broadband access at competitive prices and a secure information infrastructure. Key targets are:

- Connecting public administrations, schools and health care bodies to broadband.
- Interactive public services, accessible to all, and offered on multiple platforms.
- Online health services.
- Removing obstacles to the deployment of broadband networks.
- A review of legislation affecting e-business.
- Creating a cyber security task force.

At the same time, the Commission wants to encourage the exchange of best practice and demonstration projects, as well as sharing the lessons learned from failure, so projects will be launched to accelerate the roll out of leading-edge applications and infrastructure.

Policy measures will be monitored and better focused by benchmarking progress that is made in achieving policy objectives. Finally, an overall coordination of existing policies will encourage better links between the proposed actions.

Among the specific measures to modernise online public services, the Commission sets the following goals:

- Interactive public services by the end of 2004, including access for people with special needs.
- All Member States to carry out a significant proportion of their public procurement electronically by the end of 2005.
- Access for all to public internet access points (PIAPs) in their local authorities.
- User-friendly electronic culture and tourism information by 2005.
- A new e-learning programme by the end of 2002.
- All universities to offer online access to students and researchers by 2003.
- National action to equip unemployed adults, women returners, etc. with the key skills needed.
- Developing the use of electronic health cards throughout Europe.
- Developing health information networks between points of care (hospitals, laboratories, etc.) by 2005.
- Providing public access to online health services by 2005.

This all seems like a very good idea, but internet connection still remains the greatest problem, as can be seen from the following Figures.

Who's wired and who's not?

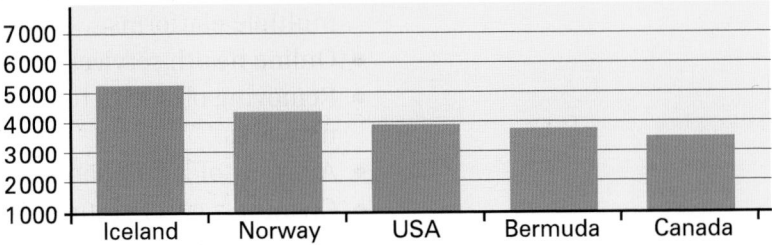

Most wired users per 10,000 inhabitants

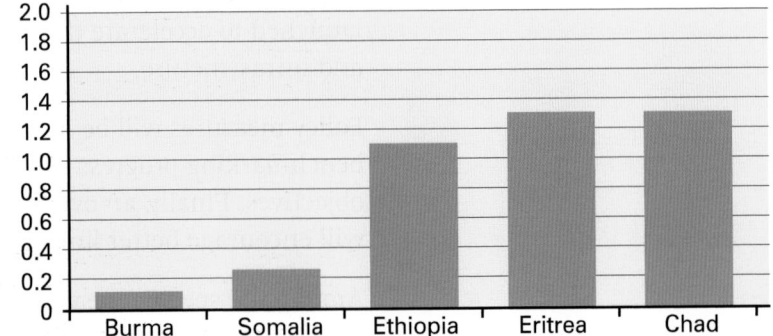

Least wired users per 10,000 inhabitants

Figure 5.3

Network systems management

The management of a business's computer network has become so complex that not only do Network Systems Managers receive considerable salaries, but whole three-year degree courses are dedicated to learning the tricks of the trade.

Many businesses have become so dependent on computers and telecommunications that they would be unable to function in the event of a network or system failure. It is important to have a business continuity plan in place that will enable staff to perform vital functions while a swift recovery program is mobilised. This may include testing that the backups of your data can be reloaded, having a backup power supply in the event of interruption to the normal supply, and manual systems that can be activated if the system is unavailable for an extended period.

In the early 1980s computer networks began to grow and be interconnected. As the size of these networks grew they became harder to manage and maintain, thus the need for network management was realised. One of the oldest forms of network management is the use of the remote login to monitor or configure a network device; however, today more sophisticated network management tools are available. Network management is a requirement for anyone who wants to control and monitor their networks.

Network management is the ability to control and monitor a computer network from a central location. The role of a Network Systems Manager falls into the following areas:

- Fault management – provides facilities that allow network managers to discover faults in managed devices, the network and network operation, to determine their cause and to take remedial action. To enable this, fault management provides mechanisms to:
  - report the occurrence of faults;
  - log reports;
  - perform diagnostic tests;
  - correct faults (possibly automatically).

- Configuration management – monitors network configuration information so that the effects of specific hardware and software can be managed and tracked. It may provide the ability to initialise, reconfigure, operate and shut down managed devices.

- Accounting – measures network utilisation of individual users or groups to:
  - provide billing information;
  - regulate users or groups;
  - help keep network performance at an acceptable level.

- Performance management – measures various aspects of network performance including the gathering and analysis of statistical data about the system so that it may be maintained at an acceptable level. Performance management provides the ability to:
  - obtain the utilisation and error rates of network devices;
  - provide a consistent level of performance by ensuring that devices have a sufficient capacity.

- Security management – controls access to network resources so that information cannot be obtained without authorisation. It does this by:
  - limiting access to network resources;
  - providing notification of security breaches and attempted breaches.

Figure 5.4 shows network management architecture.

Figure 5.4

The architecture consists of the following elements:

- Network management station(s) – the network management station runs the network management application that gathers information about managed devices from the management agent which resides within a managed device. The network management application must typically process large amounts of data, react to events and prepare relevant information for display. Some network management applications can be programmed to react to information collected from management agents and/or set thresholds with the following actions:
  - perform tests and automatic corrective actions (reconfiguration, shutdown of a managed device);
  - logging network events;
  - present status information and alerts to the operator.

- Managed devices – a managed device can be any type of **node** residing on a network, such as a computer, printer or router. Managed devices contain a management agent.

- Management agents – provide information about the managed device to the network management application(s) and may also accept control information.

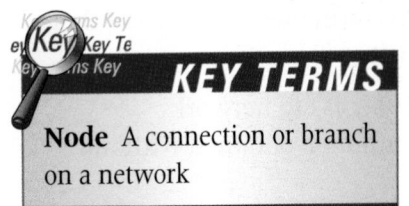

KEY TERMS

Node A connection or branch on a network

- Network management protocol – protocol used by the network management application(s) and the management agent to exchange management information.

- Management information – the information that is exchanged between the network management application(s) and the management agents that allows the monitoring and control of a managed device.

Call centres

Call centres have been around for years. If you have ever used directory assistance to get a phone number, then you have used a call centre. However, people are now becoming more aware of the power of this technology to deliver a range of dedicated services.

And if you think Call Centres are for big organisations, think again. A call centre could free you up to do much more than answer the phone when it comes to customer service.

What exactly are call centres? They are places which receive incoming phone calls on behalf of a range of organisations. Larger companies, such as banks, have their own call centres. Their services enable quick and easy access by customers to information and a range of services. Currently call centres are employed by both business and Government.

The system streamlines bill paying, queries, ordering and other such transactions. They are open 24 hours a day, seven days a week for the cost of a local call. Customers simply dial a telephone number and either speak to an operator, have their voice responses interpreted by a speech recognition system or are prompted to select services using the telephone's keypad.

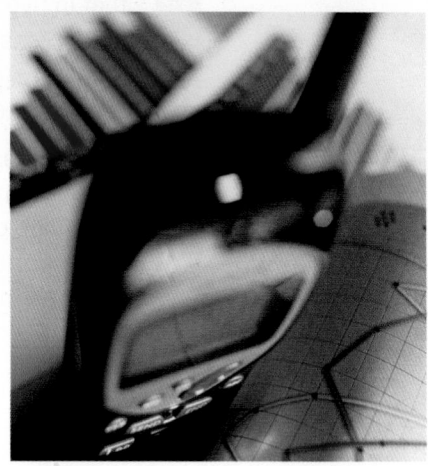

Hundreds of thousands of workers worldwide are employed by telephone call centres. On a typical day, a call centre operator may deal with inquiries from clients who are unaware of where the operator is in the world. Callers from Paris, Brussels or London may not know that they are speaking to an employee based in Ireland or India. Call centres can be based in countries that have lower wages and standards of living, thus saving large sums of money for the business running the call centres.

Regardless of where the call centre is, the operator can access information needed by the caller. The operator can access the business's computer systems instantly and give the customer the information they need without any delay. On average, a call may last only one or two minutes and on an eight-hour shift, a typical operator may have handled as many as 200 telephone calls.

Communications factories

Continually under stress, closely supervised to the extent that the supervisor often listens in to the calls, insulted by angry clients, call centre operators are a new generation of workers whose numbers are multiplying thanks both to technological innovation and the falling cost of telecommunications. Some are already comparing these 'teleadvisers' to skilled labourers and describe the call centres as 'communications factories'. Their numbers are set to increase over the next few years. While Ireland is home to many of the European call centres – and is stepping up the incentives in order to attract US companies – the UK is still by far the leader of this field in Europe.

According to a recent report, more than half of the 6,000 call centres in Europe are based in Great Britain. It is predicted that in five years call centres in the UK will have more employees than all of heavy industry put together. i.e. mines, iron and steel, the car industry, etc. The industry has 2,500,000 employees in the country.

The call centres were pioneered by the financial sector, although others were quick to copy. While banks and insurance companies have for some time offered their clients the opportunity of obtaining information or carrying out transactions from their home and outside working hours, today it is not just your banking that can be done by telephone. Travel, clothing, furniture, household equipment, after-sales services, computer support, etc. are all covered by the growing number of enterprises that offer a free telephone service for the consumer, often accessible seven days a week and 24 hours a day. The L'Oréal beauty products call centre in France gets more than 3,500 calls a day, including Saturdays. The 30 'teleadvisers', whose number is set to grow to 300, act as long-distance beauticians at the end of a phone line.

If you telephone a call centre, it will probably be a woman that answers. In most centres, three-quarters of telephonists are women and many are under 30. Based in industrialised regions where unemployment is particularly high, the call centres are a godsend for thousands of workers back on the job market. The employers' main incentives for setting up in an area are the low wages, economies of scale and the simplicity of installation. The Dublin-based call centres of the express courier giants such as Federal Express and UPS provide a service for clients in Germany, Switzerland, the Netherlands and France.

In Great Britain callers making telephone inquiries from London will probably hear a Scottish accent at the other end of the line, as British Telecom (BT) has chosen to base its service in Glasgow. Barclaycall, the Barclays Bank telebanking service, recently announced the opening of a new call centre in north-west England where it plans to employ some 2,000 people.

Everything is aimed at speeding up the pace: incoming calls must be responded to within 15 seconds, the conversation must be kept as short as possible and, to add to the stress, each operator has a console in front of them with flashing lights which indicate calls that are waiting.

1 Find a map of your local area and scan a copy on to the computer.

2 Now look in the *Yellow Pages* and find the addresses of the closest banks and building societies in your area. Place these sites on your map. How big an area does each of the branches cover?

3 Find out how many branches have closed in your local area and mark these sites on your map with a different colour.

Breaches of security

With the growing number of computer hackers and crackers, it is vital for the protection of data and personal information that you get very good protection while surfing on the web. There are many ways to protect your computer while on the net:

- Firewall – a firewall is a special type of program which monitors the access you have to the internet and the access that internet users have to your computer. For example, if you are ever infected with a Trojan horse without realising it, the firewall will stop anyone getting in and communicating with the server which is installed on your computer, thereby protecting the data stored on your computer.
- Anti-virus software – viruses are special kinds of programs that are used to cause harm and damage to a computer system. They are similar to the viruses which affect humans, for example they try to hide themselves and replicate, and they are very contagious. Sharing one file from an infected computer with another computer might spread the virus. That is where the anti-virus software comes into action. This software is used to analyse the files and check whether they are contaminated. Knowing how dangerous a virus can be, it is important to have the maximum protection. The most common virus protection software is Norton Antivirus.
- Refusal of files – the most effective way to reduce the chances of being attacked is to refuse files from the internet which come from an unknown source.

 **Action Points** Your school will need to keep a great deal of information about pupils, teachers, the local community, resources and finances to name but a few. Conduct an investigation into the systems used throughout the school to manage information.

1 Put your findings into a report.

2 Can you recommend any changes that could update the system?

Computer applications in the business environment

IN THIS CHAPTER YOU WILL INVESTIGATE ...

- **File management**
- **Word processing**
- **Spreadsheets**
- **Charts**
- **Databases**
- **Graphics and clip art**
- **Desktop publishing (DTP)**

INTRODUCTION

As we discussed in the last chapter, the ever-increasing developments in ICT have provided a number of benefits to businesses, including:

- Accuracy of information.
- Lower costs.
- More efficiency and speed.
- Increased speed of response to customers.
- Better overall control of the business activities.
- Larger volumes of work can be handled.
- Employees feel more fulfilled.

However, these benefits can only be felt by a business if the employees are sufficiently well trained in the use of the computer and the software. It is important that employees know everything there is to know about how the software works and what it can do to help them complete their various tasks.

Throughout this chapter we will be discussing the different software applications and their use, both at home and within businesses. The instructions given are for the use of Microsoft products, which are the most commonly used in business and are known as the 'business standard'.

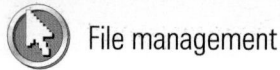

FILE MANAGEMENT

File management is all about storing your documents in the right place and being able to find them when they are needed. Efficiency in file management is very much like efficiency in any other part of our lives. For instance, if you did not tidy your room or house, then it would be more difficult to find something. Also, if that item is not stored properly then it could get damaged. It is the same with using a computer and good 'housekeeping' is just as important. In other words, if you give everything an appropriate name, then you will be able to find it. If you find it and make changes to it, then give it another name so you still have your original copy.

It is a good idea to group similar files in a FOLDER. You can give this a name, for example human resource, finance, homework, football, etc. You do this from the DIRECTORY of the drive you are using. You can get your directory by selecting FILE, OPEN. From here you should select FILE and select NEW, then FOLDER. By saving documents into a specific folder, it is easier to find them at a later date. The directory displays all folders and documents. By double clicking on a folder you then get the directory showing all of the files saved within it.

Creating files

Creating or finding a new blank document is simple. All you have to do is click on the icon shown in the Figure. That is straightforward enough. You then get a blank page and you can key in whatever information you want. However, the blank document will be called Document 1. Your next blank document will be called Document 2 and so on. Although when you close the file the information that you keyed will be saved, it would be difficult to identify what information is contained within that file from the title 'Document 1'. That is why naming a document or file is so important.

Saving files

Once your document is completed, then obviously you will want to close it. Microsoft is very good at helping to ensure that you do not lose your work. There are several options available to the user in order to save work:

- Using the icon above (an illustration of a floppy disk) you can regularly save whilst you are working on a document without having to close it. This is particularly important if the document is lengthy or if you are worried about the likelihood of an error on the computer system. However, the name of the file remains as Document 1.

- By selecting FILE, SAVE AS, you get the option to give the document a name. It is important to choose an appropriate file name here; something that relates to the content of the document. You also get the option of where the file should be saved. It may be that you want the document to go onto the hard drive of your computer (the C Drive), onto a floppy disk (A Drive) or onto a CD. You should choose from these options by clicking on the arrow next to the section at the top of this box entitled 'Save In'.

If you forget to do any of the above, then when you opt to close the file Microsoft asks you if you want to save the changes you have made. When you select FILE, then CLOSE, a box comes onto the screen. Alternatively, you could click on the icon shown in the Figure.

If you do want to save the changes made, then you should select the YES option, but if not select the NO option. If you change your mind about closing the document, you can select the CANCEL option on the box and return to the document.

Retrieving files and editing files

If you want to make some changes to a file that you have already saved, it is vital that you have named it appropriately and put it into the right place. By clicking on the above icon or selecting FILE, OPEN, you get another box on the screen. This box asks you two things:

- Where is the file saved?
- What is the file called?

By selecting the appropriate drive in the LOOK IN section of the box this will give you the DIRECTORY of that drive. In other words, everything that you have saved in that drive will be listed in alpha-numeric order. By reading down the file names and double clicking on the one you want, this will take you straight into your saved document.

If you want to make some changes to this document and the old version is no longer required, then all you have to do is save it when closing it and the changes will automatically be saved. If, however, you want to keep the original document you should save the document immediately as something else. Do this by selecting FILE, SAVE AS and then renaming it with another

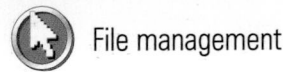

appropriate name. It may be that you just want to add a number to the original file name.

By doing this the original document is still safe and you can make as many changes as you wish to the new one.

Deleting files

Deleting files means removing them from the directory and sending them to the RECYCLE BIN. In the directory, right click on the file to be removed. A drop-down menu appears and you should select the DELETE option. Microsoft then asks you to confirm whether or not you want to send this file to the recycle bin and, if appropriate, you select the YES option. The files remain in this bin until you empty it. If you send something to the recycle bin by mistake it is possible to put the files back in their original place.

1 Have a look at the recycle bin on your computer. Do this from your desktop and double click on RECYCLE BIN.

2 What do you have to select in order to return files that have been sent there by mistake?

3 What do you have to select in order to EMPTY the bin?

The recycle bin should be emptied on a regular basis in order to maintain good housekeeping habits.

Printing hard copies

You can print a hard copy of the document by clicking on the icon shown left or by selecting FILE, PRINT from the drop-down menu. There are, however, some additional options to printing:

- You can PREVIEW the way the document will look as a hard copy by selecting the icon shown left or by selecting FILE, PRINT PREVIEW.
- You can print all or part of a document by selecting FILE, PRINT and then, in the PAGE RANGE, type in the portion of the document you want to print.
- You can print part of a page of a document, for example one paragraph, by clicking on the first letter of the paragraph and dragging the mouse down to the end. This highlights the paragraph and you should then select FILE, PRINT and click on SELECTION.

- You can print only odd or even pages of a multipage document by selecting FILE, PRINT and in the PRINT BOX select either ODD PAGES or EVEN PAGES.
- You can print more than one copy at a time by selecting FILE, PRINT and in the NUMBER OF COPIES box enter the number of copies you want.

WORD PROCESSING

This is the most popular software and is widely used in offices and homes around the world. In many businesses most employees, including those at the top of the organisation, often produce their own documents using a word-processing software package. This is because the software is easy to use and it is a simple task to make the document look professional.

With word-processing software:

- Entry and editing of text is simple.
- Errors can be easily corrected and changed.
- Changes to the size of the text and the type of font in order to improve presentation are easy.
- Text can be highlighted by using the bold, underline or italics options.
- Margins can be altered, page breaks controlled and pages can be identified by numbers and headers or footers.
- Work produced can be checked for spelling and grammar.
- An index or contents page can be created automatically.
- It will find specific words in the text and replace them if a change is needed.
- Single or multiple hard copies of documents can be printed.
- Letters can be mail merged with different addresses contained on a database.
- Labels and envelopes can be printed.

Word processing software will be used regularly for the following:

- Writing letters, memos, reports, essays and many other documents that consist of text in the office or at home.
- Developing the copy for a book or an article for a magazine, journal or a newspaper.

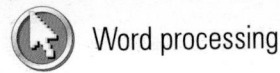

- Producing a mail merge where a standard document or letter is addressed to a number of different people.

Whether at work, school or at home there will be many occasions when it is necessary to correspond with other people through some kind of formal writing. You may need to produce a CV or a letter of application because you are applying for a job. You may have been asked to investigate a subject so that you can write up your coursework. At work you may need to put together a report on an investigation into a rival product or whether it would be a good idea to relocate or move the business to another part of the country. It may simply be that, in order to enhance the presentation of the document, you have been asked to key onto the computer something that was handwritten.

Whatever the reason, it is important that the correct amount of information is available to the computer operator in order to develop a presentation using the word processing software. The information might come straight out of an author's head, as in the production of a short story or your thoughts about a football match for the school magazine. It might be information collected through an investigation, where facts have been gathered from the internet or from books and journals.

Whatever the information, before starting to create the document it is important to ask questions to clarify what is expected. Such questions might include:

- Is the best software being used for the job?
- What size of text and font are required?
- What headings and titles need to be used?
- What sort of page layout would present the information in the best way?
- Are any other functions of the software required, such as headers, footers, page numbering or mail merge?

Action Points

Before you learn more about the importance of how a document is presented, have a look at the following letter of application. In its present form it is unlikely that Jon is going to be asked for interview.

1 You now know about business letters and how they should be presented. What is wrong, apart from the spelling mistakes, with this letter?

26 Habberley streey
The rock
Birmingham
B2 6TY

The Senior Parterne
Marches & Sons
Solicitors
The Grange
Birmingham   Re: Vacancy for an administrator
B12 5TH
23/07/02

Dear Sir

I refer to your advertisement in the Brimingham Post for an Administrator.

I have recently taken 9 GCSEs and am now looking for work where I can develop my skills. I have well developed IT skills and have already achieved my GCSE short course in IT.

I enclose a copy of my CV and look forward to hearing form you.

Yours sincerely

Jon Cash

2 Type a new letter to the solicitors putting right the mistakes and the layout issues.

Accuracy when entering text

Obviously, because communication and a good reputation are so important for a successful business, the employees have to ensure that all information contained on a document is accurate. When using word-processing software this is a relatively simple task because, in the majority of cases, the computer will highlight any errors as they are input or keyed in.

Microsoft® Word does this by:

- Underlining a spelling mistake with a red line.
- Underlining a grammar error with a green line.
- Underlining a spacing or punctuation error with a green line.

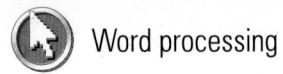

Such errors or spelling mistakes should be put right as the document is being created. If the document is particularly long, this job might get forgotten. In this case a spellchecker facility should be used. This simply involves selecting the icon on the toolbar; the computer will then scan the document, file or page. The computer will highlight any word that it does not recognise and will allow the user either to choose the correct option from the list it gives or to edit the word.

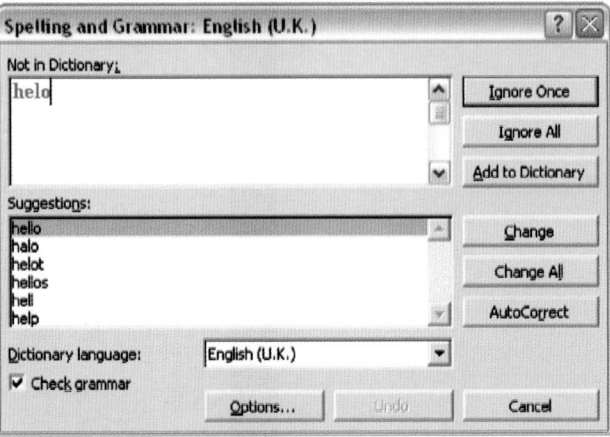

Proofreading means reading the screen for errors before you print out the document and also checking the hard copy to ensure that no mistakes have been missed on the screen. This can take some practice and it is often a good idea to read the hard copy to a colleague as this reading process often highlights errors to both individuals.

Think about it!

The following text contains several errors. Can you find them all?

Once upon a time, chopping was a labor. Sleeves were rolled up, ther was huffing and puffing, as the cook set to weilding a cleever to reduce the size of a large joint of meet. She would pound sugar or spices to a powder with a pestle and morter, and rub fruits through a clothe to make a puree.

It is little wonder that labour-saving devises were greeted so enthusisticly. Some were weird, some practicle, but they mostly helped to lighten the load of the cooks who used them.

Now we have electric servents, with blades to chop, grind and great, and I, for one, appreciate them, but we must be careful that this doesn't make for boring meals.

One useful way of correcting errors is the overtype facility which allows the user to replace the existing text with new text. This facility can be accessed in three different ways:

- By selecting the TOOLS icon on the toolbar and clicking OPTIONS.
- By hitting the INSERT key on the keyboard.
- By double clicking OVR on the status bar. (This is the horizontal bar at the bottom of the screen.)

Manuscript correction signs are something that any individual who word processes should be familiar with. They are used commonly throughout the world of book, newspaper and magazine publishing, as well as in industry, to identify any changes that need to be made to a document. The Figure below shows those that are standard throughout industry and, although you do not need to know these off by heart, it would be a good idea to familiarise yourself with them by carrying out the following activity.

Marginal mark	Meaning	Corresponding mark in text
⋎	insert space	⋎ between letters or words
#	insert space	⊱ between lines of paragraphs
⅄	insert matter indicated in margin	⅄
⊙⅄ ;⅄ ⊙⅄	substitute/insert colon semi colon or full stop	/ through character or ⅄
⅋ ⅋	insert single quotation marks	⅄ ⅄
⅋ ⅋	insert double quotation marks	⅄ ⅄
⋎	insert (or substitute) superscript character	⅄ (or encircle characters to be altered)
⋏	insert (or substitute) subscript character	⅄ (or encircle characters to be altered)
a/e/i/⊙	substitute character	/ through character to be substituted
∫	delete (take out)	/ through character(s)
∫	delete and close up	⊥ or ⊐ or through letters to be taken out

Marginal mark	Meaning	Corresponding mark in text	
⌒	close up (delete) space between characters	⌒	linking words or letters
↑	reduce space	↑	between words
⟋⟍	transpose	⟋⟍	between letters or words, numbered when necessary
[ ]	place in centre of line	[ ]	enclosing matter to be centred
⅃	move to the left or indent	⅃	enclosing matter to be moved to the left
⌐	move to the right or indent	⌐	enclosing matter to be moved to the right
⌐	begin a new paragraph	⌐	before first word of new paragraph
⌒	no fresh paragraph here (run text on)	⌒	between paragraphs
≣	change to capital letters	≣	under letters or words to be altered
＝	change to small capitals	＝	under letters or words to be altered
≢	change from capital to lower case		circle letter or word to be altered
∿	change to bold type	∿	under letters or words to be altered
⊔	change to italics	___	under letters or words to be altered
⊔	change to roman type from italic		encircle words to be altered
(×)	wrong font – replace by letter of correct font		encircle letter to be altered
×	replace by similar but undamaged character		encircle letter to be altered
⅄	make equal space	|	between words
(✓)	leave as printed (when words have been crossed out by mistake)	. . . .	under letter or words to remain

Action Points Look at the manuscript correction signs given in the next Figure. It is an itinerary, as discussed in the chapter on Communication.

1 Can you understand all of the correction signs?

2 If so, key in a copy of the corrected document and save it as ITINERARY on your computer.

ISLANDS OF THE SEYCHELLES - YOUR ITINERARY

DAY ONE Fly from London to Mahe - 08/15 from Gatwick. Arrive *of* Mahe and partake of light lunch before driving to ship for 17/00 sailing. *of*

DAY TWO Day at leisure.

DAY THREE Arrive at Aride Island for chance to explore. Time will be allowed for a visit to the coral reef and for bird watching.

DAY FOUR Sailing to Aldabra Island, during which time you will see several beautiful islands. We stop ~~for lunch~~ on an *of* uninhabited island for a barbecue lunch. ~~All the facilities of the vessel will be available to you whilst at sea.~~ *of*

DAY FIVE Aldabra Island. One of the most remote and ✱ inaccessible islands in the Indian Ocean. ~~The giant tortoise~~ *of* ~~is a regular visitor here, and they can be seen on the beaches laying their eggs.~~ There is also the opportunity of spotting the White Rail, the last flightless bird of the Indian Ocean.

DAY SIX Astove Island: Famous for its most beautiful butterflies, this coral-bound island has an almost completely land locked lagoon.

DAY SEVEN Day at leisure.

⊘ DAY ~~EIGHT~~ La Digue and Praslin Islands. Two islands today/ — *of* first of all we visit La Digue, well known for its old-fashioned charm, and then Praslin which boasts an exotic tropical rain forest.

DAY ~~EIGHT~~ **NINE** Mahe. Arrive in the morning and transfer to the Hotel Cariba for a 2-night stay.

DAY ~~NINE~~ **TEN**. At leisure.

DAY ~~TEN~~ **ELEVEN**. Mahe to London Gatwick *for* return journey. *trs*

✱ Insert:
The giant tortoise, a regular visitor to Aldabra Island, can sometimes be seen on the beach, where it lays its eggs.

Document layouts

This term refers to the way a document looks when it is completed or presented. With all word-processing software it is possible to format the document in a number of different ways, including:

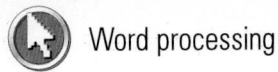

- Page orientation – this term means which way round the document should be printed on the paper. There are basically two options:
  - portrait – this means the shorter side of the paper will be at the top;
  - landscape – this means that the longer side of the paper will be at the top.

  To change the paper orientation from portrait (which is the default) to landscape click on FILE, PAGE SETUP, and select the picture of the A4 LANDSCAPE option.

- Column layout – it is very easy to make a document look like a magazine, newsletter or newspaper with two columns of text on each page. You can select the number of columns required for the whole document or for one single page within a document by selecting the column icon on the toolbar.

- Text formatting – the words or text used within a document can be amended whilst being keyed in, or at a later date. This would be done for a number of reasons, including:
  - in order to make them stand out from others;
  - to change the way the document is presented;
  - to make the text fit onto a single page;
  - to break up unused space on the page.

  The font being used means the design for the shape of the characters when printed. Each font can be selected in a variety of different sizes and can also be used in any combination of styles.

In addition to changing the font being used, it is also possible to change the way the text looks in the following ways to make it more prominent or noticeable on the page:

- **Embolden the text.**   **B**

- <u>Underline the text.</u>   *I*

- *Put the text in italics.*   <u>U</u>

- Headers and footers – there are many occasions when additional information needs to be included on each page

of a document. This information could include any or all of the following:

- page numbering;
- chapter titles;
- the date;
- a word or words which must go on each page.

If any of this information is to be shown at the top of the page, then it is known as a header. Alternatively, if it is to appear at the foot of the page, then it is a footer.

Headers and footers can consist of more than one line and can include items such as drawings or objects. Their inclusion in a document will not affect the rest of the text or any of the remaining formatting jobs carried out.

A header and footer can be included in a file or document by selecting VIEW, HEADER AND FOOTER and then keying in the information required to be shown either at the top margin or the bottom margin of the document.

Page numbering can be inserted without the use of the header and footer option by selecting INSERT, PAGE NUMBERS and then choosing the position of the number for the document.

Action Points

1 Retrieve the document you saved as ITINERARY in an earlier activity.

2 Insert your name as a header and your teacher's name as a footer.

- Indented text – indents control the space between the page margins and the paragraphs. Setting a larger left indent increases the blank space to the left of the paragraph. The use of indents helps to make the following items easier to read:
  - quotations;
  - important items which need to be made clearer.

Microsoft® Word automatically indents text from the lefthand margin when the option to either number or bullet point items is selected.

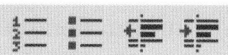

- Justification – this term refers to the margin of a document. A justified righthand margin means that each line of the text

finishes at exactly the same point, giving a straight margin like the lefthand one. Because this does not happen naturally, the computer will automatically adjust the spacing along the whole line of text to ensure that the last letters always finish in the same place. An unjustified right margin is also known as a ragged one since each line ends at a different place.

It is also possible to select the right justify icon, which starts each line from the righthand margin rather than the left, or to centre each line of text on the page.

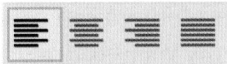

- Line spacing – the default for any new document is single line spacing. It is simple, however, to change either the whole document to a different line space or to change just one section by holding down the CTRL key on the keyboard and selecting the number of the appropriate spacing required. For instance, if double line spacing is required, then CTRL and the number two should be selected. If only a section of the text is required in different line spacing, then that section should be highlighted by clicking on the first letter and dragging the mouse down to the last letter. This will highlight the text and then the CTRL and number activity should be applied.

- Margins – these are the white space at the top, bottom, lefthand and righthand side of the paper. As we mentioned in the section on indents, the margins can be changed to adjust the distance between the edge of the paper and the beginning of the text. Often margins are changed in order to:
  - make room for long headers and footers;
  - leave space for a business letterhead when printing;
  - change the number of pages contained within a document;
  - leave room for the document to be bound together;
  - improve the look of the document.

All four margins can be changed by selecting FILE, PAGE SETUP and then clicking on the up or down arrows to either increase or decrease the amount of white space.

Rearranging information

Rearranging information on an existing document is also very easy to do with Microsoft Word. There are several options available to amend a document in the required way and these include:

- Finding and replacing words – by using the FIND and REPLACE facility on the EDIT icon on the toolbar it is possible to find a particular word that has been used on any number of occasions within a document. If, for instance, this word has been spelt incorrectly during the keying in stage, then this can be changed easily by using this facility.
- Cut, copy and paste – these clever aspects of word processing make the rearrangement of information very easy. By highlighting the text it is possible to delete it, copy it or move it to another position within the document. This is useful if a large document, say a chapter of a book, needs amending in a number of different ways.

There are two ways of carrying out these functions of the software. The first is to highlight the text and select the appropriate icon from the toolbar, as shown below. The second is to highlight the text then right click on the mouse and select the option required.

Action Points

You can practise cut, copy and paste easily yourself.

1 Open one of your existing documents which contains at least four different paragraphs in it and save it as something else.

2 Practise rearranging the text on the screen by either cutting it, copying it so that it appears two or three times, or moving sections from one position to another.

Using templates

As we discussed in the chapter on communication, many businesses use preprinted forms or templates to reduce the amount of time spent producing such items as well as to ensure their corporate image is maintained in all documents sent out. In order to ensure that this vital communication tool is maintained, the business will create a set of templates for each type of document they issue to customers, suppliers or, indeed, to the media (television, radio, newspapers, magazines, etc.).

Templates do not necessarily have to be created from scratch. Every Microsoft Word document is based on a template. A

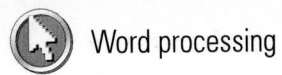

template determines the basic structure for a document and contains document settings such as fonts, page layout, special formatting and styles.

Normal templates contain settings that are available to all documents. Document templates, such as a memo or fax, contain settings that are available only to documents to which those templates are attached.

Action Points **C**reate a document template by carrying out the following instructions:

1 On the FILE menu, click NEW.

2 In the NEW FROM TEMPLATE section click General Templates.

3 Select a template that is similar to the one you want to create, then click TEMPLATE under CREATE NEW, and then click OK.

4 On the FILE menu, click SAVE AS and call the file something appropriate.

5 In the new template, add the text and graphics you want to appear in all new documents that you base on the template, and delete any items you do not want to appear. Make the changes you want to the margin settings, page size and orientation, styles, and other formats. Save the template.

Borders and shading

Borders and shading can add interest and emphasis to various parts of a document. You can add borders to:

- Pages – you can add a border to any or all sides of each page in a document, to pages in a section, to the first page only, or to all pages except the first. You can add page borders in many line styles and colours, as well as a variety of graphical borders.
- Text – you can visually separate text from the rest of a document by adding borders. You can also highlight text by applying shading.
- Tables – these are one or more rows or cells that are most often used to display numbers. These are a form of image that helps to explain something that is either complicated or which needs analysing.
- Table cells – this is the box formed where the row or columns in a table meet and into which the information is entered.

	A	B	C
1			
2			
3			
4	yellow cell		
5			red text
6			
7			
8			
9			
10		green text	
11			

- Graphic objects and pictures – when you draw an object, it appears with a border around it. You can also add borders to **text boxes**, pictures and art imported from another progam. You can change or format a border in the same way that you change or format a line. You can fill objects with a solid colour, a **gradient**, a pattern, a texture or a picture. If you want a colour or fill effect to appear behind all of the text on the page, you can use a **watermark**, background or **theme** to make it more attractive.

- Web frames – these are displayed on web pages and borders can be included to make the material contained on the page more obvious.

You can shade paragraphs and text, and apply coloured or textured fills to your graphic objects using Microsoft® Word, Excel and PowerPoint®. Just select FORMAT, BORDERS AND SHADING and then identify the colour of the line, the type of border and then move to the SHADING option to choose the colour and texture required.

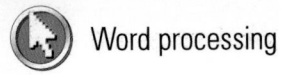
GCSE BUSINESS AND COMMUNICATION SYSTEMS

GCSE Business and Communication Systems

GCSE BUSINESS AND COMMUNICATION SYSTEMS

GCSE Business and Communication Systems

Merging files and mail merge

Because Microsoft's Word (word processing), Excel (spreadsheet), Access (database) and PowerPoint (presentation) software is compatible, it is possible to bring information from one piece of the software into another. This merging of files or pieces of information has a number of uses:

- Spreadsheet information can be imported into a Word document. This may be needed in order to illustrate a complicated piece of accounts information in a letter to a customer or supplier.

- Charts created on Excel can be imported into a Word document. These can show complicated information in a simpler chart form, for instance in a large report.
- Information held on a database using Access can be imported into a Word document. This might be done in order to list the names, addresses, telephone numbers and other details of customers for the sales representatives of a business.
- Information held on a database using Access can be imported into a standard letter so that the letter can be mail merged to any number of different customers or potential customers.

A mail merge has to start with both of the following:

- A standard letter – this can be created as a new Word document, from a template or from an existing document already saved in the directory. This is known as the MAIN DOCUMENT and should contain the text and graphics that are the same for each version to be sent out.
- A data source – this is the list of names of those who should receive a copy of the standard or main document.

Once the above have been completed, the MERGE FIELDS should be inserted into the main document. These are the places where the names, addresses and other information common to all those receiving the letter should go, for instance the heading or Dear Mr or Mrs. You do this by clicking where you want to insert the field. You should then select FILE, SAVE AS and give this document a suitable file name.

The next step is to locate the data source. We are going to look in detail at the way this database should be constructed a little later in this section. To select the right database, however, you choose the TOOLS option and select LETTERS AND MAILING. The MAIL MERGE WIZARD then takes you through the process of combining the two files to complete the mail-merged series of documents.

Basically, mail merge removes the need to type specific details into a standard letter. A business would use mail merge in order to contact a large number of existing or potential customers.

The data source created can also be useful in the mail-merge process for the printing of mailing labels. These eliminate the need to print or address individual envelopes as the addresses can be printed directly onto A4 label sheets. You can set up the labels by following these simple steps:

- Click CHANGE DOCUMENT LAYOUT.
- Click LABEL OPTIONS.
- In the LABEL OPTIONS dialog box, select the options you want, such as the label type and size, and then click OK.

SPREADSHEETS

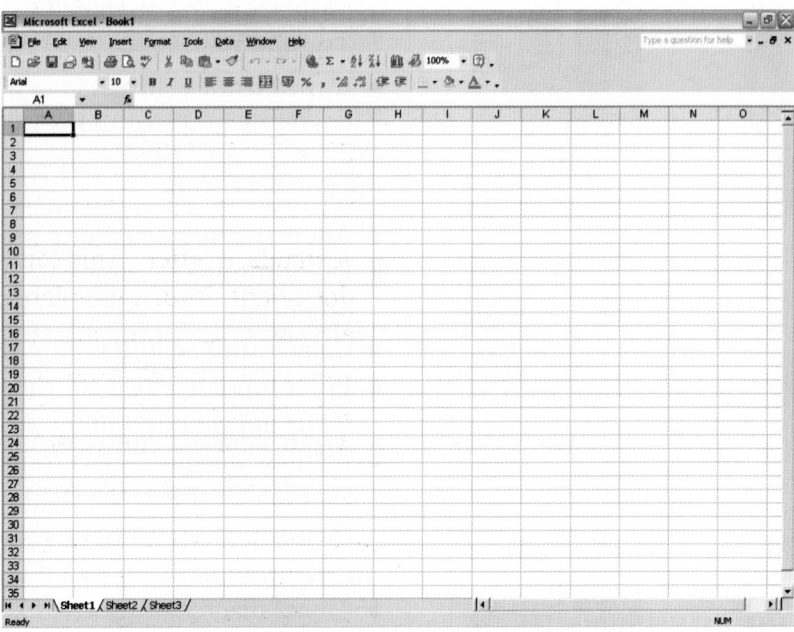

A spreadsheet package, such as Microsoft® Excel, is the computerised equivalent of a finance department's ledgers. The user can enter numbers, formulae or text into each of the cells contained on the sheet. Columns are the vertical sections of the sheet (headed A, B, C, etc. on the illustration) and rows are the horizontal sections (labelled 1, 2, 3, etc.). A cell is one square of the spreadsheet. In the illustration the cursor is in cell A1. This software is the equivalent of a calculator because it carries out calculations for the user and manipulates numeric information.

Because Microsoft® Word and Excel are compatible, many of the icons used on the toolbar are the same for both pieces of software, although others are specific to each one.

Spreadsheets can be used by a business to carry out any of the following:

- To hold records of transactions.
- To calculate future sales and costs.
- To calculate profits.
- To calculate income tax.
- To merge information from more than one department.
- To timetable employees and plan work.

The program allows the user to carry out calculations and amend data quickly and accurately. The spreadsheet is very useful when it is necessary to consider a 'what if' scenario, for instance:

- If a Finance Director wanted to see how the profit within a business might change if sales rose and costs were kept to a minimum.
- If the business invested in a new piece of technology that would incur a cost to the business over a period of time.

Spreadsheets can:

- Allow the user to enter a number, formula or text into any cell.
- Use formulae to allow calculations to be carried out in other cells.
- Copy formulae into groups of cells.
- Enter repetitive text for the user, such as where the same name appears over and over again.
- Increase a value by a certain amount at each entry. A good example of this is the football league tables where, by entering the correct formula, the calculation of the number of points each team has achieved will be automatic.
- Create macros or shortcut keys to speed up entry.

- Allow macros to be used to perform a sequence of actions or commands automatically when the macro is run. Macros save time when performing the same actions on a regular basis. Also, if you are repeating the same action again and again there is no risk of human error and you will get the exact results every time. To create a macro:
  - click on the TOOLS menu;
  - select MACRO;
  - select RECORD NEW MACRO;
  - type in a name for your macro (make sure there are no spaces and make sure it is meaningful) and press TAB;
  - select a shortcut key for this macro and press TAB;
  - click on OK;
  - carry out the actions you want to record and click on the STOP icon.

- Perform certain functions similar to a word processor, such as enhancing text and layout by using bold, underline, italics, etc.
- Create graphs and charts to display results of calculations as an image.

There are three main types of data that you will need to know about before you can use a spreadsheet effectively:

- Text – which will nearly always be labels and headings that explain what the numbers in the different cells relate to. There could be a paragraph at the end or the beginning of the spreadsheet presentation that will give an explanation or an introduction. As the text is typed, it goes across the cell width and it is not necessary to widen the columns.
- Numeric data is input under the headings to which it relates. The numbers will be the data that represent the information, such as a set of accounts or something that will help in the decision-making process.
- Formulae are instructions that the program will use to carry out any calculations.

The kind of information that might be input into the spreadsheet either as text, numbers or formulae would be:

- Accounts figures.
- Sales figures.
- Budgeting and forecasting (future predictions) information.
- Data relating to staff issues such as hours of work, wages and salaries, etc.

- Calculations using savings or borrowing information to work out interest payments to or from a bank.
- Research data and statistics used to draw conclusions or make decisions.

Designing and creating spreadsheets

When you are given the task of inputting data into a spreadsheet you will need to make sure that you have all the necessary information. Whatever the information, it is important to ask a few questions before you begin.

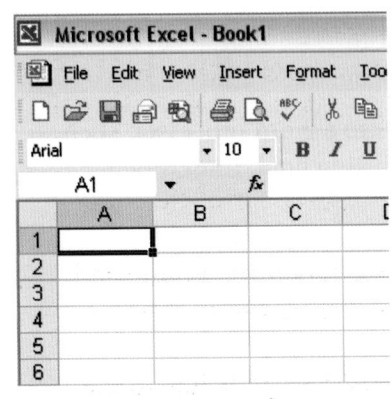

- How should the information be laid out?
- What information is required as a result of the input of the data?
- Is the data that is being input into the spreadsheet to be used for information purposes only or are there decisions to be made based on it?
- What formulae will allow you to extract the new information if this is required?
- How should the information be presented – either as a grid or as a graph or both?

As we already know, several of the icons for Excel are the same as those used for Word, so to create a new spreadsheet document you use the icon shown in the Figure on the left.

This takes you into the blank page and you now input information by moving from cell to cell using the arrows on the keyboard. When you first start to input information you need to bear the following in mind:

- When you are in cell A1 the program will accept a heading that spreads across to other cells on row 1 and will not change the width of the cell.
- You can get rid of any mistakes you make in a cell by hitting the space bar to clear the cell of information.
- The information you input into any cell also appears in the long box on the toolbar underneath the **B,** *I* and <u>U</u> icons and can be amended in this section by clicking in the box.

- You can SAVE and PRINT documents in the same way as you do in Word, by clicking on the icons or using the FILE menu.

Action Points

Create a new spreadsheet document and save it as 'Practice'. Now do the following:

1 Input the heading 'My Information' in A1 – put this into bold.

2 Put your class teacher's name in cell B3.

3 Put your favourite hobby in cell D5.

4 Put your favourite uncle's name in cell C6.

5 Print a hard copy of this.

Resizing rows and columns

If the information you want to put into a particular cell is too long, then it is possible to widen either a column or a row. You can do this by:

- Taking your mouse to the grey area at the top of the column that needs widening.
- When you move the mouse to the right of the column and hover over the dividing line, a black cross will show on the screen.
- Hold down the left mouse button and drag the line to the right to widen the column.

You can do the same for a row by:

- Taking the mouse to the grey area on the lefthand edge of the sheet.
- Hover over the dividing line.
- Hold down the left-hand mouse button and drag the line down to make the row deeper.

Formatting cells, rows and columns

It is possible to format or change the layout of a spreadsheet. It may be that you require a different font, or size of font, or that you wish to colour the background. This can be done for an individual cell, a whole row, a column or the whole of the sheet:

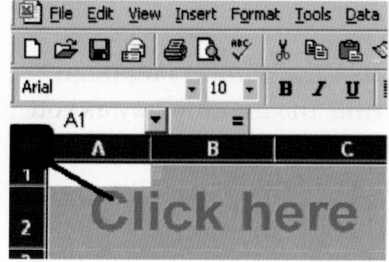

- The whole sheet can be formatted by clicking on the space shown in the corner between A and 1. This highlights the whole sheet by changing it from white to black.

When you change the format it will be applied to the whole sheet and the format options for Word also apply to Excel.

- The cell can be formatted by ensuring the cursor is positioned on the cell in question and choosing FORMAT, CELLS then selecting the appropriate layout change required from that menu.
- All cells in a row can be formatted by taking the mouse to the row number in the grey strip on the lefthand side of the sheet. Click on the row number when the small black arrow appears and that will highlight only that particular row. Once the row has been blackened then choose the FORMAT, CELLS menu and select the appropriate format change.
- All cells in a column can be formatted by taking the mouse to the column letter in the grey area at the top of the appropriate column. Click on the column letter when the small black arrow appears and the column will be highlighted black, then choose the FORMAT, CELLS menu for the appropriate layout change for the column.

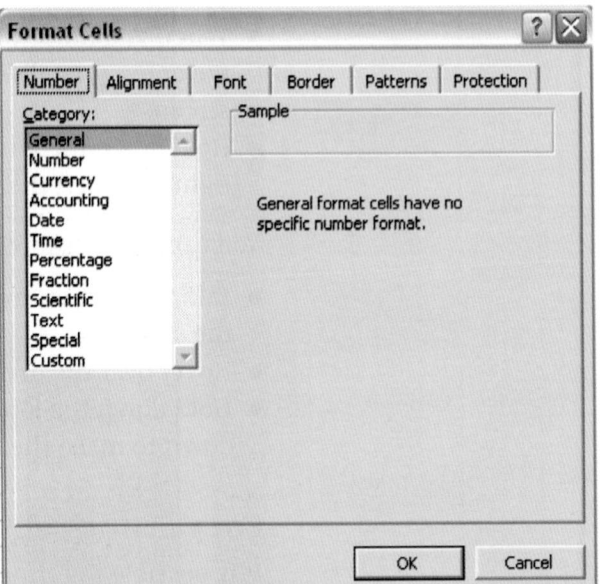

As can be seen from the 'formatting cells' drop-down menu, individual cells, rows or columns of cells can be changed in the following ways:

- Number – this refers to the way that the numbers input are displayed. It might be that each time the user inputs a number or set of numbers, these are required to be displayed as a date, or a time, or with a required number of decimal points.

- Alignment – this refers to the position within the cells that the input is placed. It could be that all information in a particular row needs to be centred, or justified on the right. This is the same option that Word gives users and the same icons can be used for this purpose.

- Font – in a similar way the font used might need to be different for a complete row of the sheet, or, perhaps just for one or two individual cells. The font can be changed as with Word.

- Borders and patterns – you can put a border around an individual cell or a block of cells. You can also border a complete column or row to make it more prominent on the sheet, or shade the cell, row or column so that it is different from the others on the sheet, as with word processing.

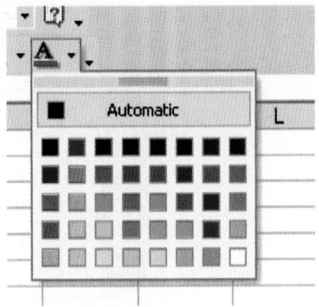

- Protection – it is possible to format an individual cell, block of cells, row or column so that it is protected. This means that the information contained within the protected areas cannot be amended or changed by another user.

Action Points **O**pen your 'Practice' file again and have a go at changing the formats and layouts. You could try all of those facilities we have covered so far by widening columns, emboldening some sections, giving one or two cells a border and shading. It is good to become familiar with the way the software works before moving on to something more demanding.

Excel also allows the user to insert headers and footers and page numbers onto a sheet or series of sheets. This facility is done in much the same way as in Word, although the header and footer insertion box is slightly different, as shown in the following Figure. After selecting the VIEW, HEADER AND FOOTER option, choose CUSTOMISE HEADER or CUSTOMISE FOOTER. You can then key in anything you wish to appear on the left of the sheet, in the centre or on the right.

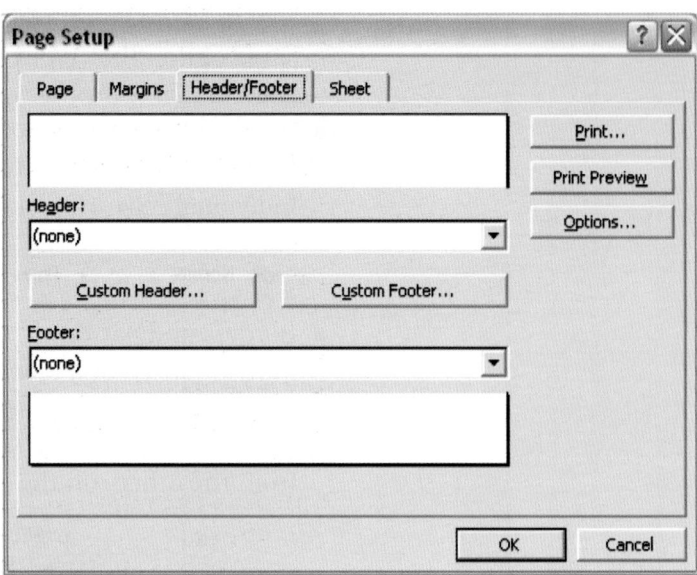

Action Points In your 'Practice' file insert your name as a header on the left of the sheet and your teacher's name centred as a footer.

Cut, copy and paste is another facility that is common to both Word and Excel. In the spreadsheet program you need to click on the cell, block of cells, row or column that you want to remove, copy or move. When you choose the EDIT menu and select CUT the desired section is deleted from the sheet. By placing the cursor in the required place on the sheet and selecting EDIT, PASTE you can move the deleted cells to another location. When you choose the EDIT, COPY option the original remains in the same place but you can PASTE into another section of the sheet so that it appears twice.

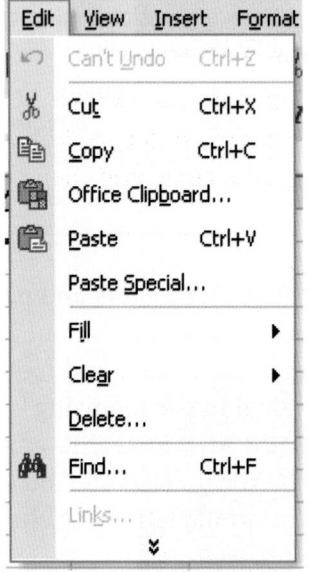

Surname	First Name	Date of Birth
Anderson	Mary	06/05/89
Dartmore	Bob	08/04/86
Caldwell	James	05/03/90
Hall	Rosemary	6/23/1969
Jade	Dernbach	04/03/64
Anthony	Jason	05/07/90
Ballwell	Rachel	6/78/78
Candy	James	3/23/76
Hannapord	Martina	03/04/65
Jane	Barbara	05/04/67

Surname	First Name	Date of Birth	Sex
Anderson	Mary	06/05/89	F
Dartmore	Bob	08/04/86	F
Caldwell	James	05/03/90	F
Hall	Rosemary	6/23/1969	F
Jade	Dernbach	04/03/64	M
Anthony	Jason	05/07/90	M
Ballwell	Rachel	6/78/78	F
Candy	James	3/23/76	M
Hannapord	Martina	03/04/65	F
Jane	Barbara	05/04/67	M
		Surname	First Name
		Anderson	Mary
		Dartmore	Bob
		Caldwell	James
		Hall	Rosemary
		Jade	Dernbach

Another way of changing how a spreadsheet is displayed is by what is known as sorting. This function allows the user to sort a list of names into alphabetical order and to include in this sort all the other information on the sheet related to that name. In other words, if column A contained the names of customers, column B their addresses and column C their telephone numbers, then by highlighting column A and requesting the sort, the data in columns B and C would also move and stay beside the right business's name.

To use the sort function, highlight the column to be sorted, select the DATA menu and choose SORT.

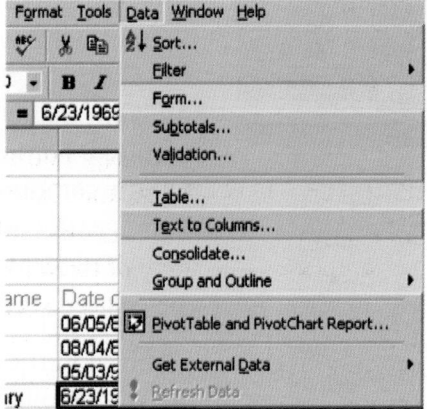

You then have the option of whether you want the names beginning with A to be shown first (ascending order) or last (descending order). Click on the appropriate circle and then click OK.

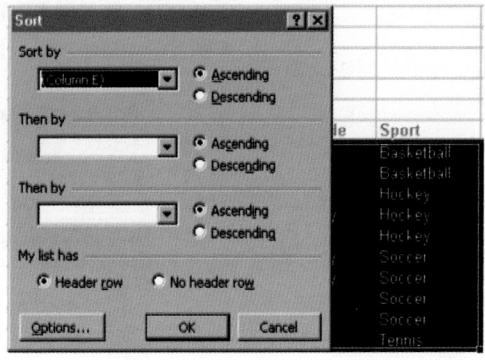

Action Points

1 Create a new spreadsheet and key in the names of everyone in your class in column A. Widen the column if necessary to ensure that all the names are going to fit.

2 Print Preview your document to make sure you have widened the column enough.

3 Now sort the names into ascending alphabetical order and print a hard copy of your file, having saved it as 'Sort'.

Sometimes you might be required to insert a picture into a spreadsheet. This might be from one you have stored on your computer or a piece of Microsoft's clip art. This is easy to do by selecting INSERT, PICTURE and then following the instructions on-screen. The picture might appear very large at first, but if you read about sizing a chart a little later in this section you will understand how to adjust the size and position within the sheet.

Formulae

Formulae are what make Excel different from Word in several ways because this is the part of the sheet that informs the program that a calculation or the manipulation of the numbers is required. For instance, at the end of a column of figures you can tell the computer that you want it to add all the figures together. This is easily done if only one column is involved, by selecting the AUTOSUM icon, as shown in the Figure.

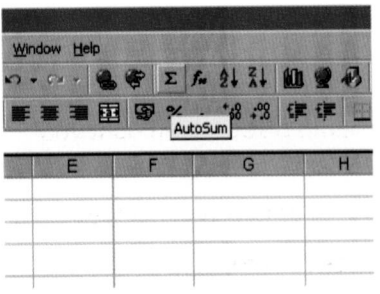

You use AUTOSUM by dragging the mouse down the cells involved in the calculation and clicking on the icon. As you will see in the following Figure, the cells involved are highlighted with a broken line around them. In addition to this highlight, the formula that the program is using is shown in the long box above the column letters. In the case of the one shown here, the formula is saying =SUM(D1:D2). The = sign indicates that a formula is about to be used, SUM means it is an addition and the (D1) is the first cell involved. The : (colon) says 'as far as' which means the final cell involved is D2.

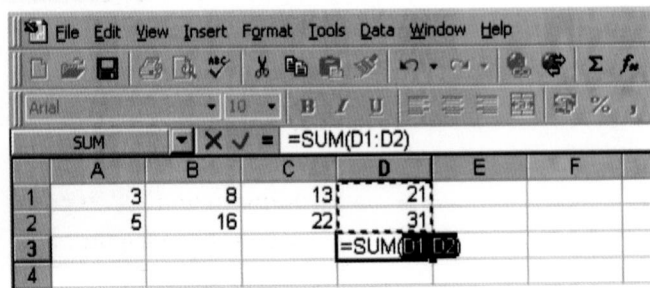

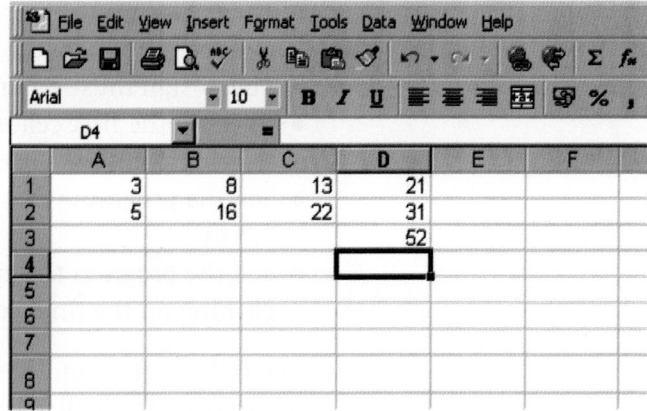

As we can now see, Excel has successfully added together 21 (D1) and 31 (D2) in order to give our total of 52 (in D3).

Action Points

1 Create a new spreadsheet and save it as 'Autosum'.

2 Give the sheet the heading 'Using the Autosum Facility' and put this heading in bold.

3 In cell A2 key in 'Item' and in B2 key in 'Amount'.

4 In column A key in all those items you tend to spend money on regularly, and in column B key the amount you spend on each.

5 Format the cells in column B so that they are centred.

6 Remember to widen columns as required.

7 Now use AUTOSUM to total your outgoings.

8 Make this cell prominent on the sheet by giving it a border and shading the cell in a colour of your choice.

9 Print a copy of your sheet.

When keying in formulae, rather than using the autosum facility you will need to use the following symbols:

● + for adding up numbers.
● – for subtracting numbers.
● * for multiplication.
● / for division.

You must make sure that you carry out any work using formulae in a logical way. Spreadsheets help you to carry out quite complicated calculations, but the computer needs exact information if it is going to do the job properly and accurately for you. The following should be borne in mind when inserting formulae:

- The cursor must be in the cell where you want the calculation to appear.
- The = sign must go first.
- Click on the first cell involved and this gives the program a starting point for the calculation.
- Tell the program what calculation is involved, for example +, −, * or /.
- Tell the program the ending point of the calculation by clicking on the final cell involved.

The following set of Figures explains this process in a much better way. As we discussed earlier in the book, images explain complicated processes in a more straightforward and easily understood manner.

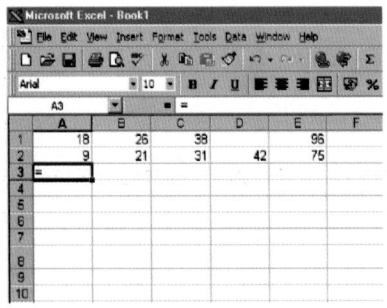

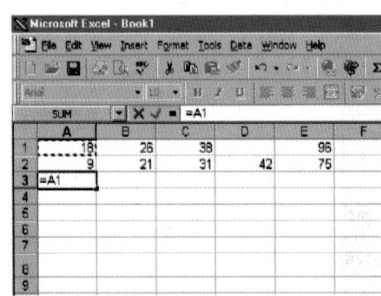

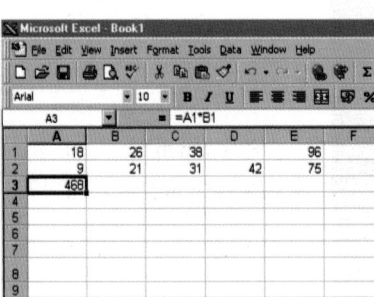

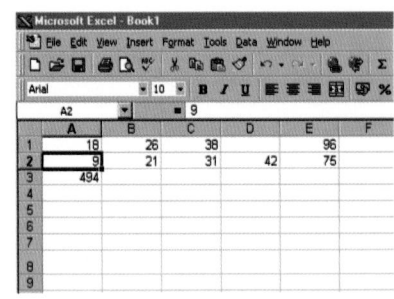

Action Points

Practise doing this for yourself.

1 Create a new spreadsheet.

2 Input the numbers in the cells given and carry out the multiplication calculation as shown in the five Figures above.

3 Save your work as 'Multiplication'.

Replicating values and formulae

Once you have understood the basic principle behind creating a suitable formula that the program will understand, it is easy to replicate (copy) this formula into other cells on the spreadsheet. You can do this by using the COPY facility if it is just a case of copying into a few cells scattered around the sheet. However, it could be that the formula is required down a whole column or across a whole row. This is done by:

- Clicking on the cell in which the formula has been inserted.
- Dragging the mouse down the column, highlighting all cells where the formula is also required.
- Clicking off at the final cell involved.

Action Points

1 Create a new spreadsheet and key in the information from the Table below.

	A	B	C	D
1	NAME	NORMAL HOURS	OVERTIME	TOTAL HOURS
2	James	37	5	
3	Williams	45	6.5	
4	Fielding	28	7	
5	Bennett	30	7	
6	Cook	45	7	
7	Samani	35	9.5	
8	Smith	28	8.5	
9	Patel J	15	5.5	

2 Adjust your column widths so that all names are shown in full.

3 In cell D2 insert a formula to give the total hours worked for James.

4 Once you are happy that your formula is correct, replicate that formula for all of the employees on the Table.

5 Print a copy of your sheet.

Displaying and printing formulae is quite straightforward should it be required. You can display a formula in a cell by choosing the TOOLS, OPTIONS, VIEW, and then clicking in the box next for FORMULAS.

Spreadsheets

Printing the formula is similar to one of the Word printing options in that you would select FILE, PRINT, and then click on the SELECTION option.

Action Points

The Table below shows the information that a payroll clerk needs to calculate the gross pay for staff employed by an employment agency. The employees are all temporary staff and their details are as shown. There are two charges involved – one that the employee receives per hour and one that the business has to pay to the employment agency per hour.

NAME	HOURS WORKED	EMPLOYEE RATE	AGENCY RATE	GROSS PAY	OWED TO AGENCY
Fry	37	5.00	7.50		
Hutchinson	45	6.50	9.00		
Freeman	28	7.00	9.50		
Bates	30	7.00	9.50		
Cowley	45	7.00	9.50		
Sutherland	35	9.50	12.00		
Stanton	28	8.50	10.50		
Prior	15	5.50	8.00		

1 Recreate the above Table in a spreadsheet.

2 The hourly rates columns should both be displayed to two decimal places.

3 The gross pay calculation should be centred in the column.

4 The 'charge to company' column should be highlighted by use of colour or shading.

5 Ensure you use the correct formulae to calculate the total amount of pay that each member of staff should receive and the amount the company owes the agency for each member employee.

6 At the end of the final column, total the individual charges to the company to give a total owed to the agency.

CHARTS   Creating charts from spreadsheets is straightforward using the chart options icon.

There are 14 chart types and a further 73 sub-chart types. So you have a large selection of charts to choose from. To create a chart from the spreadsheet you need to do the following:

- Select the data from your sheet by highlighting the cells to be involved in the chart.
- Click on the icon or choose the INSERT drop-down menu.
- You then have two options in the box that appears – either choose the STANDARD TYPE of chart or the CUSTOM TYPE. There is a very good selection in the standard type which should be sufficient to meet your needs, but it is worth looking at what else is available.
- From the list given you can choose the sort of chart you want to use to display your information.
- If you want to preview what your chart will look like, you can do this by holding down the button shown on the left.

Press and Hold to View Sample

This will display a preview of what your graph will look like. When you are happy with the graph you have created, click on NEXT to go to the next screen.

- You will then be shown the highlighted data that you selected for your graph with running dots around it. If this is the data you want to use, click NEXT. If it is not the right data, highlight the correct data from your worksheet, then click on NEXT.
- On this screen you can enter a TITLE for your chart and then, to continue with the labelling of the diagram, press TAB.

If required, you can now label the different axes of the chart (the vertical line (X axis) and horizontal line (Y axis) before completing this by clicking on FINISH.

Now your chart will be displayed on your spreadsheet page. You can move and resize the chart, as if this were a picture or a piece of clipart.

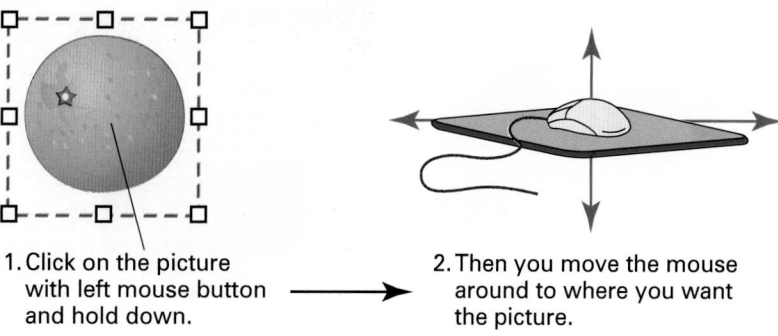

1. Click on the picture with left mouse button and hold down.
2. Then you move the mouse around to where you want the picture.

Figure 6.1

To resize your chart or a picture you click on it to select it. It will be obvious when this has been achieved as little square boxes appear around the chart or picture. Now you click on one of the little square boxes and move the mouse until you have achieved the desired size.

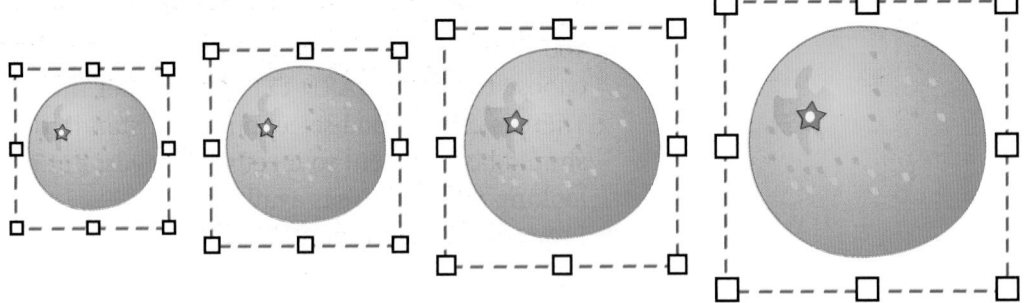

Chart formats

Bar charts are a good way to display information in an easy-to-read format. They use bars of different blocks of colour which can be displayed either horizontally or vertically (as shown). Bar charts have a vertical and a horizontal axis, and for the purpose of clarifying the information contained it is a good idea to label these when the chart is being created.

Figure 6.2

A different form of graphic representation of data is the pie chart. A pie chart is always shown in a circle with each slice showing the portion of the whole that it represents. There are a number of features which can be associated with the construction of a pie chart:

- The circle consists of 360 degrees.
- Each of the slices or sections of the pie which you allocate to a value of the data should have a percentage or the relevant number of degrees shown clearly.
- The pie chart should be titled and given a name.

1990 US Population Statistics by Race

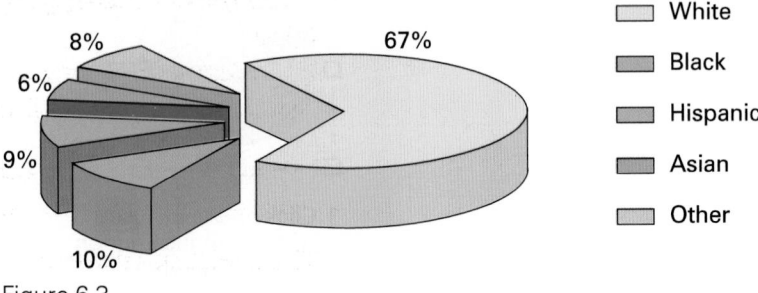

Figure 6.3

In general, line graphs have a number of rules regarding the way in which they are constructed:

- The horizontal line is known as the X axis and the vertical line is known as the Y axis.
- Each axis should have a clear scale which allows the information to be displayed plainly on the graph. This means that you should take advantage of all of the space available on the page so that the labels are easy to read when the graph is printed out.
- A line graph should have the points that are plotted on the graph joined together.
- The line graph should always be titled.

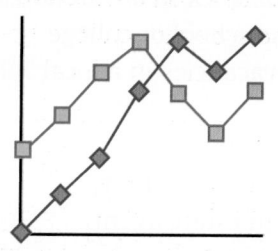

Figure 6.4

DATABASES

There must be millions of databases around the world containing masses of information on each and every one of us. The old-fashioned way of keeping records was to put all the details onto cards and to place the cards in some kind of filing system. This worked quite well. It had its advantages and disadvantages and many people clung to this way of working for a number of years. The computerised database software has some distinct advantages over this now old-fashioned way of working, as we discovered in the previous chapter.

Microsoft® Access database software has the following features:

- The user can store data in the form of records relating to one individual or item.
- By creating fields, the person who sets up the database can define exactly what will be included.
- Information entered into the database can be sorted in a variety of different ways, much the same as information stored on a spreadsheet.
- Information can be taken from the database as a list, an individual record, a group or category of records.
- It can provide statistical information about the data that it has.
- The data can be combined to form the basis of a report for inclusion in other documents.

Microsoft Access can be used when it is necessary to collate large amounts of information about groups of people, for example:

- The details of customers of a business.

- Patients' details in a surgery.
- Members' details at a golf club.
- Information about the amount of stock in a warehouse.
- Records of students or pupils in a school or college.
- A careers database or list of job vacancies in a local Job Centre or employment agency.
- Lists of suppliers that a business might wish to use.
- A collection of books, CDs or videos in a library.
- Properties for sale or to rent by an estate agent.

The components of a database

When we consider the entries in a telephone directory, it is obvious that all of the information contained in it is related since it is possible to obtain the following details about subscribers:

- Their name.
- Their address.
- Their postcode.
- The area where they live.
- Their telephone number.

Each of these pieces of information in a database is known as a field. Each field will be given a title and it will then be necessary to estimate the amount of information that is likely to be input into that field. Having identified the title of the field and the length it is required to be, it is then necessary to identify the type of information that will be inserted into this field. By type of information, we mean what the computer will be able to recognise and deal with effectively. When deciding on the size of fields to be included, it is best to remember that the computer has only limited memory. For this reason it is not advisable to make the fields too long but to allow sufficient space for the information to be entered. The following are field types:

- Text – in the case of a telephone directory this will be the name and address of the subscriber.
- Number – again, in the telephone directory this will be the area code and telephone number of the subscriber.

It is also possible to create fields which accept the following types of information:

- Surnames
- First names
- Addresses
- Postcodes
- Dates of birth
- Telephone numbers
- Age

Having decided on the fields to use within the database, it is now time to start to create the individual records, each of which will contain the same fields. Obviously, if some of the information is unavailable for one particular record, then the field will be left blank.

When creating the telephone directory, each of the subscribers will have their own record. All of the available information for each of them will have been inserted into the relevant fields and then all the records are joined together to form the telephone directory database. The information input into each field of a record is known as the data.

A table will be used to design the layout of the database. The layout can be amended at different stages of the design, and can be viewed either in its blank form or with some of the information inserted. In a business situation each table could contain information about one area or department. These tables are then linked together so that the information from one can be combined with the information from another.

When tables are related in some way and then combined, this is known as a relationship database. These are particularly useful when the database holds a lot of information.

Data types

We need to look in a little more detail at the type of data that each field would contain. The following are the most common types of data:

- Text – letters, numbers and symbols. It is possible to sort this information into both alphabetical and alpha-numeric order. We looked at these methods of filing paperwork in Chapter 2. You might want to refresh your memory on this before continuing.
- Numbers – it is possible to restrict the number of digits which can be inserted into a number field by removing any decimal points and 'rounding up' to the nearest whole number. It is possible to sort data into numerical order and to ask for information above (>) or below (<) a certain figure.
- Dates – it is possible to insert dates into a field so that searches for birthdays and diary entries can be made. You could then search for all those born on a certain date. A date format will appear as: – –/– –/– –.
- Time – these fields will be used by a business to insert start and finish times of employees. They will appear in the same way as the date format.

Creating a database

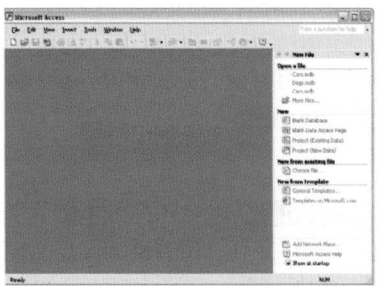

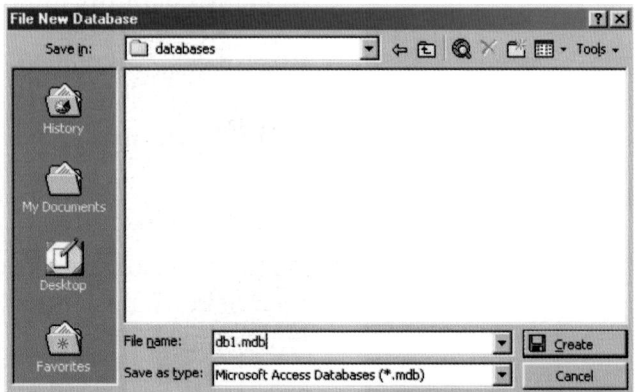

Action Points

Before going any further, have a look at Chapter 4 – Communication, where you learnt about designing a questionnaire. On page 166–167 it was suggested that you create a questionnaire to find out if there is a murket for a school shop and what you might sell in it. This information may be useful again to help with decisions about your database design. You may wish to conduct a new survey using a newly designed questionnaire.

When you open Access you will be presented with the window shown on the left. Select one of the first two options if you are creating a new database. Unlike Word documents, you must save an Access database before you start working on it. After selecting BLANK ACCESS DATABASE you will be asked to specify a location and a name for the database, as shown below.

Find the folder where you want to save the database in the SAVE IN drop-down menu, then key the name of the database in the FILE NAME line and click on the CREATE button. You then get the screen shown on the left and you should select CREATE TABLE IN DESIGN VIEW.

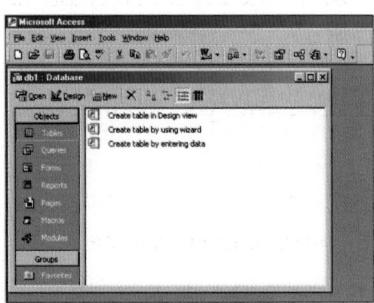

Design view customises the fields in the database so that the data can be entered.

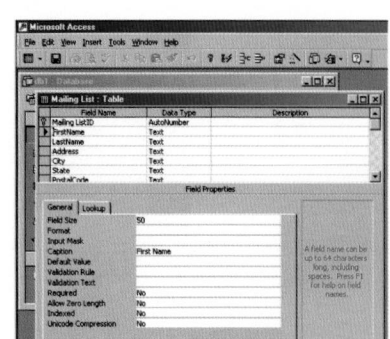

You are going to set up a school shop and you want to create a database of potential customers; these might be pupils, teachers, parents, the general public, friends and relatives.

1 Consider your potential market and create some field headings. These might include name, address, age group, income. Think about this very carefully and ensure the length of the field is adequate.

2 Construct your database in design view, having saved your database as 'Market research'.

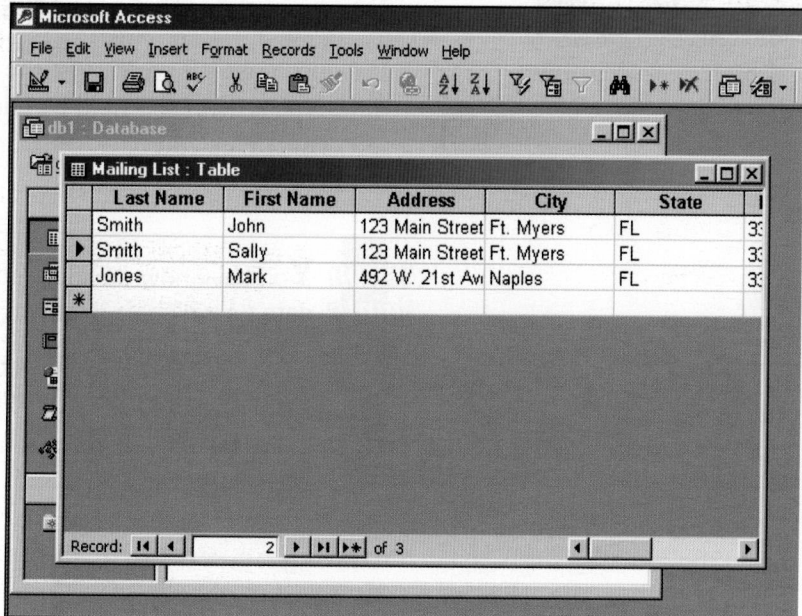

The DATASHEET (as shown above) shows the FIELD NAMES as column headings (in the grey section at the top of each column). The rows are the same as those in Microsoft Excel and each row is an individual RECORD. The datasheet allows you to enter details onto the database.

You can now enter your information onto the datasheet.

1 You should attempt to include at least 20 records in the database. In other words, include at least 20 responses to your questions.

2 Word process a memo to your teacher giving an explanation of the data types used for each field that you created.

3 Identify in the memo any mistakes you made whilst creating the fields for your database and any changes you had to make.

4 Print a copy of your table and your memo.

Adding and editing fields

If, having created the database, you decide you want to make amendments to the field names, this can be done by selecting the FORMAT/RENAME column from the menu bar or by highlighting the column, right clicking on it with the mouse and selecting RENAME COLUMN from the shortcut menu.

 It is also possible to change the title of a field or to reselect the data type within the field by clicking on the icon shown on the left. This takes you back to your original DESIGN VIEW in order to edit your datasheet layout.

 **Action Points** **Y**ou have now decided that you should have included the date on which each of your interviews took place.

1 Go back to your database design view and add another field to allow this information to be included.

2 Print a copy of your table.

Inserting, editing and deleting records

You can add new records to the table in datasheet view by typing in the record beside the asterisk (*). This marks the new record. You can also click on the NEW RECORD button at the bottom of the datasheet to move to the last empty record.

To edit records, place the cursor in the record that is to be edited and make the necessary changes. Use the arrow keys to move through the record grid. You can also use the FIRST, PREVIOUS, NEXT and LAST buttons at the bottom of the datasheet to help you move through the datasheet.

You can delete a record on a datasheet by placing the cursor in any field of the record row and selecting EDIT/DELETE RECORD from the menu bar or by clicking the DELETE RECORD button on the datasheet toolbar.

You can also add and delete columns, although it is best to add new fields in DESIGN VIEW because there are more options available to you. You can add them quickly in DATASHEET VIEW by highlighting the column that the new column should appear to the left of, by clicking its label at the top of the datasheet. You then select INSERT/COLUMN from the menu bar. Entire columns can also be deleted by placing the cursor in the column and selecting EDIT/DELETE COLUMN from the menu bar.

Search, sort and select records

Using Access it is possible for you to view records in a table in a different way. You can reorder the records and you can view only those records in a table that match what you are looking for.

Sorting is one of the most common ways of reordering your records as, for example, it allows you to sort records by date or by alphabetical order. In order to do this you need to be in TABLE VIEW and place the cursor on the column that you want to sort by. Select RECORDS then SORT then SORT ASCENDING or DESCENDING from the menu bar. Alternatively you can click on either of those buttons on the toolbar. Notice that these are the same as those used in Microsoft Excel.

You can sort by more than one column by highlighting the columns, by clicking and dragging the mouse over the field labels and selecting your sort method. In this way you could organise your records by date and alphabetical order.

You can select particular records from your database that include only the information you require. For instance, you might want to filter out just those people who live in a certain area of the country or who regularly shop at Marks and Spencer. In order to select specific records you should place your cursor in the field that you want to filter the records by and click FILTER BY SELECTION on the toolbar or select RECORDS, FILTER, FILTER BY SELECTION from the menu bar.

Queries select records from one or more tables in a database. To create a query in design view, from the QUERIES PAGE on the database window, click on the NEW button, then select DESIGN VIEW and click OK. Then select TABLES AND EXISTING QUERIES from the TABLES AND QUERY TABS and click the ADD button to add each one to the new query.

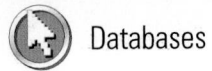
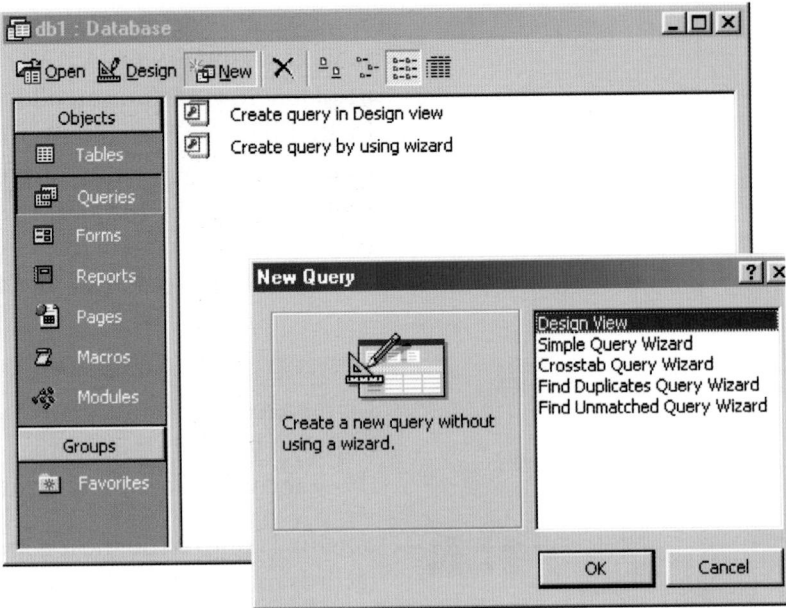

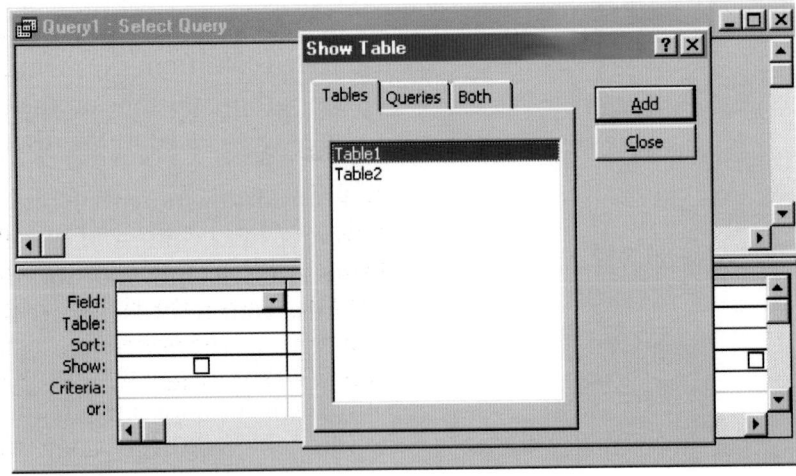

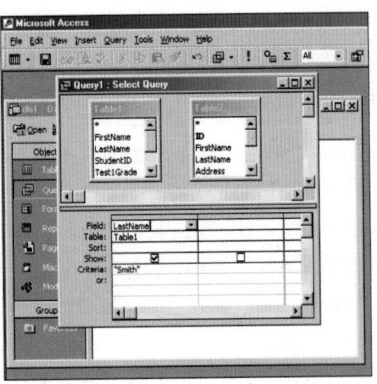

Click CLOSE when all of the tables and queries have been selected.

You can add fields from the tables to the new query by clicking on the field name in the TABLE BOX or by selecting from FIELD and TABLE.

Enter your query in the CRITERIA field.

1 Decide on at least six different queries that you want to apply to your database. You could, for instance, choose any of the following as queries, but make sure they are not all simple queries; at least half should be more complex:

- All those pupils in the first year at your school.
- All those who wanted crisps to be sold in the shop.
- All those who wanted chocolate to be sold in the shop.
- All those who shop regularly at Woolworths before Christmas.
- All those who have more than £5 disposable income.
- All those who have more than £2.50 disposable income.
- All those who have less than £2.50 disposable income.

2 Print a copy of each of your queries.

Creating and printing reports

Reports will help you organise and group information from a table or query and will provide you with a way to print the data. One of the easiest ways to do this is to use a WIZARD. Double click on the CREATE REPORT BY USING WIZARD option on the REPORTS DATABASE WINDOW. Select the information source for the report by selecting a TABLE or a QUERY from the TABLES/QUERIES drop-down menu. You then need to select the fields that you want in your report by transferring them from the available fields menu to the selected fields menu. You can move the fields using the single right arrow button to move them one at a time, or the double arrow button to move them all at once. You then click the NEXT button to move to the next screen.

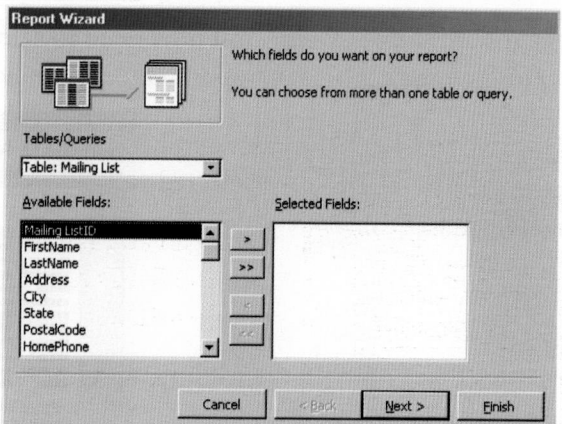

Select the fields from the list that the records should be grouped by and click the right arrow button to add those fields to your

diagram. You can use the PRIORITY buttons to change the order of the grouped fields if you wish. Then click NEXT to continue.

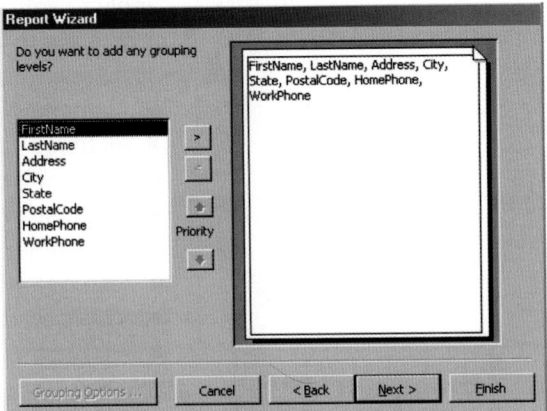

If you wish to sort the records, identify your sort order here. Select the first field that records should be sorted by, click the A–Z sort button and choose ascending or descending order, then click NEXT to continue.

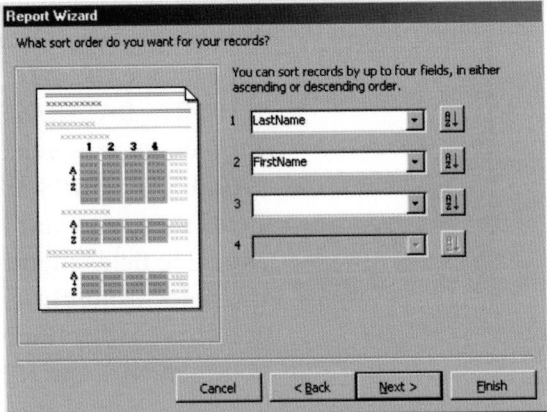

You now need to select a layout and page orientation for your report. Once you have done this, click NEXT.

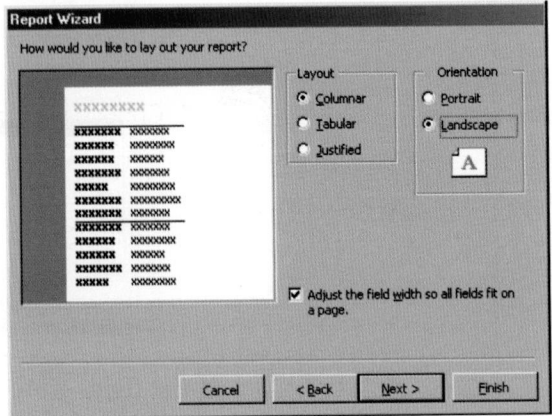

You can now select the colour and graphics style for your report. Once you have done this click NEXT.

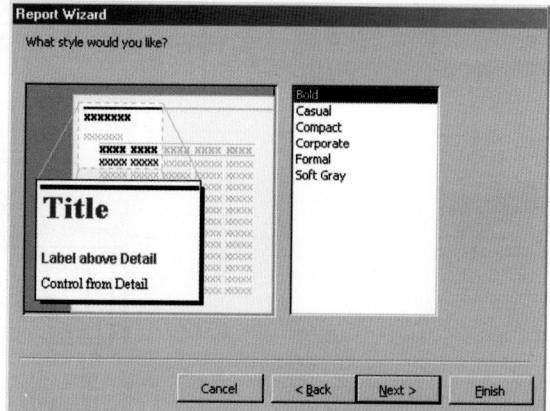

You are now on the final screen, where you need to name your report and decide whether to preview it or modify it before printing.

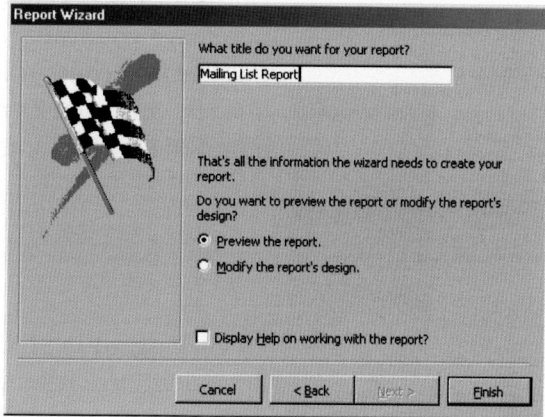

In order to print your report you need to select FILE and PRINT or click on the printer icon as you do normally.

 **You** should now change the way your research is displayed by creating a report format for it.

1 Choose your own report style and layout but include all necessary fields.

2 Print a copy of your report.

GRAPHICS AND CLIP ART

As we have already discovered, the use of pictures, images and charts, of whatever kind, can help make something that is complicated more easy to understand. The use of these items can also make a document more interesting and colourful to read.

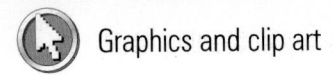

One of the easiest ways to add graphics to a document is to use a clip art image. Your school should have a number of clip art images in a library. From the Word toolbar, select INSERT, PICTURE, then CLIP ART. You will then see something like this:

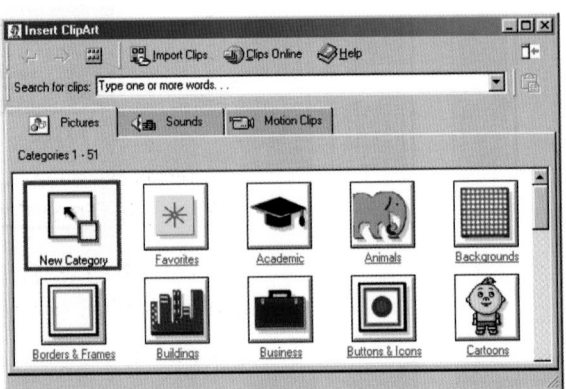

You can find an image by clicking in the white box following the words SEARCH FOR CLIPS. Enter any keyword which describes the image you want to use. You can also click on one of the CATEGORY icons and browse through the different clip art images. Once you have found the image that you want, click on it and the following menu will appear:

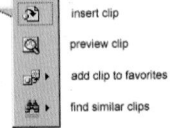

By clicking on INSERT CLIP, the image will be placed into your document. By clicking on PREVIEW CLIP you will see a full-size image before you add it. You can resize the image to make it bigger or smaller here before you insert it into your document. ADD CLIP TO FAVOURITES puts this image into your Favourites directory, which means it will be easier to find next time. FIND SIMILAR CLIPS will ask the program to look for images like the one that you have just chosen. You can continue to add images until you click on the CLOSE button in the top righthand corner of the INSERT CLIP ART window.

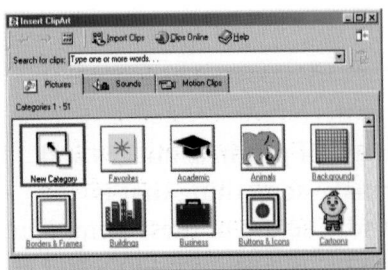

The other way of adding an image to a document is to add it from a file. This means that your computer must already have images other than clip art stored on it. To do this select INSERT, PICTURE, FROM FILE. Click on the down arrow on the right of the LOOK IN window to find the image on your computer, then click on the file name (a preview of that picture will appear on the righthand side of the box) and simply click INSERT to place the image into your document.

DESKTOP PUBLISHING (DTP)

Microsoft® FrontPage is one of the many programs available to those wishing to publish on the internet. There are some common words which will crop up in these instructions and you will need to remember them:

- Hyperlink – which is a text or graphics hotspot that you can click on to move to another web page.
- Pixel – this is a unit of measurement on the web.
- ULR (universal resource locator) – which is the address of a website.
- Web – in FrontPage your website is called a web.

You can change the view of the opening page by selecting a different view option. The basic view options are:

- Page view – which is one of the most useful options because it is known as a WYSIWYG (what you see is what you get) and this shows you exactly what your web page will look like.
- Folders view – lists all the files and folders in your web.
- Reports view – which identifies problems within pages and links in your web.
- Navigation view – which lists the navigation order of your site.
- Hyperlinks view – which enables you to organise the links on your web pages.
- Tasks view – which provides you with a grid for doing the tasks you need to complete your web.

You can, of course, create a web using a web wizard. On the opening page select FILE, NEW, WEB.

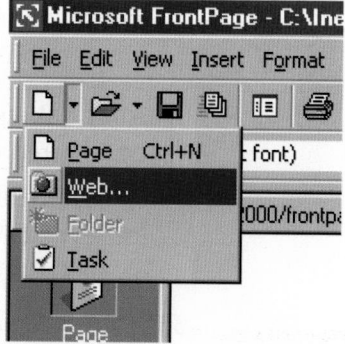

You must then choose the type of web that you want to create. It is usually simpler to choose a one-page web as this allows you to add additional blank pages later. You must enter a location for the web in the box which begins with 'http://:' as this is where you will be able to preview your web on your computer.

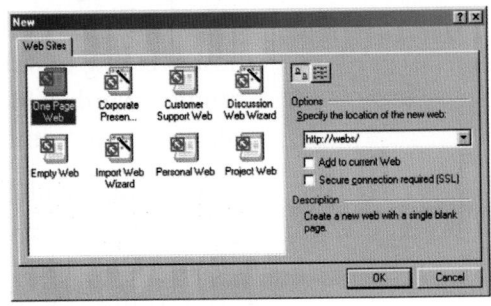

You must then click on OK. You will see that in FOLDERS VIEW the initial page that was created is shown and there is another, which is the images folder where you will place all of your photographs and graphics.

You can create web pages from templates. Select FILE, NEW and PAGE and choose the template that will dictate what the page looks like.

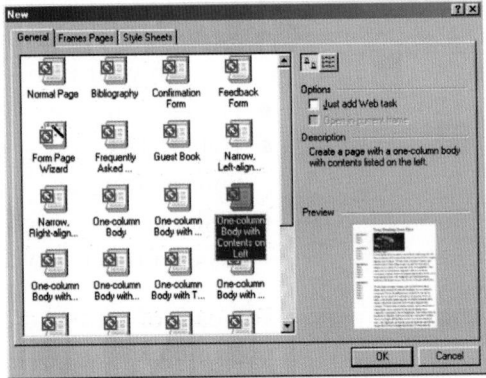

Select a template and click OK. You can then replace the text and photographs with your own text and images.

All the skills learned whilst using Microsoft® Word can be transferred to FrontPage. In other words, you can embolden, italicise, change fonts, copy and paste any of your text using the same icons or drop-down menus.

Action Points

1 Create a web page for a shop. Get together with some of the other members of your group and decide what information would need to be included.

2 Small groups could prepare the text and graphics that you would use. Obtain images from the internet to use on your web page or use some clip art images.

3 Another group could do some research to find out what images are available.

Index